Arbatax

S. Priamo

THE EASTERN COAST

Nurallao

Quartu S. Elena

CAGLIARI AND THE SOUTH

Cagliari

Pula

Fordongianus

Sanluri

THE WESTERN COAST

Tramatza

Oristano

Fluminimaggiore

Iglesias

Carbonia

S. Antioco

Isola di Sant'Antioco

Isola San Pietro

0 kilometres   20

0 miles   20

EYEWITNESS TRAVEL

SARDINIA

EYEWITNESS TRAVEL

SARDINIA

Main Contributor **Fabrizio Ardito**

LONDON, NEW YORK,
MELBOURNE, MUNICH AND DELHI
www.dk.com

Produced by Fabio Ratti Editoria Libraria e Multimediale, Milano, Italy

Project Editor Diana Georgiacodis
Editors Anna Lia Deffenu, Giovanni Francesio, Renata Perego, Laura Recordati
Designers Paolo Gonzato, Stefania Testa, Studio Matra
Maps Paul Stafford
Picture Research Fabio De Angelis, Riccardo Villarosa

Dorling Kindersley Ltd
Project Editor Fiona Wild
Editor Francesca Machiavelli
DTP Cooling Brown
DTP Designer Ingrid Vienings

Main Contributor Fabrizio Ardito
Additional Contributors Patrizia Giovannetti, Raffaella Rizzo

Illustrators Giorgia Boli, Alberto Ipsilanti, Daniela Veluti, Nadia Viganò

English Translation Richard Pierce

Printed and bound in China by L. Rex Printing Co. Ltd

First published in Great Britain in 1998 by Dorling Kindersley Ltd,
80 Strand, London WC2R 0RL

14 15 16 17 10 9 8 7 6 5 4 3 2 1

Reprinted with revisions 2000, 2001, 2002, 2003, 2006, 2008, 2011, 2014

Copyright 1998, 2014 © Dorling Kindersley Limited, London
A Penguin Company

MIX
Paper from
responsible sources
FSC
www.fsc.org   FSC™ C018179

Front cover main image: Seascape with yacht, Olbia-Tempio district, Costa Smeralda

◀ The 12th-century castle overlooking the village of Burgos

Contents

How to Use this Guide **6**

Sheep grazing in pastures filled
with spring flowers

Introducing
Sardinia

A prehistoric tower of the Santu Antine
nuraghe at Torralba

The beach at Stintino on the tip of the northwestern coast

Flamingo, one of the many birds that
winter in the wetlands of the western coast

Knight on horseback during the Sa Sartiglia
festival at Oristano

A bird's-eye view of
the city of Alghero

HOW TO USE THIS GUIDE

This guide helps you get the most from your visit to Sardinia, providing comprehensive expert recommendations as well as detailed practical information. *Introducing Sardinia* sets the island in its geographical, historical and cultural context. The five area chapters in *Sardinia Area by Area* describe the main sights and monuments in detail, with maps, pictures and illustrations. *Travellers' Needs* offers recommendations for hotels, restaurants and bars, as well as features on what to eat and drink and where to shop. The *Survival Guide* contains practical information on everything from transport to safety.

Sardinia Area by Area

Sardinia has been divided into five main sightseeing areas, each coded with a coloured thumb tab for quick reference. A map illustrating how the island has been divided can be found on the inside front cover of this guide. The sights covered within the individual areas have been plotted and numbered on a *Regional Map*.

1 **Introduction** The landscape, history and character of each region is described here, showing how the area has developed over the centuries and what it has to offer visitors today.

Each area can be identified quickly by its colour coding.

A locator map shows the region in relation to the other areas of Sardinia.

2 **Regional Map** This gives an illustrated overview of the whole area. All the sights covered in the chapter are numbered and there are useful tips on getting around by car and public transport.

Features and story boxes highlight special or unique aspects of an area or sight.

3 **Detailed Information** All the important towns and other places of interest are described individually. They are listed in order, following the numbering on the *Regional Map*. Within each entry there are details on the important buildings and other major sights.

4 **Major Towns** All the important towns are described individually. Within each entry there is further detailed information on important buildings and other sites. The *Town Map* shows the location of the main sights.

A Visitors' Checklist gives you the practical details to plan your visit, including transport information, the address of the tourist office, market days and festivals.

The Town Map shows all major and minor roads. The key sights are plotted, along with train and bus stations, parking areas, churches and tourist information offices.

5 **Street by Street Map** Towns or districts of special interest to the visitor are given a bird's-eye view in detailed 3D with photographs and descriptions of the most important sights.

A suggested route for a walk covers the most interesting streets in the area.

Opening hours, telephone number and transport details for the sight are given in the Visitors' Checklist.

6 **The Top Sights** These are given two or more pages. Historic buildings are dissected to reveal their interiors, while the photographs highlight the most interesting features.

INTRODUCING SARDINIA

DISCOVERING SARDINIA

The following leisurely itineraries enable you to experience as many of Sardinia's highlights as possible. First comes a themed three-day tour, which delves into the island's archaeological heritage, revealing the rich legacy of the Phoenician, Carthaginian and Roman periods. Next comes a two-day tour of Sardinia's capital city, Cagliari, showcasing its rich artistic wealth and historical importance. Finally there are two seven-day tours. The first follows the northern coast, taking in deluxe resorts and medieval towns, then swinging south to Spanish-flavoured Alghero and inland to the mountain town of Nuoro. The second explores the southwestern coast, with forays into the interior taking in major historical sites. These two seven-day tours can be combined to create a two-week itinerary. Or simply dip in and out of these itineraries and be inspired.

Archaeological Tour

- Visit the archaeological museum in **Cagliari**, which boasts the largest collection of artefacts on the island.
- Marvel at the remains of the ancient city of **Nora**, right by the sea.
- Relax in the bucolic surroundings of the **Temple of Antas**.
- Climb up to **Tiscali**, a nuraghic village located within a mountain.
- Seek out the scattered group of monuments around **Arzachena**.

Cagliari
The island's bustling capital, Cagliari, with its rich history, lies in a sheltered gulf on Sardinia's southwestern coast.

Arzachena
Situated at the centre of Sardinia's glitzy resort destination, the Costa Smeralda, Arzachena is famous for a clutch of prehistoric monuments nearby.

◀ Painting of *Sardinian Landscape* (1900–1910) by Guglielmo Micheli

Castelsardo

Sassari

Palmavera Nuraghe

Grotta di Nettuno

Alghero

Santissima Trinità di Saccargia

San Salvatore
San Giovanni di Sinis
Tharros

Oristano

Santa Giusta

Golfo di Oristano

Gùspini

Temple of Antas

Iglesias

Portovesme

Carloforte
San Pietro

Calasetta
Sant'Antioco

Sant' Antioco

0 kilometres   30

0 miles   30

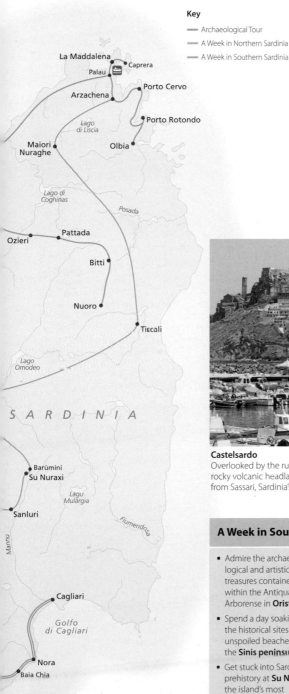

Key

— Archaeological Tour
— A Week in Northern Sardinia
— A Week in Southern Sardinia

A Week in Northern Sardinia

- Explore the spectacular northeastern coast, which includes the five-star hotels and beaches of the **Costa Smeralda** and the **Maddalena archipelago**.

- Wander the medieval lanes of **Castelsardo**, dominated by an impressive castle.

- Enjoy the shops, restaurants and beaches of **Alghero**.

- Savour the traditional atmosphere of **Nuoro**, an inland centre with rich cultural heritage.

Castelsardo
Overlooked by the ruined *castello* (castle) that sits atop a rocky volcanic headland, the town of Castelsardo lies not far from Sassari, Sardinia's second city.

A Week in Southern Sardinia

- Admire the archaeological and artistic treasures contained within the Antiquarium Arborense in **Oristano**.

- Spend a day soaking up the historical sites and unspoiled beaches of the **Sinis peninsula**.

- Get stuck into Sardinia's prehistory at **Su Nuraxi**, the island's most important nuraghic site.

- Get a taste of the charming offshore isles of **Sant'Antioco** and **San Pietro**, full of historical interest and boasting some excellent beaches.

- Drive along the Costa del Sud and **Baia Chia** for magnificent views, superlative swimming and interesting archaeological sites.

Archaeological Tour

- **Duration** Three days
- **Airports** Arrive at Cagliari's Elmas airport and depart from Olbia-Costa Smeralda.
- **Transport** You'll need your own transport to visit the places on this itinerary.

Day 1: The Southwest

Start off in Cagliari's **Museo Archeologico Nazionale** (p62), the most comprehensive collection of archaeological finds on the island. Head south-west to explore the Roman and Carthaginian ruins at **Nora** (pp78–9), then continue along the south coast to Chia, site of the Phoenician settlement of **Bithia** (p78), ending up in **Sant'Antioco** (pp76–7), with its extensive Punic remains.

Day 2: Tharros and Tiscali

Visit the well-preserved Carthaginian and Roman **Temple of Antas** (p72), en route to **Tharros** (pp136–7), another important Roman and Carthaginian site on the Sinis peninsula. Devote the afternoon to the mountain cave-village of **Tiscali** (pp108–109), preferably on a guided walk.

Day 3: Gallura

Maiori Nuraghe (p155), in the mountains of Gallura, is a fascinating relic of Sardinia's ancient nuraghic civilization, lying in dense woods outside

Ruins of the Carthaginian and Roman Temple of Antas, near Fluminimaggiore

Tempio Pausania. End the tour on the coast to see the cluster of nuraghic remains in the countryside around the village of **Arzachena** (p149).

Two Days in Cagliari

Sardinia's capital has a rich selection of sights, mostly located in the atmospheric old town.

- **Arriving** Cagliari's Elmas airport lies 6 km (4 miles) northwest of the city. A half-hourly bus service takes you to Piazza Matteotti in the city centre, where taxis are available.
- **Moving on** The railway station is also in Piazza Matteotti, and close to the port for mainland ferry connections.

Day 1

Morning The best-preserved area of Cagliari is the **Castello** district (pp60–61), crowning the city and girdled by stout walls. Here, seek out the **Cathedral** (p59), which vividly displays its 12th-century Pisan origins.

An imposing gateway at the far end of Piazza Palazzo leads to the **Cittadella dei Musei** (p62), a complex of museums that include important archaeological finds, Renaissance art and Asian treasures.

Afternoon Climb up either of the two defensive towers that punctuate the old city walls: **Torre di San Pancrazio** (p60) and **Torre dell'Elefante** (p61), for some of the best views over the city and out to the sea. From here, saunter to the northern end of Castello for more sweeping vistas from

Vineyards surrounding the nuraghic village of Tiscali

the **Bastione San Remy** (p58), a wide esplanade constructed in the 19th century and now furnished with elegant bars. The view over the port and Cagliari's salt flats and marshes is especially magnificent at sunset.

Day 2
Morning Head up Viale Sant'Ignazio for the **Orto Botanico** (p59), a botanical garden planted with more than 500 exotic species. A shady sanctuary from the summer heat, it also contains grottoes and Roman remains. Just above it is the **Roman Amphitheatre** (p58), once a grand arena for popular entertainment. If the site is closed (for ongoing restoration work), you can still appreciate the scale of the site from the outside. Carry on over the brow of the hill to visit the **Galleria Comunale** (p62), which contains a fine collection of modern Sardinian art.

Afternoon Visit the modern Villanova district, where a former slaughterhouse has been converted into an arts centre. The venue, **Exma** (p63), hosts exhibitions and has a bookshop and café. A short walk west, **San Saturnino** (p63) is one of Sardinia's oldest churches, dating from the 5th century. The building

The Costa Smeralda, known for its exclusive resorts

suffered bomb damage during World War II, but retains some Roman remnants. Buses pass nearby that will take you to the sands of **Poetto** (p25), a seaside resort that makes the perfect place to unwind, with full beach facilities available.

A Week in Northern Sardinia

- **Airports** Arrive at and depart from Olbia-Costa Smeralda airport, or use the ferry service, with frequent connections between Olbia and the mainland.

- **Transport** A car is essential for this trip.

Day 1: Costa Smeralda
Travel north out of Olbia and turn off towards **Porto Rotondo** (pp146–7) for your first taste of the stretch of coast known as the **Costa Smeralda** (pp147–9). As well as a yacht marina, chic boutiques and pricey bars, it also boasts a selection of granite-backed sandy beaches. Continuing along the coast with its seductive vistas over creeks and bays, you'll soon reach **Porto Cervo** (p148), the stylish centre of the Costa Smeralda, where you can indulge in leisurely window-shopping among the famous fashion outlets. Inland **Arzachena** (p149) is more down-to-earth and worth

a stop for the nearby archaeological sites of Albucciu Nuraghe, Tomba di Giganti Coddu Vecchju and Li Muri Necropolis.

Day 2: Maddalena archipelago
From Palau, board a ferry for **La Maddalena** (p152), the main island of the Maddalena archipelago, and wander around the port's alleys and squares. In the afternoon, take a boat tour of the uninhabited islands, these often include swimming stops. Alternatively, explore the **Compendio Garibaldino** (p153), a museum dedicated to the life of the Italian hero Giuseppe Garibaldi, situated on the small island of **Caprera** (p152).

Day 3: Castelsardo
Head down Sardinia's panoramic northwestern coast to the town of **Castelsardo** (p168), built on a promontory that is capped by the remains of a formidable stronghold. Explore the town's steep lanes, stopping at its ancient churches and the castle, which houses a museum displaying a collection of typical basketwork. You can find home-made examples for sale in the town.

Day 4: Sassari
A short drive inland, Sardinia's second city, **Sassari** (pp164–7), has most of its major sights

Flamingoes in flight over the salt marshes on the outskirts of Cagliari

Watchtower at Alghero, with the azure Mediterranean Sea below

located within its medieval core. Seek out the flamboyant, Spanish-inspired Duomo and the graceful Fontana del Rosello, which was carved by Genoese craftsmen, before crossing the grandiose Piazza d'Italia to the Museo Archeologico on Via Roma, which contains a wealth of nuraghic and Roman finds.

Day 5: Alghero and environs
The port and resort of **Alghero** *(pp122–3)* has long attracted visitors for its pretty lanes, lively atmosphere and Catalan culture. In the morning, walk the stout city walls, browse the shops selling jewellery and visit the Cathedral. After a lunch al fresco, travel north out of town to enjoy gorgeous sandy beaches and explore the

The picturesque Grotta di Nettuno on the Capo Caccia promontory

archaeological remains at **Palmavera Nuraghe** *(p123)*. If there's time and the weather permits, take a boat tour to view the fascinating natural rock formations in the **Grotta di Nettuno** *(p127)*.

Day 6: Santissima Trinità di Saccargia to Nuoro
Located in open countryside southeast of the city of Sassari, the Romanesque church of **Santissima Trinità di Saccargia** *(pp162–3)* is striking, with its black-and-white design recalling its Tuscan workmanship. Look out for the carved animals, the ornate decoration of the façade and the frescoes in the apse. From here, head east, taking in the traditional villages of **Ozieri** *(p159)*, **Pattada** *(p158)* and **Bitti** *(p104)* on the road to Nuoro.

Day 7: Nuoro
On a hill in the centre of the island, **Nuoro** *(pp102–103)* provides fascinating insights into Sardinia's culture and traditional way of life. Explore the **Museo Etnografico**, a repository of traditional masks, costumes and objects relating to rural culture. A walk through the old town will bring you to the **Museo Deleddiano**, devoted to the town's literary star Grazia Deledda, and to the **Museo Archeologico**, both worth a visit.

A Week in Southern Sardinia

- **Airports** Arrive at Olbia-Costa Smeralda and leave from Cagliari's Elmas airport (both cities also have a ferry service to the mainland).
- **Transport** You'll need your own vehicle to explore this area.

Day 1: Oristano and Santa Giusta
On Sardinia's west coast, the town of **Oristano** *(pp138–9)* has a long and glorious history, championing the opposition to the Spanish in the Middle Ages. You can see evidence of its cultural wealth at the superb **Antiquarium**

Oristano's cathedral, with its unusual octagonal belltower

Arborense *(p138)*, one of the island's foremost museum collections, and in its **cathedral**, with its octagonal bell tower. Just south of town, the Romanesque cathedral and the nearby lake at **Santa Giusta** *(p140)* merit a stop.

Day 2: Tharros and the Sinis peninsula

West of Oristano, the **Sinis peninsula** *(pp134–5)* is a low-lying, sparsely populated area boasting a cluster of historic sites and some of Sardinia's finest beaches.

The ancient Punic and Roman site of **Tharros** *(pp136–7)* is the most prominent sight, best seen on a guided tour. Close by are **San Giovanni di Sinis** *(p135)*, one of the oldest churches on the island, and **San Salvatore** *(pp134–5)*, a double-level church surrounded by *cumbessias* –simple white-painted houses used as pilgrims' lodgings. Spend the rest of the day enjoying the secluded sandy beaches of Sinis.

Day 3: Su Nuraxi and Sanluri

Turn off the Carlo Felice highway (SS131) to reach the village of Barùmini, outside which lies Sardinia's largest nuraghic site, **Su Nuraxi** *(pp68–9)*, whose origins date to 1500 BC. Visit the museum for an overview before taking in this extensive complex of

Salt pans on Sant'Antioco, harvested since Roman times

palace, huts and fortifications on a guided tour. Heading south, you'll find yourself back on the SS131 at **Sanluri** *(p66)*, the site of a decisive battle in 1409 that led to the Aragonese takeover of the island. The castle still stands, and is now home to an entertaining collection of militaria and quirky historical items, including a museum of wax.

Day 4: Temple of Antas to San Pietro

Head west to **Gùspini** *(p71)*, then follow the S126 south to visit the **Temple of Antas** *(p72)*, which mixes nuraghic, Carthaginian and Roman elements. Further south, stop at **Iglesias** *(pp72–3)* if you have time, otherwise carry on to

Portovesme for the car ferry to **San Pietro** *(pp74–5)*, whose Ligurian origins can still be detected in the local dialect and cuisine.

Day 5: Sant'Antioco

A ferry crosses from San Pietro's only town, Carloforte, to **Calasetta** *(p75)* on the neighbouring, larger island of Sant' Antioco. The main town, also called **Sant'Antioco** *(pp76–7)*, was once the centre of the Carthaginan region of Sulki, and still holds a concentration of Phoenician and Punic finds, including a *tophet*, a type of pre-Christian shrine, and a necropolis. Save some time to see the museum here and the catacombs below the nearby basilica of Sant'Antioco.

Day 6: The Costa del Sud and Nora

Crossing the land causeway that connects Sant'Antioco with the Sardinian mainland, follow the southern coast road past scenic coves and rocky promontories, pausing for a dip at one of the beaches of **Baia Chia** *(p78)*. Continuing north from here, you'll come to **Nora** *(pp78–9)*, one of Sardinia's most important Carthaginian and Roman archaeological sites.

Day 7: Cagliari

Round off your tour with a day spent exploring the island's capital: pick a day from the two-day city itinerary on pp12–13.

The town of Sanluri on the Campidano plain, scene of a famous battle

Putting Sardinia on the Map

Sardinia lies west of the Italian mainland, surrounded by the Mediterranean Sea. The island is flanked by the Tyrrhenian Sea to the east and by the Sardinian Sea to the west. Sardinia's population of 1,700,000 lives in an area of 24,000 sq km (9,300 sq miles), divided into eight provinces: Cagliari (surrounding the island's capital city), Carbonia-Iglesias, Medio-Campidano, Oristano, Ogliastra, Nuoro, Olbia-Tempio and Sassari.

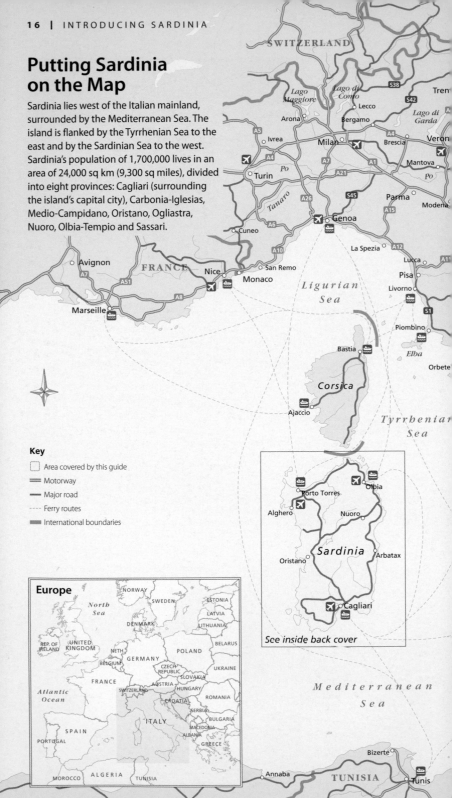

Key

- ☐ Area covered by this guide
- ═══ Motorway
- ─── Major road
- ---- Ferry routes
- ▬▬ International boundaries

See inside back cover

Europe

AUSTRIA

Bolzano
Cortina d'Ampezzo
Belluno
Klagenfurt
Dráva
Maribor
Varazdin
HUNGARY
Pecs

SLOVENIA
Udine
Ljubljana
Zagreb
CROATIA

Treviso
Vicenza
Venice
Trieste
Rijecka
Karlovac
Slavonski Brod

Padova
Adige
Ferrara
Pula
Banja Luka
Zenica

Bologna
Ravenna
Zadar
CROATIA
BOSNIA AND HERZEGOVINA
Sarajevo

San Marino
Rimini
Pèsaro
Sibenik
Mostar

Florence
Ancona
Split
Dubrovnik

Siena
Gubbio
Perugia
Ascoli Piceno

Orvieto
Terni
Adriatic Sea

Viterbo
L'Aquila
Pescara
Isole Tremiti

Civitavecchia
Sulmona
Manfredonia
Greece, Egypt

Rome
ITALY
Foggia
Barletta

Anzio
Benevento
Bari
Greece

Naples
Potenza
Matera
Brindisi

Isola d'Ischia
Amalfi
Taranto
Lecce

Isola di Capri
Lauria

Rossano

Cosenza
Crotone

Ustica
Isole Eólie o Lípari
Vibo Valentia
Catanzaro

Palermo
Messina
Reggio di Calabria
Ionian Sea

Isole Egadi
Trapani
Marsala
Enna
Sicily
Catania

Agrigento
Gela
Siracusa

Isola di Pantelleria
Malta

0 kilometres   125
0 miles   125

For additional map symbols *see back flap*

A PORTRAIT OF SARDINIA

The very isolation of this large island, set in the middle of the Mediterranean, has shaped its unique character. For thousands of years Sardinia has stood on the sidelines of mainstream Mediterranean historical events, remaining a singular world to itself. Even the Romans found it a difficult place to subdue.

The experience of invasion from across the water over the centuries has left a legacy which is still evident today. The roads tend to follow valleys inland rather than tracing a scenic path along the beautiful coastline. There are yachting marinas and harbours, but fishing is not a mainstay of the economy and, even in peacetime, Sardinia has never really become a seafaring nation. Over the years Sardinia's shores have seen the arrival of Phoenicians, Romans, Genoans battling for supremacy with Pisans and Arabs, the Spanish, and finally the House of Savoy. The different cultures have all contributed to the art, architecture and cultural life of Sardinia and evidence is scattered throughout the island: prehistoric dwellings and fortresses from the earliest known inhabitants, ancient rock-cut tombs, and Romanesque churches which resemble those of Pisa or Lucca. Introduced artistic styles were often taken up and developed with distinctive Sardinian character – the altar paintings in the Spanish *retablo* tradition, for instance. In 1848 this untamed island became part of the newly created nation of Italy.

The 20th century brought with it dreams of industrialization and newfound prosperity, as well as the beginnings of a tourist industry.

However, the Sardinia that brings the visitors is a land of white beaches and deep blue sea, which does not really represent the essence of the place. The coastline is certainly beautiful, apart from some stretches

The stately procession of Sant'Efisio passing through Pula

◀ Cala Gonone, a popular resort on the eastern coast of the island

where random building has spoilt the views. But the interior is stunningly beautiful too, and deserves further exploration. The natural scenery is extremely varied, providing totally different environments and habitats for plants, animals and birds. In some areas there are fertile alluvial plains, in others steep mountains of granite and limestone, and flat landscapes drop suddenly into steep ravines within the space of a few kilometres.

People, Language and Music

Human settlements have existed in the interior for thousands of years, and Sardinia is studded with the traces of ancient pastoral civilizations, further

Hand loom at the Museo Etnografico in Nuoro

Fishermen at work on Isola Rossa

proof that the people have always tended to prefer to live in the comparative safety of the mountainous interior rather than along the coasts. The passing of the seasons is still marked by the stages in the agricultural year, and by celebrations of successful harvests. Ancient traditions – now deeply rooted in Catholicism but showing traces of far older religions –

Decanting ewes' milk after the morning milking

are manifested in numerous festivals, which are often based on the very close relationship between the people and their natural environment.

A number of very different dialects can be heard in the interior of the island, and the Sardinian language still has a clear Latin base – the word *domus* is used to mean a house, for instance, instead of the Italian *casa*. Years of Spanish rule mean that in Alghero, on the west coast, you can still hear Catalan spoken on the streets, and, on the island of Sant'Antioco in the southwest, the traditions and the cooking reflect a Ligurian and Tunisian influence.

Music features strongly in Sardinian life, at feast days and weddings, and even everyday events, especially in the interior, are always celebrated with music. Musicologists and musicians – such as Peter Gabriel, who recorded the music of the Tenores de Bitti group in his world music series – have described traditional Sardinian music as unique in Europe. Today it is undergoing something of a revival. There is a great deal of vocal and instrumental variety; based on the sound of the *launeddas*, a cane wind instrument, and polyphonic music for four voices. The most well-known example is the Canto a Tenores.

Economic Development

In an uneasy position between the past and the future, the economy of Sardinia is complex. Agriculture and shepherding used to be the key factors in the economy, and there was also a mining boom in certain areas after unification, particularly around Sulcis, an abundant source of both coal and metals. But the Sardinian mining industry declined, especially after World War II, and is unlikely to recover. Other schemes for promoting industry have badly affected the environment, and have been abandoned. However, attempts in the 1950s to eradicate malaria, by treating marshy areas with pesticides, produced impressive results: in a short space of time the coast became habitable.

Tourism in Sardinia Today

Sardinia possesses some of the most unspoilt scenery in Europe which, like its other special qualities, can only be fully appreciated by visiting the island. Interest in creating the facilities needed for tourism in Sardinia was initially subdued, and services were slow to take off. The gradual development of

Traditional bread from the Sulcis region

tourism has, however, made the island famous, opening up Sardinia to the outside world, as well as increasing awareness of its history, local culture, arts and handicrafts.

The island's varied wildlife was perhaps bound to be affected by increasing numbers of visitors, and a number of wildlife and marine reserves have now been established to protect unique habitats and their flora and fauna. The vast, wild Gennargentu range is also now a protected National Park. The rare monk seal, previously thought to be extinct, has been sighted once again off Sardinia's western coast, an indication that it is possible for tourism and ecology to co-exist in comfort.

Limestone stacks rise from the sea off the headlands of the Masua and Nebida coastlines

Marine Life of Sardinia

The waters around Sardinia are considered to be the cleanest in Italy and are rich in flora and fauna. The generally healthy sea beds are havens for both scuba divers and naturalists. The sheer cliffs along the coast are home to dozens of species of nesting birds and birds of prey. Years of marine research in the Golfo di Orosei, on the eastern coast, have finally confirmed the return of the fabled monk seal, once so widespread in the area that caves and inlets were named after it. Dolphins and other large sea mammals, such as small whales, can occasionally be seen in the northwestern waters and the Straits of Bonifacio. The area has been declared an international marine reserve.

Neptune grass *(Posidonia oceanica)* is a sea plant with shaggy leaves that grows down to a depth of 30–35 m (100–115 ft). Sea grass, as it is also known, has flowers, which is unusual for a marine plant.

Rocks of volcanic origin

The striped sarago, quite a common fish in the Mediterranean, combs the sea bed in search of prey.

Rocks are covered with seaweed such as *Cystoseira.*

Sardinian coral can be various shades of red or white and lives on the rocky sea bed, at depths of 15–100 m (50–330ft) below sea level.

The lobster is a crustacean that lives mostly along the rocky shores, but can also be found at depths of up to 100 m (328 ft). The meat is a local delicacy.

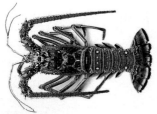

The sea anemone attaches itself to rocks in shallow water. Its deceptively delicate tentacles contain stinging cells, enabling it to capture small fish and crustaceans.

Gorgonian coral survives because the water is so clean. The flexible branches may be white, yellow or red, and can grow to be 1m (3 ft) tall.

Birds of the Coastline

The cliffs along the Sardinian coastline provide an ideal habitat for birds. Wild pigeons build safe nests here and raise their young without being disturbed. Herring gulls, Audouin's gulls and cormorants perch on the rocks between bouts of fishing. Further up the cliff edge, birds of prey such as the peregrine falcon, the red kite and the rare griffon vulture, build their nests.

Cormorants on the cliff ledges

Audouin's gull

Herring gull

Peregrine falcon

Red kite

Underwater Mediterranean

The Mediterranean Sea has a rich and varied ecosystem, sustained by warm currents and clean waters. There is coral and myriad species of seaweed, a wide variety of fish, crustaceans and molluscs and marvellous rock formations for snorkellers and scuba divers to enjoy

Cracks and crevices in the rocks make an ideal habitat for the moray eel.

Fronds

Brown meagres move in schools to defend themselves from predators by day. At night they hunt molluscs, small fish and prawns.

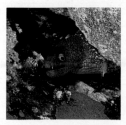

Dolphins are frequently seen riding the waves at the bow of a boat in the warm waters around Sardinia, particularly in the clear seas around Maddalena along the northern shore.

The moray eel has powerful teeth and poisonous mucus. It also has an excellent ability to camouflage itself, making it one of the most dangerous creatures in the Mediterranean Sea.

Monk seals, once thought to be extinct, have returned to the Golfo di Orosei where they live in grottoes and solitary caves.

The Sardinian Coastline

Washed by the clear blue waters of the Mediterranean, Sardinia offers a varied coastline of sculpted cliffs and coves. Secluded inlets alternate with golden sand dunes, where wild lilies and cistus bloom, or rugged cliffs that plummet into the sea. One of the most well-known resorts is the world-famous Costa Smeralda where visitors come to enjoy luxury villas and pretty, sandy beaches. Other popular areas are the coast south of Olbia, including the sheltered Cala Gonone, and the southeastern tip of the island, near Villasimius (easily accessible from Cagliari). Several stretches of coastline have remained untouched, such as the isolated coves between Orosei and Arbatax, and the southwestern area between Baia Chia and Oristano.

At Capo Caccia, sheer limestone cliffs, 186 m (610 ft) high, jut out from the sea.

Between Bosa and Alghero the spectacular coastline is punctuated by cliffs of volcanic origin, covered with mastic trees.

Around Piscinas the coast is known for its impressive wind-carved sand dunes. The sand is an ideal habitat for juniper and tamarisk.

The cliffs on the island of San Pietro, eroded by sea and wind, are of pink and grey trachyte. Crevices and ledges offer useful shelter to rare birds like Eleonora's falcon.

Trinità d'Agultu

Golfo dell'Asinara

Porto Torres

THE NORT AND THE COSTA SMERALD

Sassari

Alghero

Mar di Sardegna

⑤ Bosa Marina

Macomer

Ottana

THE WESTERN COAST

Is Arutas ④

Oristano

Nuralla

S. Nicolo d'Arcidano

Sanlu

③ Piscinas

Villa

② Cala Domestica

Siliqua

Cagli

Carbonia

San Pietro

CAGLIARI AND THE SOUTH

S. Antioco

The Costa Smeralda is characterized by granite cliffs shaped by wind and water erosion, and by inlets with clear water – paradise for scuba divers, snorkellers and surfers.

°to
°lo
⑦ Isola di Budelli

Porto Cervo

achena

Olbia

La Cinta ⑧

Budduso   Siniscóla

Berchida ⑨

Orosei

Nuoro

ENTRAL
RDINIA
AND
RBAGIA

⑩ Cala Luna

Golfo di Orosei

Arbatax

THE
EASTERN
COAST

In the Golfo di Orosei the limestone cliffs plunge into the sea. Isolated coves can be reached only by boat or a long hike on foot through the maquis.

0 kilometres   30

0 miles   30

S. Priamo

artu S. Elena

Poetto

fo di
liari

The Arbatax coast is famous for the reddish colour of the porphyry rock and the steely grey colour of the older granite, jutting out in pinnacles from the sea.

Sardinia's Ten Best Beaches

① Most lively
Poetto, near Cagliari, is one of the liveliest beaches on the island. Locals throng here at weekends and through the summer.

② Most hidden beach
Cala Domestica, protected by a Saracen tower, is invisible from the sea. In World War II it was used as a German military base.

③ Best dunes
At Piscinas there are 7 km (4 miles) of sand dunes covered with maquis vegetation. Some are as high as 50 m (164 ft), the highest found in Europe.

④ Most tropical
The beach at Is Arutas is made of tiny "grains" of quartz. A forest of pine trees forms a green backdrop to the sand.

⑤ Cleanest sea
Bosa Marina, unchanged since the 1950s, has won medals for being the cleanest beach in Italy.

⑥ Best windsurfing
A strong and constant breeze from the mouth of the Liscia river makes Porto Pollo (*Porto Puddu* in Sardinian dialect) perfect for windsurfing.

⑦ Best coral beach
The beach on the island of Budelli consists of pieces of shells, coral and marine micro-organisms. Now, however, landing on the island is forbidden.

⑧ Best beach for young people
La Cinta, 4.5 km (3 miles) long, is a favourite with the trendy younger set. It is ideal for soaking up the sun and for windsurfing.

⑨ Most remote beach
Berchida, with its white beach and red rocks, can only be reached via a long sandy track through the shrubby maquis.

⑩ Most inaccessible beach
The secluded Cala Luna, with its white beach, pink oleanders and green mastic trees, is only accessible by boat or on foot.

The Flora and Fauna of Sardinia

From the rugged Gennargentu massif to the Campidano plains, and from the Nurra hills to the wind-eroded rocks of the Gallura area, Sardinia offers a great variety of natural habitats for wildlife. The forests, especially in the north, are dominated by cork oaks, for centuries a useful source of raw material. The Mediterranean maquis is permeated with the scents of lentiscus, cistus, myrtle and strawberry trees. Despite decades of farming, the fauna is still varied and interesting. Deer and wild boar abound in the scrub and forests and the rocks are home to the moufflon. The small Monte Arcosu reserve retains a tiny population of rare Sardinian deer, and the island of Asinara is the home of wild donkeys. In the spectacular Giara di Gesturi plateau, unbroken horses graze freely. Assorted reptiles can also be found, but no vipers.

The moufflon is an ancient inhabitant of the island. It has a thick coat and impressive curving horns.

Sardinian deer are stocky, with smaller horns than their mainland counterparts.

Foxes can be seen throughout all regions of Sardinia.

Mountain

Woods

Marshla

The Sardinian horse is a compact animal native to the island. The horses only roam on the Giara di Gesturi plateau.

The Kermes oak *(Quercus coccifera)* thrives mostly on the southern coastline.

The cork oak *(Quercus suber)*, important to the economy, dominates the forest of Gallura *(see p155)*.

Sardinian boar live in various parts of the island. They are smaller and stouter than species on mainland Italy.

The holm oak *(Quercus ilex)* predominates in almost all medium-altitude woods.

The Mediterranean Maquis

The thick, often impenetrable covering of shrubby vegetation known as maquis *(macchia* in Italian) thrives in the coastal and mountainous regions of Sardinia. The shrubs – including myrtle, arbutus (strawberry tree) and blackthorn – flower in spring, rest in summer and revive again in autumn. Even in winter the island looks green, with splashes of colour from berries. In recent years the area of maquis has increased, as a result of forest fires which encourage plenty of new growth.

Myrtle in flower

Strawberry tree

White cistus flowers

The kite's habitat is the wooded upland valleys.

The Sardinian Terrain

The southwestern corner of Sardinia began to emerge from the sea over 500 million years ago.

Turtles, which may grow up to as much as 1 m (3 ft) in length, are dying out because their eggs are highly prized.

Mastic trees *(Pistacia lentiscus)* grow on the coast, on Monte Limbara and the Gennargentu.

Plain

The flamingo winters in the coastal marshes and lagoons, and now nests on Sardinia.

The white-headed duck, which nests among reeds, is quite a rare sight on Sardinian marshland.

Prickly pears *(Opuntia)* are a characteristic feature everywhere along the coastline.

The Nuraghi

There are over 7,000 nuraghi in Sardinia, their distinctive truncated cones a familiar part of the landscape. Little is known about their builders, a civilization that flourished on the island from 1800 to 500 BC (in some areas the nuraghic peoples resisted the Romans long after this date). Initially a nuraghe consisted of a single tower made of huge blocks of stone laid without mortar. Later, more towers were added, with connecting ramparts, resulting in more complex structures such as the Losa nuraghe at Abbasanta, the Santu Antine at Torralba and the Su Nuraxi at Barùmini. Nuraghi served as both dwelling and fortress, and the towers were often surrounded by a village and wall. There is no trace of any written language, but over 1,500 bronze figures have been found in tombs and near holy wells. The figures, and other finds, are now on display in Sardinia's archaeological museums.

Tribal chief
This bronze figure comes from the nuraghic village of Santa Vittoria, at Serri, one of the largest in Sardinia. It is a portrait of a prince at prayer.

Simple nuraghe
This is the most commonly seen and simplest form of nuraghe, consisting of a single tower with a chamber made of inwardly stepped circular tiers of stones. At times these nuraghi had more than one storey.

The central tower
is in the shape of a truncated cone.

The rampart
incorporates three defence towers.

Outer defence wall

Map of Sardinia showing principal nuraghic sites

SASSARI
NUORO
ORISTANO
CAGLIARI

• Principal Nuraghic Sites

The Losa Nuraghe at Abbasanta
This nuraghe is in three parts and is surrounded by a rampart with small towers. The oldest tower dates from before 1500 BC. There is a fine panoramic view of the Gennargentu mountains from the terrace.

Maiori Nuraghe at Tempio Pausania
This ground-floor room of the Maiori nuraghe in northern Sardinia could only be illuminated by light filtering in from the outside.

Nuraghic Burials

The nuraghic peoples built monumental tombs known as Tombe dei Giganti (Tombs of Giants) to bury their dead. Each tomb consisted of a long covered corridor constructed with huge slabs of stone. The shape represented the horn of the Bull God. A monolithic oval stele, with an opening at the base, formed the front face. Two rows of stones on either side, forming an arch, completed the burial chamber. The central, arched stele could sometimes be as much as 3 m (10 ft) tall. The area around a typical Tomba dei Giganti was often surrounded by long rows of menhirs.

The Tomb of Giants at Li Lolghi is one of the most famous prehistoric sites in Sardinia

The central tower had three super-imposed chambers.

The side towers were built at a later stage, in the early Iron Age.

The rampart created a solid defence system.

Santu Antine Nuraghe

The central tower of this roughly triangular nuraghe is surrounded by a three-sided rampart with three towers. It was built in different stages in the 9th–8th centuries BC. The huge complex was later dedicated to the Roman emperor Constantine.

This reconstruction
shows the original layout of Santu Antine. The central tower was the main fortress and dwelling, protected by the external towers.

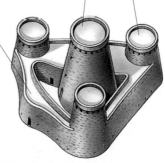

Arrubiu Nuraghe
This consists of a massive fortress built in red stone covering an area of about 3 hectares (7 acres) at the edge of a plateau dominating the Flumendosa valley. Imposing external ramparts with five towers protected the inner courtyard and the central nuraghic construction, which was 16 m (52 ft) high.

SARDINIA THROUGH THE YEAR

Spring is by far the best season to visit Sardinia. Perfumed flowers are in bloom in the maquis thickets, the woods and meadows are still green and, although the weather is warm enough for swimming as early as May, it has not reached the scorching temperatures of summer. Easter, with its colourful processions, marks the religious high point of the island. During the rest of the year, towns and villages organize festivals to commemorate the feast day of the local patron saint and sanctuaries are enlivened by celebrations and banquets.

The summer months are dedicated to activities along the island's stunning coast, such as bathing, sailing and windsurfing. Inland, it can get stiflingly hot in summer, but the higher mountainous areas provide a cool retreat from the crowds and an ideal place for walking. Grape harvesting begins in the autumn, and in early winter there is heavy snowfall on the Mount Gennargentu massif. At times snow can even fall on the lower areas covering the rocky landscape of the Supramonte.

Narcissus in bloom, a typical flower of the Mediterranean

Spring

Once the warm spring weather sets in, the sheep and goats grazing on the hillsides will be moved to higher pastures. The aromatic plants and strongly scented flowers of the maquis are in full bloom, and bees abound. They produce the rather bitter honey used in many traditional Sardinian cakes.

In the flatlands and on the hills of the Anglona and Montiferru regions the fruit trees are in blossom, while in the countryside young artichokes are almost ready to be picked. These are shipped to vegetable markets on mainland Italy and are traditionally the first on the market.

March and April

Holy Week and **Easter** *(Mar or Apr)* are a time of great religious celebrations, with colourful processions taking place throughout the island. In Cagliari there is an important procession through the streets on Good Friday. A representation of the *Iscravamentu*

and *Incontru* mystery plays is performed at Iglesias. At Oliena the costume procession known as *S'Incontru* takes place on Easter Sunday. *Su Concordu* in the town of Santu Lussurgiu features 15th-century psalms sung in Gregorian chant. On Holy Monday at Castelsardo, there is the *Lunissanti*, a religious feast of Spanish origin.

Sagra del Riccio di Mare *(early Mar)*. A festival of the sea urchin in Alghero.

The **Livestock Festival** *(25 Apr)*, at Ollastra Simaxis, is held in honour of St Mark.

Festa Patronale *(2nd Sat after Easter)*. The island of Sant' Antioco celebrates its patron saint's feast day.

May

Sant'Efisio *(1–4 May)*, in Cagliari, offers a grand procession commemorating the end of the plague in 1656. The saint's statue

is carried through the city and is then taken to Nora on an ox-drawn cart. During this splendid display of religious feeling the faithful cast flowers onto the street as the statue passes by.

San Francesco's feast day *(second Sun)*. Held at Lula, this is one of the most popular celebrations in the Baronie and Nuoro areas.

Festa dell'Annunziata *(third Sun)* at Bitti. A pastoral celebration of the Annunciation.

San Bachisio *(29 May)*. This feast day consists of three days of *Ballu Tundu* (round dance) in the squares of Onanì.

Cavalcata Sarda *(Ascension Day)*. A celebration of spring, the "Sardinian Horseride" has become one of the island's major folk festivals. Handicraft stalls and general festivities fill the streets of Sassari's old town centre. People from all over the

The *S'Incontru* procession in the streets of Oliena on Easter Day

Average daily hours of sunshine

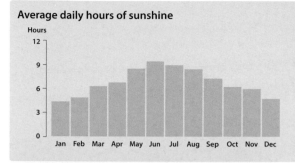

Sunshine Chart
Summer is the sunniest, as well as the hottest time, and June has the maximum hours of sunshine daily. The least sunny month is January, but the weather varies a great deal between inland and coastal regions, and in general, coastal areas will be brighter.

The Ardia horse race in front of the Sant'Antine sanctuary at Sedilo

island crowd into the town on horseback or dressed in colourful costumes to hear traditional songs and poetry from the different towns and regions of the island until the early hours of the morning.

Summer

The high temperatures and stunning coastline attract locals and visitors alike to the seashore during the summer months. The coastline is filled with bathers and windsurfers, and yachts and sailboats from all over Europe dock at the small, picturesque harbours. For snorkellers and scuba divers there are underwater beds of posidonia to explore. Sailing, windsurf and scuba diving clubs organize lessons throughout the summer months (see pp200–1). The cooler temperatures on the slopes of Gennargentu make it excellent for hikers, and the climb down the gorges of Su Gorroppu is also popular with experienced mountaineers.

This is the period of rural festivals, when small religious sanctuaries hidden among the valleys and hills come to life with pilgrimages and feasting. **Pani, Pisci, Pezza e Piricchittus** (Jun–Sep), meaning "bread, fish, meat and almond pastry", is a food festival held in the restaurants of Quartu. Cagliari offers a programme of music, theatre and cinema during the summer. At San Gavino Monreale there are concerts and other cultural events as well as sports activities at night.

June

Horse Festival (2 & 3 Jun). Santu Lussurgiu holds an important agricultural festival with a handicrafts exhibition.
Sagra delle Ciliegie (first Sun of month). Festival celebrating the cherry harvest at Villacidro, Bonarcado and Burcei.
San Leonardo (11 Jun). An evening of music, dance and food in Villanova Monteleone.

July

Ardia (5-8 Jul). This characteristic rural festival is held at San Costantino a Sedilo in front of the Santu Antine sanctuary. A lively horse race accompanies celebrations honouring the saint.
Madonna of the Shipwrecked (third Sat in Jul) at Villasimius. A procession takes the Madonna from the church to the port, and there are festivities in the piazza.
Sagra delle Pesche (17 Jul), is a peach festival held at San Sperate on the feast day of the town's patron saint.
Estate Musicale (Jul–Aug), at Alghero, with concerts in the Chiostro di San Francesco.
International Folklore Festival (end of Jul), held in Tempio Pausania, during the summer Carnival.
Carpet Fair (two weeks in Jul or Aug) at Mogoro. This is one of the leading displays of Sardinian handicrafts, in particular carpets, tapestry and hand-made furniture.
Music in Antas Valley (Jul–Aug). Classical music concerts held in the splendid setting of the Temple of Antas at Fluminimaggiore (see p72).

Advanced sailing lessons off the Costa Smeralda

Average monthly rainfall

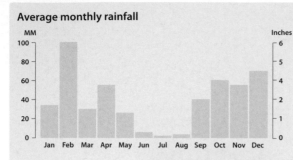

Rainfall Chart
In Sardinia most of the rainfall occurs in the autumn and winter. The rainfall is heavier in the mountainous regions of the interior, with precipitation as high as 1,000 mm (39 inches) per year. The driest season is during the summer months, particularly in the coastal regions.

August
Mauretanian Wedding
(1–15 Aug) at Santadi.
A ceremony dating back to the ancient traditions of the North Africans who inhabited the Sulcis region in Roman times.
Dieci Giorni Sulcitani
(1–15 Aug) in Sant'Antioco.
This consists of ten evenings of traditional local entertain-ment, including plays in dialect, recitals of Sardinian poetry, traditional folk dances and local choral music.
Carpet Show *(first Sun of Aug)*.
Traditional hand-made carpets and blankets are exhibited at Aggius.
Madonna della Neve feast day *(first Sun of Aug)*. The hardships of winter are exorcised in the Tascusì sanctuary at Desulo.
Sagra della Vernaccia *(first Sun of Aug)*. Festival of the local wine at Baratili San Pietro, near Oristano.
Sagra del Vino *(4 Aug)*. Wine festival at Jerzu with costume parades, dances, traditional songs and Cannonau wine.
Sagra del Pomodoro
(11 Aug). The tomato festival offers tomato-based dishes

Men and women parading in the Processione del Redentore in Nuoro

served outdoors at Zeddiani. There is also an exhibition of local farm produce.
Faradda de li Candelieri
(14 Aug). Candles *(candelieri)*, weighing between 200–300 kg (440–660 lbs) are carried by members of the ancient guilds in Sassari. Each candle is decor-ated with the coat of arms of the guild and its patron saint.
Time in Jazz *(the week incor-porating Ferragosto)*. Berchidda hosts an annual jazz festival.
Processione del Redentore
(29 Aug). Nuoro hosts one of Sardinia's most popular cele-brations with a procession through the streets in honour

of Christ the Redeemer, and performances of local folklore.
Launeddas Festival *(fourth Sun)* at San Vito. This festival features performances by leading musicians of the traditional triple-piped wind instrument *(see p94)*. The music is accompanied by the *Ballu Tundu*, a circular dance.
Rassegna di Musica Leggera *(Aug–Sep)*. Performances of popular music and theatre in Piazza Peglia, Carloforte.
Regata Vela Latina *(end of Aug)*. A regatta for traditional Sardinian fishing boats held in Stintino *(see p124)*.
Mostra del Tappeto *(mid-Aug–late Sep)*. Carpet fair held at Nule.

Autumn

It is still possible to swim in the sea well into September, but the air becomes cooler in the evening. October is grape harvest time and autumn marks the beginning of the hunting season. The favourite game is wild boar, a tasty meat used in the strongly-flavoured Sardinian cuisine. The chestnut harvest in the mountains often ends with lively festivals.

September
Pilgrimage to the Madonna di Gonare Sanctuary *(8 and 16 Sep)*. Departures to this hilltop church alternate between the centres of Sarule *(see p107)* and Orani.
Fiera del Bestiame *(third Sun of month)* at Serri. A livestock fair on the day of Santa Lucia.
San Cosimo *(27 Sep)*. The *Mamuthones (see p106)* parade through the streets of Mamoiada in sheepskins.

Traditional costumes worn for the Madonna della Neve festival at Desulo

Average monthly temperature

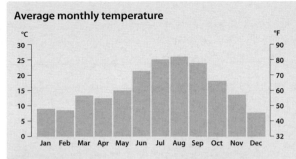

Temperature Chart
The summer months between June and September are hot and dry, with temperatures above 20° C (68° F), and at times reaching 30° C (86° F). In winter the temperatures are mild, rarely dipping below 5° C (41° F). January generally has sunny days and cold nights.

Masked figures *(Boes)* with cowbells during carnival at Ottana

October

Santa Vitalia Festival *(first Mon of month)*. A festival dedicated to agriculture held at Serrenti, with stalls selling local handicrafts.

Sagra delle Castagne e delle Nocciole *(last weekend)*. Festival to celebrate the harvest of chestnuts and hazelnuts at Aritzo. There is also a handicrafts fair.

November

Festa della Madonna dello Schiavo *(15 Nov)*. A statue of the Madonna is worshipped as it passes through the town of Carloforte. The statue is said to have been sculpted by citizens from Carloforte, who had been kidnapped by pirates and held in Tunis.

Santa Caterina *(25 Nov)*. The saint's feast day is celebrated in Abbasanta.

Winter

Winter is a fairly cold season throughout the island and snow covers the mountainous interior. Livestock is returned to its lower winter pastures and pens, and the chill wind puts an end to fishing activity along the coast.

As well as **Christmas**, which is very important in Sardinia, there are many other feast days and local festivals in the Carnival period before Lent.

December

Sagra delle Salsicce *(first Sun of month)* held at Siligo. After the pig slaughter, preparation and curing of the meat, the sausage festival is an opportunity to taste the year's new delicacies.

Christmas is celebrated at home with presents and by preparing traditional sweets.

January and February

Feast of Sant'Antonio Abate *(16–17 Jan)* is celebrated at Mamoiada and Fluminimaggiore *(see p72)* with huge bonfires.

Carnival *(the ten days before Shrove Tuesday)* is extremely popular in Sardinia, especially in the Barbagia region. Masked and costumed figures parade on Shrove Tuesday and the last Sunday of Lent. At Mamoiada, the *Mamuthones*, men dressed in sheepskins with heavy bells strapped to their backs, are driven through the town by the *Issohadores (see p106)*. Similar

festivals during carnival are the *Thurpos* at Orotelli, and the *Merdules* and *Boes* at Ottana *(see p105)*. At *Sa Sartiglia* in Oristano, masked horsemen spear a silver star hanging from a tree. There are cakes and free wine at Iglesias *(see p72)* and food is served in the main square at Perfugas. At Tempio Pausania an effigy of "King George" is burned and at Santu Lussurgiu *(see p132)* there is the *Sa Carrela 'e Nanti* horse race.

Processo a Su Conte *(Ash Wednesday)*. At Ovodda the stuffed figure of "Su Conte" is tried in the main square and burned at the stake.

Public Holidays

New Year's Day (1 Jan)
Epiphany (6 Jan)
Easter Sunday and Monday (Mar or Apr)
Liberation Day (25 Apr)
Labour Day (1 May)
Republic Day (2 Jun)
Ferragosto (Assumption Day, 15 Aug)
All Saints' Day (1 Nov)
Immaculate Conception (8 Dec)
Christmas Day (25 Dec)
Santo Stefano (26 Dec)

Snow-covered mountains of the Gennargentu in winter

THE HISTORY OF SARDINIA

The origins of Sardinian history go back thousands of years. The first people to settle are thought to have reached the island by crossing over a natural causeway which once linked Tuscany and Sardinia, perhaps between 450,000 and 150,000 years ago. A succession of different cultures led up to the rise of the nuraghic civilization. These tribes of shepherds and warriors lived in round stone dwellings called nuraghi, defended by walled fortresses, and their occupation left exceptional megalithic ruins across the island. Of the 7,000 nuraghi left in Sardinia, some are in an excellent state of preservation: the Su Nuraxi settlement at Barùmini, the Santu Antine complex and the nuraghi at Losa.

The Phoenicians arrived in 1000 BC, settling along the coastline at Tharros, Nora, Bithia and Cagliari and, after winning the Punic Wars, the Romans occupied the island. Roman dominion lasted 700 years despite strong resistance from Sardinians, and evidence can still be seen in the many ruins. When the Roman Empire fell, Sardinia again fell prey to various conquerors.

For centuries the Vandals, Byzantines and Arabs fought for possession of the strategic harbours, until the maritime republics of Pisa and Genoa made their appearance on Sardinian waters. A golden age of Sardinian Romanesque architecture was introduced, which gave way to Gothic when the House of Aragon conquered the island. After 400 years of Spanish rule, control of the island passed to Austria, which ceded it to the House of Savoy in 1718. The Kingdom of Sardinia survived up to the unification of Italy. A long period of neglect was ended only after World War II, with the reclamation of the malarial marshes. The scheme's success opened up possibilities for a tourist industry and the development of an autonomous, modern Sardinia.

Calaris, modern-day Cagliari, in a print dating from 1590

◀ The Roman Temple of Antas at Fluminimaggiore, built over a 6th–5th century BC Phoenician temple

Prehistoric Sardinia

Although some stone tools found at Perfugas show that Sardinia was inhabited from the Paleolithic period (150,000 years ago), it was only around 9000 BC that the island began to be settled by populations from Asia Minor, the African coasts, the Iberian peninsula and Liguria. The fertile, mineral-rich land and the obsidian mines at Monte Arci were a major factor in the island's prosperity. By around 3000 BC the Sardinians had grouped into tribes. They lived in villages with thatched-roof huts and buried their dead in rock-cut tombs called *domus de janas* (house of fairies). By about 1800 BC this rural society had evolved into the warrior nuraghic civilization, who built thousands of circular stone towers *(nuraghi)* across the island. Many of these remarkable prehistoric constructions are still visible.

Necklace with Tusk
This ornament was found in a tomb dating from 2000–1800 BC, the bell-shaped pottery era.

Earthenware
These jugs and vases were everyday objects used to store water and grain.

The motifs on the prow have more to do with the land than the sea.

Monte d'Accoddi ruins
These traces reveal the ruins of a tiered, terraced construction, probably a temple, dating from the 3rd millennium BC. It looked remarkably similar to the famous ziggurat temples of Mesopotamia and the Aztec pyramids.

6000 BC Sardinian peoples make tools and weapons from the obsidian found at Monte Arci

Obsidian arrowhead

A typical example of domus de janas

6000 BC	5000 BC	4000 BC

Boar tusk, an ornament from the early Neolithic period

4000–3000 BC The age of the Bonu Ighinu culture – small communities living by raising sheep and goats. Distinctive, high-quality grey pottery with incised decoration is produced

Bronze Artifacts from Abini

These spears were part of a hoard of 100 kg (220 lb) of objects hidden in large clay vessels, perhaps to conceal them from the Roman invaders.

Candelabrum

These bronze figurines were made using the melted wax technique.

Ex Voto with Deer Motif

This ex voto lamp in the shape of a ship was one of 70 or so found at Is Argiolas near Bultei. It dates from the 8th–7th centuries BC, and is now in the Museo Archeologico Nazionale in Cagliari. In the nuraghic age, Sardinians had a love-hate relationship with the sea, which ended with the arrival of the Carthaginians, Romans and later conquerors, who forced the local inhabitants to live in the interior.

Where to see Prehistoric Sardinia

Pre-nuraghic ruins include a ziggurat at Monte d'Accoddi and rock-cut tombs *(domus de janas)* at Pranu Muteddu (Goni). Nuraghic villages survive at Su Nuraxi *(see pp68–9)*, Serra Òrrios *(see p88)*, Tiscali *(see pp108–9)* and Abini. Burial chambers, or "Tombs of Giants", can be seen at places such as Sa Ena'e Thomes, and holy wells can be visited at Santa Cristina (Paulilàtino) and Santa Vittoria (Serri).

The nuraghic village of Serra Òrrios is one of the best preserved in Sardinia. It consisted of about 70 dwellings *(see p88)*.

The Montessu necropolis houses *domus de janas* of the Ozieri pre-nuraghic era.

3000 BC Era of Ozieri or San Michele culture. Villages are established throughout the island and the dead are buried in the *domus de janas*

Replica of the goddess Mater Mediterranea of Senorbi

1800 BC Rise of nuraghic civilization, characterized by truncated cone-shaped buildings erected at the edges of upland plateaus

The Santa Barbara nuraghe at Macomer

3000 BC	2000 BC	1000 BC

Dolmen at Luras

2000–1800 BC Civilization known for its bell-shaped pottery. Rectangular or round dwellings constructed

1500 BC The first simple forms of nuraghe appear

1000 BC Phoenician ships moor along coast

The Phoenicians, Carthaginians and Romans

Around 1000 BC Phoenician ships began to use the inlets of the Sardinian coasts as harbours. When commerce intensified about 200 years later, they founded the cities of Nora, Sulcis, Tharros, Olbia and, later on, Bithia and Karalis (today's Cagliari). But good relationships with the local chiefs soon waned. After a brief period of peace, the nuraghic populations attacked the Phoenician settlements which, in 509 BC, asked Carthage for help. In 238 BC the Carthaginians, defeated in the first Punic War, ceded Sardinia to the Romans, who made it their province. For over a century the Sardinians put up fierce resistance, a situation which ended in 215 BC with the battle of Cornus *(see p133)*. The Romans never succeeded in subduing the entire island and rebellion in the interior continued for years. However, Roman civilization gave the island a network of roads, as well as baths, temples, aqueducts and amphitheatres.

Gold Bracelet
Decorated with palmettes, lotus flowers and a scarab beetle, this bracelet came from Tharros *(pp136–7)*.

This shape of nose is typical of the Phoenicians.

Glass Vase and Perfume Bottle
In Roman times glass was used to make ornamental vessels as well as practical objects like cups, bowls and bottles. Numerous glass pieces have been found in burial grounds and examples can be seen in the Museo Archeologico Nazionale in Cagliari *(p62)*.

Lines on the face imitate tattoos.

Carthaginian Necklace
Carthaginian jewellery was often quite elaborate, as shown by this necklace with pendants carrying human and animal symbols.

Grinning Mask
This mask dates from the 4th century BC, when the island was under Carthaginian rule. Masks like these were used to ward off evil, to protect children or ensure the sleep of the dead. This mask was found in the settlement beneath the town of San Sperate (see p66).

900 BC Nuraghic villages, bronze figures and stone sculptures

Phoenician ship

500–400 BC Sardinians flee to Barbagia after losing battles against Carthaginians

900 BC	750 BC	500 BC

730–700 BC
First Phoenician harbours built: the future Nora, Tharros, Bithia and Karalis

ca. 550 BC
The Carthaginians arrive and found the first Punic cities

509 BC The nuraghic peoples attack the coastal cities, who ask Carthage for help

**Statue of Drusus Junior
(13 BC–AD 23)**
The portrait of the Roman consul, son of the emperor Tiberius, was found at Sant'Antioco *(see p76)*, together with other busts from the early Empire.

The incisions show lotuses and rosettes.

**Where to see
Punic–Roman Sardinia**

The best preserved Punic-Roman cities are Nora *(see pp78–9)* and Tharros *(see pp136–7)*. The ruins at Sulki, present-day Sant'Antioco *(see p76)*, are wholly Punic. Roman ruins include the amphitheatre in Cagliari *(see p58)*, near the Villa of Tigellio *(see p63)*, and baths at Fordongianus *(see p140–41)*.

Roman amphitheatre at Cagliari, 2nd century AD.

The Roman theatre at Nora is still used for summer cultural events.

Punic Inscription
This inscription was engraved on the base of the pedestal of a 4th-century BC statuette, found in the Temple of Antas.

Glass Bowl with the Figure of Christ
This beautiful early Christian piece was found inside a tomb near Ittiri. Christ is depicted in the role of both legislator and emperor.

The nose-ring is shaped like a leech.

---

238 BC The Carthaginians lose the first Punic War

227 BC Sardinia, together with Corsica, becomes Roman province

Mosaic found at Nora

AD 200–300 Full of disease, Sardinia becomes a deportation site

250 BC

AD 1

AD 250

Temple of Antas dedicated to Sardus Pater

27 BC Sardinia is divided from Corsica and becomes a senatorial province

AD 66 Roman Sardinia becomes an imperial province and is occupied by legions

The Middle Ages: from the Vandals to the Aragonese

In AD 456 the Vandals conquered Sardinia. Shortly afterwards, liberated by Byzantium, the island became one of the seven African provinces of the Eastern Roman Empire. The subsequent power vacuum, aggravated by Arab invasions, gave rise to the four autonomous *giudicati*, or principalities, of Torres, Gallura, Arborea and Cagliari. Around AD 1000 the Pisans and Genoese, after fierce campaigns against the Arabs, took over parts of the island. The long relationship with Aragon was formalized in 1295, when Pope Boniface VIII signed the papal bull naming James II of Aragon as King of Corsica and Sardinia. On 12 June 1323 the Infante Alfonso landed in Sardinia with his army.

The Castello quarter, Cagliari
Built during the era of Pisan rule, the fortified Castello quarter in Cagliari was the heart of the city until the 1800s.

Eleonora of Arborea
This remarkable woman inherited Arborea from her father Mariano IV in 1383. After two wars against the Aragonese, Eleonora gained control of most of Sardinia in 1394. Known as the Giudica, she remains a symbol of Sardinian independence.

Papal coat of arms

Benedetto Caetani was the real name of Pope Boniface.

Boniface VIII
In 1295, Pope Boniface VIII (depicted here while celebrating the Jubilee of 1300) signed the papal bull giving control of the Regnum Sardiniae et Corsicae *to James II of Aragon, in exchange for relinquishing Sicily. The Aragonese continued to annexe Sicily, ignoring the agreement.*

Barison I's seal
In 1038 the Pisans, after wresting Sardinia from the Arabs, helped Barison I of Arborea to take possession of its four *giudicati* (principalities).

534 Byzantium liberates Sardinia which, together with Corsica, becomes one of its seven African provinces

Pope Gregory the Great

AD 500	600	700	800

Earthenware from Vandal tombs

600 Pope Gregory the Great sets out to convert Sardinia to Christianity

711 Arab invasions begin

815 Sardinian diplomat ask France for aid in war against Arabs

Capo Falcone
This tower was part of a defence system which finally put an end to barbarian raids on Sardinia in the 16th century.

Pope Boniface VIII

Where to see Medieval Sardinia

The medieval conquerors often infiltrated the interior, influencing local architecture. San Saturnino in Cagliari *(see p63)* and San Gavino at Porto Torres *(see p124)* are two of the earliest medieval churches in Sardinia. Evidence of artistic contact with the mainland can be seen in the Romanesque churches of Logudoro *(see pp160–61)*, the cathedral of Oristano *(see pp138–9)* and the cathedral of Santa Maria in Cagliari *(see p59)*. Some castles remain: the Rocca at Castelsardo *(see p168)* and the Castello complex in Cagliari *(see pp60–61)*.

Santissima Trinità di Saccargia is Pisan Romanesque *(see pp162–3)*.

The Castello Malaspina dominates the town of Bosa *(see pp130–31)*.

Boniface VIII, despite this serene pose, was a highly controversial pope.

Alghero city walls
The massive walls and their towers date from the 14th-century period of Catalan rule.

Spanish Rule

The Spanish conquest of Sardinia was slow: the rulers of Arborea waged a lengthy war against the invaders, there were determined revolts in Alghero and, in 1355, the Spanish crown was forced to grant a form of parliament to the six largest cities. The Aragonese took power definitively only in 1409, when the principality of Arborea was eliminated after the bloody battle of Sanluri and replaced by the marquisate of Oristano. Spanish domination of Sardinia was strengthened in 1479, with the marriage of Ferdinand of Aragon and Isabella I of Castile and Leon. The Spanish era also saw the founding of the first universities: Sassari in 1562 and Cagliari in 1620. Following the Peace of Utrecht in 1714, the island was ceded to Austria who then, in the Treaty of London, passed it over to King Vittorio Amedeo II of the House of Savoy.

The upper part shows scenes from the life of St Peter; below are the saints with St Peter in the centre.

Vittorio Amedeo II of Savoy
Vittorio Amedeo became king in 1718 when Austria gave Sardinia to him in exchange for Sicily. The Cagliari parliament swore allegiance to the new king on 2 August 1720.

VICTOR AMÉDÉE.

Decorated border

Four Moors Coat of Arms
Of Catalan origin, the coat of arms with four Moors first appeared in Sardinia after the arrival of Alfonso of Aragon in 1323. It has become one of the symbols of the island.

The Four Evangelists are depicted in the elaborately bordered predella. Sardinian artists put their own stamp on the Catalan *retablo* style.

1355 Sardinian parliament established

1409 Battle of Sanluri; end of Arborea as a principality

1541 On his way to Tun Charles V stops at Alghe

1350

1400

1500

1402 *Anno de Sa Mortagia Manna,* the year of the great plague

Ferdinand of Aragon and Isabella of Castile

1509–1520 Repeated Arab pirate raids on Sardinia

Alghero Cathedral
The interior of the cathedral of Santa Maria, begun in the 16th century, is a splendid example of the Catalan Gothic style in Sardinia.

Where to see Spanish Sardinia

The first Spanish building in Sardinia was the Gothic-Aragonese chapel in the cathedral in Cagliari *(see p59)*, followed by San Francesco in Iglesias, San Giorgio in Perfugas, and San Francesco and the cathedral in Alghero *(see p122)*. The cathedral in Sassari was built in the style known as "Colonial Baroque". Baroque influence is also evident in Àles cathedral. A notable school of *retablo* painting developed. There are 15th- and 16th-century paintings in the Art Gallery in Cagliari.

The St Peter *Retablo*

The retablo is a religious panel painting that was quite often used as an altarpiece. It was one of the most important artistic genres in 16th-century Sardinia under Spanish rule. This work, Madonna and Child with Saints Peter, Paul and George of Suelli, is by Pietro and Michele Cavaro (1533–5). It is now in the church of San Giorgio at Suelli (Cagliari). The elaborate frame and wealth of decorative elements reveal its Flemish derivation.

This Aragonese house at Fordongianus was built in the 15th–16th centuries.

Retablos often combined painting, sculpture and carved decoration.

San Francesco in Alghero (14th century) was rebuilt in the Gothic-Aragonese style.

Philip V (1683–1746)
Forced to relinquish France and Sardinia, Philip tried to reconquer Sardinia in 1717 with the help of his chief minister Alberoni.

Charles V

1620 Under Philip III the University of Cagliari is founded

1688 Discontent and uprisings: the Spanish viceroy is assassinated

1600

1700

Cardinal Alberoni, Philip V's chief minister

1717 Philip V of Spain tries to reconquer Sardinia and Naples

1718 Treaty of London: Sardinia ceded to the House of Savoy

The Kingdom of Sardinia

One of the first acts of the Savoyard government was to reinstate the island's universities. However, a serious economic and social crisis led to unrest and the spread of banditry. After the Revolution of 1789, France made vain attempts to conquer Sardinia, but, by 1795, the island was overwhelmed by revolutionary fervour of its own and a "Sardinian revolution" broke out in Cagliari. In 1799 the Savoys took refuge on the island after losing their other territories to Napoleon. In 1847, in Cagliari and Sassari, huge crowds persuaded the Savoys to link the kingdom of Sardinia with Piedmont in *"fusione perfetta"*. In 1861 both became part of the Kingdom of Italy.

The Harbour at Cagliari
The port was developed after the arrival of the Savoy rulers. Together with Porto Torres it became the island's principal harbour.

The University of Cagliari
The university was founded as part of a cultural reorganization and development policy adopted by Carlo Emanuele III (1730–73), who set up a committee for Sardinian affairs in Turin.

Carlo Emanuele IV
King of Sardinia from 1796 to 1802, Carlo Emanuele took refuge here after losing his mainland territories to Napoleon in 1798. His brother Vittorio Emanuele I became King of Savoy.

The Absolutist Viceroy
Carlo Felice, seen here receiving the keys of Cagliari, was viceroy of Sardinia from 1799 to 1821, when he became king. Unchallenged, he nonetheless governed the island as an absolute monarch.

1720 Filippo Pallavicino becomes the first Savoyard viceroy of Sardinia

Throne of the Kingdom of Sardinia in Turin

1793 Anti-Savoy rebellion

1720	1740	1760	1780

1764–5 Re-establishment of Cagliari and Sassari universities

1788 The court of the House of Savoy flees Turin and remains in Cagliari until 1815

Memorial Tablet
This tablet, embedded in Palazzo Viceregio in Cagliari, was dedicated to Carlo Felice by Vittorio Emanuele I, his brother, who abdicated in his favour in 1821.

Where to see Savoyard Sardinia

Important Savoy buildings are the theatres in Cagliari, Sassari and Alghero, the provincial administration buildings and Cagliari Town Hall *(see p62)*. Many of Sardinia's railway lines were laid down in this era. Statues of prominent Savoy figures, like the one of Garibaldi at Caprera, were put up everywhere. The Villa Aymerich at Làconi was one of many country houses to be rebuilt.

Giuseppe Garibaldi
After years in exile because of his republican ideas, Garibaldi came to Caprera in 1857. He settled here permanently after conquering the Kingdom of Two Sicilies for the House of Savoy with his army of 1,000 volunteer soldiers, the Redshirts *(see p152)*.

The Galleria Comunale d'Arte di Cagliari, *the capital's art gallery.*

Monument to Carlo Emanuele III *at Carloforte, the town he founded.*

House of Savoy Coat of Arms
Dating back to the 11th century, the dynasty first ruled Savoy and Piedmont, then the Kingdom of Sardinia and finally the Kingdom of Italy.

Vittorio Amedeo III, king of Sardinia (1773–89)

1847 Sardinia and Piedmont join forces

1857 Garibaldi settles on Caprera and then buys part of the island

| 1800 | 1820 | 1840 | 1860 |

1826 Alberto La Marmora's *Voyage to Sardinia* published

Tomb of Carlo Emanuele IV of Savoy, Cagliari

Alberto La Marmora

1861 Sardinia, together with Piedmont, becomes part of Kingdom of Italy

Sardinia and a United Italy

Industrialization in Sardinia began to make progress after unification: in 1871 the first railway line was built and the mines in Sulcis and Iglesiente became fully operational. The first daily newspapers were founded and Nuoro became the centre of a cultural movement that included the Nobel Prize-winning novelist Grazia Deledda. In World War I the heroism of the Brigata Sassari emerged as a symbol of the island's new confidence, and led to the foundation of the Partito Sardo d'Azione political party in 1921. Between the wars the mining industry continued to develop, and the town of Carbonia was founded in 1938. A wide-ranging programme of land reclamation and artificial lakes – such as Lake Omodeo, created by a dam on the Tirso river – was carried out, significantly altering the health of previously malarial areas. On 31 January 1948 the island became an autonomous region of Italy.

The Monteponi mine
A 19th-century print shows the huge plant at this important Sardinian lead and zinc mine.

The crowd consisted of the social groups suffering most from the high cost of living.

Carbonia
In 1938 Mussolini himself inaugurated the newly built town of Carbonia *(see p75)*. The town was meant to become the leading mining centre in Sardinia.

Brigata Sassari
The brigade consisted entirely of Sardinians. They distinguished themselves in World War I by their heroism, winning two gold medals of honour.

Emilio Lussu (1890–1975) This author recorded his World War I experiences in the Brigata Sassari in *Un anno sull'altopiano* (One Year on the Plateau).

1871 Writer Grazia Deledda is born

1889–1899 Arrival of army task force to combat rampant banditry in Sardinia

1897 First ever special restrictive laws passed in Sardinia

1870   **1880**   **1890**   **1900**

1889 The first daily newspaper in Sardinia, *Unione Sarda*, is founded

Quintino Sella, Minister of Finance in 1862, 1865, 1869–73

1891 Political writer Antonio Gramsci born in Ales

Antonio Gramsci

The Cagliari-Arbatax Railway

As part of a unified Italy, Sardinia embarked on a programme of modernization. The first railway lines were laid in 1871; by 1881 Cagliari and Sassari were linked by rail. The line connecting Cagliari and Arbatax passes through lovely scenery and is now an attractive tourist route *(see pp96–7)*.

The strikers attacking the customs and excise office to protest against the bread tax.

The Dam on the Tirso River

This dam, 70 m (230 ft) high, with a 40-m (130-ft) drop, was begun in 1918, creating Lake Omodeo. At 20 km (12 miles) long, it was the largest artificial lake in Europe of its time.

The Cabras Marsh

The marsh, extending over 20 hectares (49 acres), is one example of the wide-ranging land reclamation schemes carried out in Sardinia. These public works freed the island from malaria, paving the way for the development of a tourist industry.

The Strike In Cagliari

At the turn of the century, social conflict and tensions were so strong in Sardinia that the first special restrictive laws were enacted. The unrest of miners at the Buggerru mine on 3 September 1904 led to the first general strike in Italy. In 1906, distress at the high cost of living led to a wave of riots in Cagliari which were brutally repressed; ten people died and many others were injured.

1915–18 The Sardinians make a significant contribution to the war effort

1924 The "billion lira law" finances vast public works programme in Sardinia

Flag of the Region of Sardinia

1943 Allied bombings seriously damage Cagliari

1910   1920   1930   1940

1921 Partito Sardo d'Azione founded

1926 The Sardinian writer Grazia Deledda wins Nobel Prize

1938 Mussolini founds mining town of Carbonia

1948 Sardinia declared an Autonomous Region

Modern Sardinia

The reclamation of Sardinia's coastal marshes was crucial to the modern development of the island. Sardinia's lovely coastline, abandoned and shunned for millennia, could now be developed and seaside resorts built. New luxury villas and holiday villages sprang up, and the Costa Smeralda, or Emerald Coast, became world-famous as an exclusive holiday area. Reclaimed land could also be used for agriculture for the first time, and market gardens and orchards could be planted. The economy has started to shift as a result. Sheep-rearing is on the decline, while industry and services are developing, sometimes adversely affecting the environment. Sardinia at present appears to be at a crossroads, modern life competing with the most precious resource: unspoilt nature and habitat diversity.

1972 The first mines are abandoned, signalling the decline of the Sardinian mining industry

1979 Revolt of terrorists in maximum security prison on island of Asinara

1980 The Caprera National Park is founded

1971 The Cagliari football team of star striker Gigi Riva wins the Italian championship for the first time

1974 The oil crisis in the Middle East damages the Sardinian petrochemical industry

1962 Antonio Segni, a Christian Democrat from Sassari, is elected President of the Italian Republic

1950	1960	1970	1980

1950	1960	1970	1980

1956 Sardinia starts receiving television broadcasts from RAI, the Italian state TV

1970 Pope Paul VI visits Sardinia

1971 Industrial workers outnumber farmers for the first time

1979 Cases of kidnapping increase: well-known Italian singer/ songwriter Fabrizio De André and his wife Dori Ghezzi kidnapped

1953 First island kidnapping at Orgósolo, marking the beginning of one of Sardinia's most serious postwar problems, one which has fortunately decreased in recent years. Vittorio de Seta's film on Sardinian banditry was awarded a prize at the 1961 Venice Film Festival

1962 Creation of the Costa Smeralda syndicate, promoted by Karim Aga Khan (above), which triggers development in the Costa Smeralda and a consequent tourist boom in north-eastern Sardinia. That same year a law is passed with the aim of stimulating all business sectors

1985 Francesco Cossiga from Sassari, former Prime Minister and Home Secretary, is elected President of the Italian Republic

1950 No Sardinian cases of malaria, for the first time. The American Rockefeller Foundation's public health programme eliminates the *Anopheles maculipennis* mosquito, which transmits the disease

1972 Enrico Berlinguer from Sassari (centre) elected secretary of the Italian Communist Party, a post he holds until his death (1983), promoting a "third way to socialism" and the "historic compromise" between Communists and Christian Democrats

1989 Fires, mostly cases of arson, kill ten tourists on the northeastern coast

2001 Gold Mines of Sardinia and the Homestake Mining Company of California agree to open up Sardinia's gold deposits. The metal was first detected in the 1980s, when traces were discovered in streams

2002 The euro replaces the lira, becoming Italy's new currency

2006 Luxury tax on second homes, yachts and private aircraft introduced for non-residents

2000 Together with tourism, the livestock industry (cattle breeding, dairies, tanning) is the leading force in the island's present-day economy

2011 The Italian president, Giorgio Napolitano, visits Sardinia as part of the celebrations of 150 years since the unification of Italy

1990	2000	2010	2020
1990	2000	2010	2020

1990 Sardinia struck by a terrible drought

1995 The mining industry crisis worsens; the Sulcis coal mines are put up for sale

2009 Ugo Cappellacci is elected president of Sardinia, defeating Renato Soru

2004 Renato Soru, founder of successful ISP Tiscali SpA, is elected president of Sardinia

2000 The island's marinas, especially those at Porto Cervo, are rated among the best in the entire Mediterranean

SARDINIA AREA BY AREA

Sardinia at a Glance

Famous mostly for its sea and coastline, Sardinia also abounds in spectacular natural scenery and numerous archaeological ruins. Prehistoric nuraghi are scattered throughout the island, from Su Nuraxi to Orroli, Santu Antine and Silanus. Besides the Costa Smeralda, northern Sardinia is dotted with Romanesque churches in the Logudoro and Gallura countryside. In the Barbagia region and the eastern coast, which are dominated by the large Gennargentu National Park *(see pp86–7)*, the maquis vegetation reigns in the isolated valleys and on inaccessible hilltops. The south and west have interesting Punic ruins (Nora, Sant'Antioco, Tharros), as well as a relatively wild and undiscovered western coastline.

Ardara's Romanesque church, Santa Maria del Regno *(see p160)*

Flamingoes wintering in the marshes around Oristano *(see pp138–9)*

The impressive ruins of Tharros *(see pp136–7)*

The rugged coast near Buggerru *(see p72)*

◀ The quayside at La Maddalena, principal town of the Maddalena archipelago

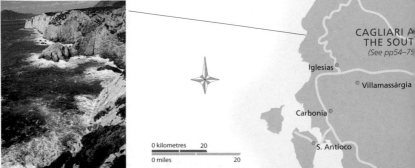

Tr
d'Ag

Porto Torres

Sassari

Alghero

Bosa

Mac

THE WESTERN COA
(See pp116–41)

Tramatza

Oristano

S. Nicolo
d'Arcidano

Sanlu

**CAGLIARI A
THE SOUT**
(See pp54–7

Iglesias

Villamassárgia

Carbonia

S. Antíoco

0 kilometres   20

0 miles   20

Porto Cervo

Arzachena

Golfo Aranci

Olbia

THE NORTH AND
THE NORTH AND
THE COSTA SMERALDA
(See pp142–69)

Oschiri

Alà dei Sardi

Siniscola

Orosei

Nuoro

Ottana

CENTRAL
SARDINIA AND
BARBAGIA
(See pp98–115)

Arbatax

Nurallao

THE EASTERN
COAST
(See pp80–97)

S. Priamo

Sestu

Cagliari

Capo Testa lighthouse near Santa Teresa di Gallura,
on the north coast *(see pp148–9)*

Wild moufflon in the woods of central Sardinia
(see pp26–7)

Part of the route around the island followed by the
Trenino Verde (little green train, *see pp96–7*)

View of Cagliari, the ancient Roman city of Kàralis, capital of the region of Sardinia
(see pp58–65)

CAGLIARI AND THE SOUTH

Southern Sardinia has a varied landscape, with tall sand dunes along the coast, marshland where pink flamingoes build their nests and abundant maquis where rare Sardinian deer still survive. It is also an area of interesting prehistoric sites, such as Nora and Su Nuraxi, and it was once the mining heartland of the island.

The mining history of the area dates back to 5000 BC, when the island's inhabitants discovered how to extract and smelt copper and silver. The Phoenicians used the area as a base for trade and shipped local ores across the Mediterranean. In the Middle Ages the Pisans brought new wealth to the region with expansion of the silver mines. During the Fascist era, Mussolini exploited the island's coal in an attempt to make Italy self-sufficient.

Today, after years of decline, the industrial buildings of the Sulcis and Iglesiente areas are being converted into tourist attractions with mines and museums to visit. The area's natural beauty merges with the 19th-century mining buildings, which look like Gothic castles among the maquis.

The island's capital, Cagliari, was founded by Phoenician sailors, but it was the Aragonese who left the most enduring mark. The Spanish fortification, or Castello district, still dominates today's city. North of Cagliari lies the Campidano plain, bordered by prickly pears and eucalyptus. This has long been Sardinia's "bread-basket", but farm labour now combines with factory work, especially around Cagliari. In the uplands to the east are the ruins of Sardinia's largest prehistoric site, Su Nuraxi, chosen for its vantage point over the surrounding plains.

The islands of San Pietro and Sant' Antioco are separate from the mainland culturally as well as geographically: the towns of Calasetta and Carloforte are inhabited by the descendants of Ligurian coral fishermen who were held hostage in North Africa by Muslim pirates and, once freed, were offered a home on the islands. Today, their dialect, cuisine and traditions remain little changed.

Volcanic rock framing Cala Fico (Fig Bay)

◀ The ramparts of Bastione San Remy in old Cagliari

Exploring Cagliari and the South

The southwestern coast is one of the most unspoiled on the island, with undisturbed coves and beaches. Few roads run along the coast, so the best way to explore is by sea or on foot. Inland, the wild maquis of the rugged Iglesiente and Sulcis terrain contrasts with the derelict 19th-century industrial buildings of this former mining area. In the north, excavations at Su Nuraxi have revealed a complex nuraghic settlement. Cagliari offers the city's sights and a wildlife sanctuary in the salt flats, and is also a good base for the ancient site of Nora.

18th-century walls at Carloforte on the island of San Pietro

Sights at a Glance

Key

━━━ Major road
━━━ Secondary road
═══ Minor road
━━━ Scenic route
╍╍╍ Main railway
─── Minor railway
△ Summit

0 kilometres   10

0 miles   10

For additional map symbols *see back flap*

Las Plassas hill with its castle

Cagliari's tourist marina at Poetto, at the foot of the Sella del Diavolo (Devil's Saddle)

Getting Around

The state railway (Trenitalia) offers services to towns in the Campidano plain along the Cagliari-Oristano line. The local railway, Ferrovie della Sardegna, connects Cagliari to Mandas. Coaches will take you almost everywhere. The roads are usually winding, except for those in the Campidano plain and the dual carriageways (statali) SS130 and SS131.

❶ Cagliari

The city's sheltered position, tucked into the Golfo di Cagliari, has long made Cagliari an important harbour. The Phoenicians chose the eastern shore of Santa Gilla lagoon in the 8th–6th centuries BC, as a stopover for trade ships en route between the Lebanon and the Iberian peninsula. Kàralis ("rocky city") soon became one of the leading Mediterranean centres of trade. The city's present appearance was the work of the Pisans, who developed the Castello district. Local inhabitants, who could only enter the city during the day, lived in the walled villages of Stampace and Villanova. These fortifications were demolished in 1862 and the areas are now part of the city. Modern-day Cagliari, capital of the region, is flanked on three sides by sea and marshes and has only expanded northwards.

Arcaded 19th-century buildings on Via Roma

Exploring Cagliari

For those arriving by sea, the elegant boulevard of Via Roma, parallel to the quay and lined with 19th-century buildings and long arcades, is the first view of the city. During the day crowds throng along this busy shopping street, stopping at the cafés to relax and chat. Stretching out behind are the narrow streets and alleys of the old Marina district. Formerly inhabited by fishermen and merchants, this area is now filled with trattorias and rustic taverns as well as shops selling antiques and local food and handicrafts. Heading northeast from Via Roma, Largo Carlo Felice is a wide, tree-lined avenue dating from the mid-1800s, with a statue of Carlo Felice, the viceroy of Sardinia (see pp44–5).

City's coat of arms

🏛 Palazzo Comunale

Via Roma. **Tel** 070 67 71.
📞 Call 070 677 72 35/6.

At the corner of Via Roma and Largo Carlo Felice is the Palazzo Comunale (town hall). Built in the early 20th century in Neo-Gothic style, the building was restored after World War II. Its façade is decorated with double lancet windows and turrets. Paintings by Filippo Figari and Giovanni Marghinotti hang in the Sala della Rappresentanza, and in the Sala del Consiglio Comunale depicting key moments in Sardinain history.

🏛 Bastione San Remy

Terrazza Umberto I.
Built in the late 19th century over the Spanish ramparts, the bastions can be reached from Piazza Costituzione up a

Sala del Consiglio Comunale, Palazzo Comunale

stairway that leads to a wide terrace, Terrazza Umberto I (also accessible from Porta dei Leoni if the stairway is closed). From here, there is a magnificent view over the seafront to the surrounding marshes.

🏛 Roman Amphitheatre

Viale Sant'Ignazio. **Tel** 338 277 47 90.
Open currently closed for restoration; check the website for details of reopening. 🅦 **anfiteatroromano.it**

Northwest of the city centre is the most significant evidence of Roman Cagliari. The 2nd-century AD amphitheatre was hewn out of the rock, in the style of Greek theatres. Circus acts with wild beasts were performed here, as well as naumachiae, popular recreations of naval battles. A canal system made it possible to fill the arena with water.

Much of the brick masonry collapsed during the Middle Ages and stone was taken from the tiers to build the Castello district. Of what remains, still visible are the cavea, the pit that held the wild beasts, the corridors behind the tiers and underground passageways, as well as some of the tiers where the spectators sat.

The ruins of the 2nd-century AD Roman amphitheatre

🏛 Orto Botanico

Viale Sant'Ignazio 13. **Tel** 070 675 35 12. **Open** Apr–Oct: 8:30am–6pm Mon–Fri; Nov–Mar: 8am–1:30pm Mon–Fri. 🌐 🎫 (070 675 35 22). ♿

South of the amphitheatre, the Botanic Gardens extend over an area of about 5 hectares (12 acres). Founded in 1865, the gardens contain over 500 species of tropical plants from the Americas, Africa, Asia and the Pacific, as well as from the Mediterranean region.

The Orto Botanico is full of small caves such as the Grotta Gennari, used to cultivate ferns because of its ideal temperature and high levels of humidity. There are also remains of Roman tunnels, constructed to improve the water supply to the gardens, a Roman gallery and a well.

🏛 Cathedral

Piazza Palazzo. **Open** 8am–noon, 4–7pm daily. **Museo del Duomo**: Via Fossario 5. **Tel** 070 68 02 44. **Open** 4:30–7:30pm Tue–Fri, 10am–1pm & 4:30–7:30pm Sat & Sun. 🌐 **museoduomodicagliari.it**

Cagliari's Cathedral of Santa Maria was built by the Pisans in the 11th and 12th centuries. Gradually transformed over the

The Baroque marble interior of the Cathedral of Santa Maria

centuries, particularly with 17th-century additions, today's façade is the result of radical restoration in the 1930s, which reinstated the original Romanesque style.

Four lions guarding the entrance date from this period. Inside, Santa Maria retains much Baroque decoration, as well as some original detail. Close to the entrance are two pulpits by Mastro Guglielmo, sculpted in 1162 for the cathedral of Pisa and donated to Cagliari by the Tuscan city. A marble basin for holy water is decorated with the image of an angel.

Holy water basin detail

A crypt under the altar houses the tombs of the princes of the House of Savoy. In the chapterhouse, paintings include a *Flagellation of Christ* attributed to Guido Reni. The **Museo del Duomo** (Treasury) displays precious church items such as chalices and amphoras, as well as a large gilded silver cross.

VISITORS' CHECKLIST

Practical Information
Road map C6. 🚗 177,000.
🛈 Molo Sanità (338 649 84 98).
🚌 Sun, Sant'Elia district (general). 🎉 1 May: Sant'Efisio Feast Day. 🌐 **cagliariturismo.it**

Cagliari Town Centre

① Roman Amphitheatre
② Orto Botánico
③ Villa di Tigellio
④ Bastione San Remy
⑤ Cathedral
⑥ Cittadella dei Musei
⑦ Torre dell'Elefante
⑧ Exma
⑨ San Saturnino
⑩ Palazzo Comunale

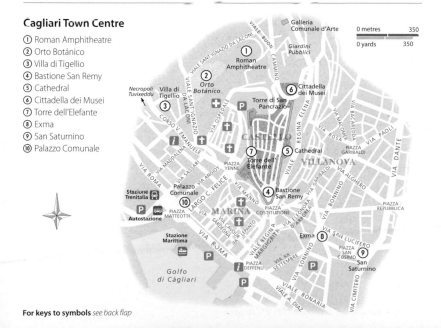

For keys to symbols *see back flap*

Street-by-Street: Castello

The Castello district, the oldest part of Cagliari, was built by the Pisans and Aragonese. Positioned at the top of a hill, and protected by ancient city walls, it consisted of aristocratic mansions and the city's Cathedral. With time its function as a centre of power waned, and the elegant buildings gradually deteriorated. At the centre of the district is Piazza Palazzo with the Palazzo Arcivescovile (Archbishop's Palace) and the Cathedral. Surrounding the ancient citadel, imposing watchtowers dominate the entrance gates, and parts of the fortifications have been transformed into a museum complex and an esplanade.

★ Cathedral
Santa Maria Cathedral, rebuilt several times, combines Pisan, Aragonese and Baroque features. The multi-coloured marble interior has fine sculptures (see p59).

★ Cittadella dei Musei
This modern complex, converted from the former Savoyard arsenal, houses the city's most important museums (see p62).

Palazzo Arcivescovile

PIAZZA PALAZZO

VIA MARTINI

PIAZZA ARSENALE

VIA D

Torre di San Pancrazio
The northern gate of the Castello district was built in 1305 by Giovanni Capula. It is dressed on three sides with limestone ashlar, while the inner face is open, exposing the stairs and wooden balconies of the interior.

Via La Marmora
A number of craft workshops and antique shops line the characteristic Via La Marmora.

★ Bastione San Remy
In the early 1900s the Spanish defensive walls were transformed into the bastions of San Remy, opening out onto a wide esplanade with spectacular views.

Porta dei Leoni
The gate that leads into the lower Marina district owes its name to the two Romanesque lions' heads (leoni) above the arch.

| 0 metres | 50 |
| 0 yards | 50 |

Palazzo Boyl
Overlooking the bastions of San Remy, this palazzo was built in 1840. It incorporates the remains of the Torre dell'Aquila (Eagle's Tower), one of the large Pisan towers that stood over the entrance gates of the ancient city.

Key

 Suggested route

Torre dell'Elefante
The "Elephant's Tower" was built by local architect Giovanni Capula in 1307. The mechanism for opening the gates is still visible and an elephant statue, after which the tower was named, can be seen on the façade.

Cittadella dei Musei, the modern complex in the Castello district

Cittadella dei Musei

Piazza Arsenale. 🖳

At the northern end of the Castello district is this modern museum complex. Fashioned from the former royal arsenal which had been built on the site of the Spanish citadel, the complex houses the Museo Archeologico Nazionale, the Museo Civico d'Arte Orientale Stefano Cardu and the Pinacoteca Nazionale.

🏛 Museo Archeologico Nazionale

Cittadella dei Musei, Piazza Arsenale.
Tel 070 65 59 11. **Open** 9am–8pm
Tue–Sun. 🈂 🕭

The National Archaeological Museum is devoted to the history of Sardinia. The ground-floor exhibits are arranged in chronological order, from the Neolithic era to the Middle Ages; the other floors are organized by archaeological site. In the Neolithic hall are fine alabaster statues of female divinities, including one in the shape of a cross from Senorbi. Objects from the late Bronze Age include axes with raised edges. There is an exceptional collection of nuraghic bronze figurines *(see pp36–7)*, found in the Tempio di Teti at Abini. The collection includes votive swords decorated with the head of a deer, a tribal chief or a warrior. In the third hall is a statuette of a musician playing the Sardinian flute, the *launeddas (see p94)*.

The Phoenician and Roman periods are represented by objects found mostly at sites around Cagliari, Tharros and

Nora. These include jewellery and amulets, small coloured glass heads and terracotta votive statuettes. Among the loveliest pieces of jewellery are an embossed golden bracelet and gold earrings from Tharros.

The Early Christian pieces, such as jugs, lamps and gold jewellery, give an insight into the island's medieval culture, and influences from Byzantine, Vandal and Moorish invaders.

🏛 Museo Civico d'Arte Orientale Stefano Cardu

Cittadella dei Musei. **Tel** 070 65 18 88.
Open 10am–6pm Tue–Sun (to 8pm mid-Jun–mid-Sep). 🈂

The Museum of Oriental Art exhibits most of the 1,300 objects donated to the city in 1917 by Stefano Cardu, a Sardinian who served at the court of the King of Siam. The collection includes imperial gold and silver objects, ivory statues and vases, mostly dating from the 11th century.

🏛 Pinacoteca Nazionale

Cittadella dei Musei. **Tel** 070 67 40 54.
Open 9am–8pm Tue–Sun. 🈂 🈂 (buy
ticket at the Museo Archeologico). 🕭

The entrance to this three-storey gallery is on the upper floor. Here, 15th- and 16th-century

paintings include Catalan and Sardinian altarpieces, like the *Annunciation* by Juan Mates (1391–1431), *Sant'Eligio* by the Master of Sanluri (early 16th century), and *Nostra Signora della Neve* (1568) by Michele Cavaro.

The middle floor houses 17th- and 18th-century paintings and reveals the original Spanish fortification wall (1552–63). The lower floor features the restored *Retablo di San Cristoforo*, rescued from the Chiesa di San Francesco di Stampace, which was damaged by lightning in 1871.

🏛 Galleria Comunale d'Arte

Giardini Pubblici, Viale Regina Elena.
Tel 070 67 77 598. **Open** 10am–9pm
Mon, Wed–Sun (to 6pm mid-Jun–mid-Sep). 🈂 🈂 🕭 🈂

The Municipal Art Gallery has a collection of significant works by Sardinian artists from the late 19th century to the 1970s. On the ground floor are works by Francesco Ciusa. The first floor features contemporary art.

🪦 Necropoli Tuvixeddu

Via Falzarego. **Open** Mar–Sep:
8am–sunset.

The hundreds of underground burial chambers of the Punic necropolis, west of the Botanical Gardens, are overgrown with brambles. The funerary paintings on the tombs, however, are worth a visit, especially the *Tomba del Guerriero* (Warrior's Tomb) and the *Tomba dell'Ureo*.

🪦 Grotta della Vipera

Viale Sant'Avendrace. **Tel** 070 41 108 or
070 6771. **Open** 9am–5pm Tue–Sun.

One of the tombs in the necropolis is that of Atilia Pomptilla, wife of Cassius Philippus, exiled here in the 1st century AD. Two snakes adorn the façade of the "viper's cave" and on the walls are inscriptions in Greek and Latin.

Marble sarcophagus (4th century AD) from the Archaeological Museum

The early Christian church dedicated to San Saturnino, patron saint of Cagliari

🏛 Subterranean Cagliari

Viale Sant'Ignazio. **Tel** 070 66 30 52.
Open for conducted tours only; see
🌐 cagliaritour.com

In the area below the Roman amphitheatre, the hospital and the Orto Botanico there are underground chambers and passageways cut out of the rock by the Phoenicians. The most spectacular of these is the vast chamber named after King Vittorio Emanuele II. From the Casa di Riposo in Viale Fra Ignazio, it is accessed via a dingy stairway which leads into the eerie chamber. The walls, around 2,500 sq m (26,900 sq ft), are covered with thick facing to protect them from the humidity.

The Phoenician underground chamber, "Vittorio Emanuele II"

🏛 Villa di Tigellio

Via Tigellio. **Closed** to the public.
Situated southeast of the Botanical Gardens, Villa di Tigellio is a group of three aristocratic Roman villas and baths dating from the Imperial era. The first house has a *tablinum*, the room used to receive guests, which opens onto the central atrium.

🏛 Exma

Via San Lucifero 71. **Tel** 070 66 63 99
Open 9am–1pm, 4–8pm Tue–Sun
(Jun–Sep: 9am–1pm, 5–9pm).

On the eastern side of the Castello district stands the former municipal slaughterhouse, built in the mid-19th century and closed in 1964. The dark red building, decorated with sculpted heads of cows, has been restructured to house the city's arts centre.

A cow's head on the Exma building

The centre's cultural calendar offers temporary exhibitions of photography, painting and sculpture, as well as courses for children and adults. Classical music concerts are held in the courtyard in the summer and in the auditorium in the winter.

🏛 San Saturnino

Piazza San Cosimo. **Tel** 070 201 03 01.
Open for Mass (11am Sun) and by arrangement May–Oct. ♿

East of the Exma building is the church of San Saturnino, also known as Santi Cosma e Damiano. Reopened after 18 years of restoration, and still not completely refurbished, this simple church is one of the oldest Christian buildings on the island. It was begun in the 5th century to commemorate the martyrdom of Saturno, the city's patron saint.

In the Middle Ages, San Saturnino, together with its adjacent monastery, became an important religious and cultural centre. The Greek cross plan of the church was enlarged in the 11th century by French Victorine friars from Marseille, who built three aisles with barrel vaults. Inside, a marble ex voto holds the oldest representation of San Saturno.

Glass windows have been placed in the sturdy tufa construction to prevent further damage and decay from humidity and air, and this has given the church a rather modern appearance. Nonetheless, it is still a fascinating place to visit.

The Marshes and Salt Flats

A network of marshes and lakes extends around the outskirts of Cagliari, particularly along the western shore of the bay. The vast lagoon of the Santa Gilla marsh stretches over 4,000 hectares (9,800 acres), including the ancient Macchiareddu salt flats. These saltworks are now the only ones in operation in the area. After years of neglect and environmental deterioration, the marshy areas around Cagliari have finally become reserves, and the area once again has a rich and varied fauna. To the east of the city, the Molentargius marsh is a favourite refuge for migratory birds. At least 170 species have been identified here, which is one-third of the entire bird population of Europe. Between August and March, flamingoes attract dozens of naturalists. Since 1993 these creatures have begun once again to nest along the banks of the Molentargius marsh.

A Naturalist's Paradise
In autumn the marshes are filled with migratory birds and are a favourite with bird-watchers.

The Saltworks
Of the numerous saltworks that once operated around Cagliari, only those in the Macchiareddu industrial area are still active.

Macchiareddu Salt Flat

Fishing port of Giorgino

Stagno di Santa Gilla

Nesting Grounds
In recent years, flamingoes have begun to use the marshes as a nesting ground again.

Key
- ▬ Major road
- ▬ Minor road
- 🔲 Salt flat
- 🔲 Marsh

Wildlife of the Marshlands

Many migratory and endemic bird species populate the marshes around Cagliari. These feed upon the small creatures, such as the brine shrimp *Artemia salina*, which thrive in the salt-rich water. As well as the colony of flamingoes, which sometimes exceeds 10,000, you will also see many other species of water birds such as blackwinged stilts, avocets, cormorants and teals. The waters of Macchiareddu salt flats, on the other hand, are populated by mallards, coots and pintail ducks, which hunt peacefully among the islets and inlets.

Flamingo

Blackwinged Stilt

Avocet

Cormorant

Teal

Cat's-tail flowers

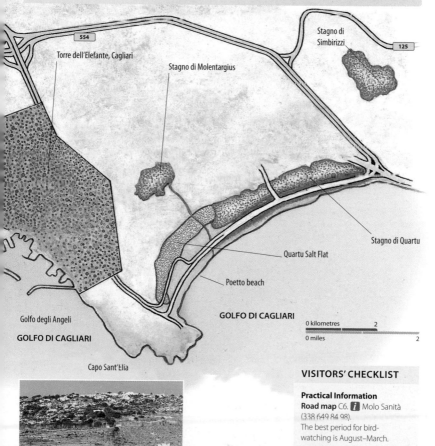

554

Torre dell'Elefante, Cagliari

Stagno di Molentargius

Stagno di Simbirizzi

125

Stagno di Quartu

Quartu Salt Flat

Poetto beach

Golfo degli Angeli

GOLFO DI CAGLIARI

GOLFO DI CAGLIARI

0 kilometres   2

0 miles   2

Capo Sant'Elia

Molentargius Marsh
This is an ideal stopping place for migratory birds from Africa.

VISITORS' CHECKLIST

Practical Information
Road map C6. 🛈 Molo Sanità (338 649 84 98).
The best period for bird-watching is August–March.

Transport
🚌 P from Via Roma for Poetto; 8 for Santa Gilla.

The Romanesque church of Santa Maria at Uta

❷ Uta

Road map C6. 🔼 7,000. 🚌 🚆
ℹ️ Via Umberto I (070 96 66 02 01).
🎭 26–31 Aug: Santa Lucia.

The flourishing agricultural town of Uta is situated at the edge of the Campidano plain, a vast fertile corridor that stretches northwards from Cagliari to Oristano. On the outskirts of town is the church of **Santa Maria**, built in 1140 by French Victorine friars from Marseille. The façade is made of light-coloured stone, with blocks of a darker hue, and is decorated with blind arches and a small bell gable. Sculptures of human heads, deer, calves and geometric patterns adorn the arches.

Environs:
The village of **San Sperate**, 8 km (5 miles) northeast of Uta, is a living museum with murals, and sculptures by local artist Pinuccio Sciola.

🏛 **Santa Maria**
Via Santa Maria. **Tel** 070 96 82 16.
Open by appt only.

❸ Sanluri

Road map C5. 🔼 9,000. 🚌 🚆
ℹ️ Piazza Mazzini 74 (070 937 05 05).
🎭 10 Aug: San Lorenzo.
Ⓦ prolocosanluri.it

An important town in the Campidano plain, Sanluri grew up around the 14th-century castle of Eleonora d'Arborea (*see p40*). This stronghold changed hands several times before it was taken by the Aragonese in 1409. The massive square structure has towers on its four corners and an ornate wrought-iron gate.

Today the castle is owned by the Villasanta family and houses the **Museo Risorgimentale Duca d'Aosta**. The historical exhibits include fine furniture such as a 16th-century bed. A sculpture of San Michele (St Michael) stands in the entrance hall. On the upper floor is the **Museo della Ceroplastiche** in which there are 343 pieces of wax from 1500 to 1800.

In the restored 16th-century Convento dei Cappuccini (still a working monastery), on a hill overlooking the town, the **Museo Storico Etnografico** displays a collection of tools and archaeological finds.

🏛 **Museo Risorgimentale Duca d'Aosta**
Castello di Eleonora d'Arborea.
Tel 070 930 71 05 (morning), 070 930 71 07 (afternoon). **Open** May–Sep: 9am–1pm, 4–8pm daily; Oct–Apr: 9:30am–1pm, 3:30–7pm daily.
📷 📹

🏛 **Museo Storico Etnografico**
Via San Rocco 6. **Tel** 070 930 71 07.
Open by appt only. 📷 📹 ♿

❹ Serri

Road map C4. 🔼 810. 🚌 🚆
ℹ️ Via Municipio 1 (0782 80 50 09);
Pro Loco, Via Roma 36 (0782 80 51 42).
🎭 Third Sun of Sep: Santa Lucia.

This sheep-farming centre lies on the edge of a rocky plateau dominating the Trexenta hills. Right on the spur of the promontory is the **Santuario Nuragico di Santa Vittoria**, one of Sardinia's most fascinating nuraghic sites. The archaeological ruins here have yielded some important bronze votive statuettes, now housed in the Museo Archeologico Nazionale in Cagliari (*see p62*).

Pilgrims came here to worship the God of Water at the sacred well. The temple well, which is in an excellent state of preservation, is reached via 13 amazingly precise basalt steps. A short walk from the entrance leads to the *Recinto delle Feste* (festivities area). This elliptical building has a porticoed courtyard surrounded by rooms for the pilgrims. This is possibly a predecessor of the many rural sanctuaries (*cumbessias* or *muristeni*) found today in Sardinia's country churches.

Wax statue in Sanluri's Museo della Ceroplastica

🏛 **Santuario Nuragico di Santa Vittoria**
7 km (4 miles) NW.
Tel 0782 80 51 42/43.
Open by appt only.

A modern mural in the village of San Sperate

The 16th-century parish church of the Beata Vergine Assunta at Sàrdara

❺ Sàrdara

Road map C5. 🗻 5,000. 🚌
ℹ️ Town Hall (070 93 45 02 00).
🎭 22 Sep: Santa Maria is Acquas.

Situated at the northern edge of the Campidano plain, the town of Sàrdara lay on the border between the medieval principalities of Arborea and Cagliari *(see pp40–41)*. Stone houses from this period, with large arched doorways, have been preserved in the district around **San Gregorio**. This Romanesque church was built in the 6th century. Its tall, narrow façade, however, shows the initial influence of Gothic architecture. On the western outskirts of town is the 16th-century parish church of **Beata Vergine Assunta**, interesting for its sculpted columns and arches, and vault patterned with stars.

Near the Assunta church are the remains of a nuraghic well-temple. This underground chamber, from the 9th–10th centuries BC, has walls of basalt and limestone and a domed ceiling. Also known as the *Funtana de is Dolus* (fountain of pain), it is where worshippers came to take the curative spring waters. The source of the temple water was an ancient underground well, and a canal carried the mineral water from the spring to the temple. Decorated earthenware votive objects found in the temple are now in the Museo Archeologico Nazionale in Cagliari *(see p62)*.

Sàrdara is also famous for its carpet-weaving and woollen and cotton tapestries. These are colourfully embroidered with traditional animal and floral decorative motifs.

Environs

Ruins of the medieval **Castello di Monreale**, a fortification of the principality of Arborea, stand on a hill 1 km (half a mile) southwest of town. A little further west are the remains of the **Aquae Neapolitanae**, Roman baths, and nearby is the Gothic church of **Santa Maria is Acquas**, where a festival takes place in September.

❻ Villanovaforru

Road map: C5. 🗻 730. 🚌
ℹ️ Piazza Costituzione (070 93 31 009). 🎭 15 Jul: Santa Marina
🌐 comune.villanovaforru.ca.it

This agricultural centre was founded in the 1600s by the Spanish and has retained much of its original layout. Many houses have kept their decorative features. Today, the Monte Granatico building (formerly a grain store), in the town's central square, houses a small but well-run **Museo Archeologico**. Finds from the nearby nuraghic site of Genna Maria are on display, including bronze, iron and ceramic objects from the 9th century BC on the ground floor. On the first floor are votive items dedicated to Demeter and Persephone from the Roman era.

Environs

On the road to Collinas, 1 km (half a mile) west of the town, is the nuraghic village of **Genna Maria**. Discovered in 1977, the site, which is still being excavated, is on a prominent hilltop. This nuraghe has a typical design *(see pp40–41)*. Thick walls with three towers form a triangle which encloses a central tower and courtyard with a well. Another wall with six corner towers surrounds the entire village area.

🏛 **Museo Archeologico**
Piazza Costituzione. **Tel** 070 930 00 50. **Open** 9:30am–1pm, 3:30–6pm (Apr–Sep: to 7pm) Tue–Sun. ♿ & 🔲

🏛 **Genna Maria**
1 km (half a mile) W. **Tel** 070 930 02 32. **Open** 9:30am–1pm, 3:30–7pm (2:30–5pm Oct–Mar) Tue–Sun. ♿ 🎧 call in advance. 🔲

The Saffron of Sardinia

The production of Sardinian saffron, prized throughout Europe, is based around San Gavino in the Campidano plain. Saffron is obtained by drying the dark red stigma of *Crocus sativus*, a purple flower that carpets the barren fields in autumn. The harvest, however, is very brief as the stigmas must be collected the day the flower comes into bloom. Saffron, once considered as precious as gold, was used to make dyestuff for fabrics and rugs, as a colouring agent for sweets and as a spice for savoury dishes. It is still used in today's cooking *(see p182)*.

Saffron

Crocus flowers

❼ Su Nuraxi

Excavations east of Barùmini have brought to light the largest nuraghic fortress in Sardinia, Su Nuraxi. The original settlement dates from 1500 BC, during the Middle Bronze Age. Built on a hill, the 19 m (62 ft) high fortress occupied an excellent vantage point, with clear views over the surrounding plains. In the 7th century BC, with the threat of Phoenician invasion, the central section of the fortress, consisting of a tower connected to four external nuraghi, was further protected by a thick outer wall with turrets and a sentinel's walkway. The village gradually developed outside the main fortifications with single- and multi-room dwellings, including a flour mill and bakery. The area was inhabited for almost 2,000 years although, after the Carthaginian conquest, the upper parts of the fort were demolished and the site lost its strategic importance.

Single dwellings
The oldest living quarters were circular with a single room.

Defences
In order to defend themselves from Carthaginian invasions, the Nuraghic inhabitants built an outer bulwark. This consisted of seven towers connected by a wall with a walkway for sentinel patrols.

KEY

① **The circular assembly hall** was built against the outer wall. During meetings the elders sat on a long stone bench that ran along the inside of the wall. Objects found here are held in Cagliari's archaeological museum (see p62).

② **The outer wall** was added in the 7th century BC.

③ **The "keep"**, or central section, was the highest part and the centre of military operations.

④ **The four main towers** were connected by a central courtyard.

⑤ **Sentinel's walkway**

Multi-room Dwellings
These living areas were made up of seven or eight square or trapezoidal rooms which opened onto a courtyard or vestibule, often with a well.

Building Techniques
Huge irregular blocks of stone, laid in "dovetail" fashion without mortar, were used to build the nuraghi. The inner walls of the towers were often reinforced by another wall of stone.

Northeastern Tower
The outer corner towers of the fortress were pierced by a double row of radially arranged fissures through which light could penetrate.

The Village
The dwellings were built outside the fortress walls between the 8th and 6th centuries BC. There were about 200 circular houses with roofs made from wooden beams and branches.

❽ The Piscinas Dunes

The hills of sand at Piscinas and Is Arenas ("the sands" in Sardinian) are "moving" dunes, sometimes as much as 50 m (164 ft) high, that rise up around the estuary of the River Piscinas. Wind erosion by the mistral, the cold north wind that blows in from France, continually changes the landscape, while strongly rooted pioneer plants work their way across the sand. The robust roots of marram grass *(Ammophila arenaria)* gradually stabilize the dune slopes, which are then covered by other salt-resistant plants such as juniper and lentiscus. This unique ecological niche is also the habitat for many animals, and footprints of foxes, wild cats, partridges and rabbits are a common sight on the sand. Remains of the 19th-century mines that were once the mainstay of the Sulcis regional economy are also still visible.

Piscinas beach
The sandy beach at Piscinas is 7 km (4 miles) long. Exposed to the strong mistral wind in winter, the shape of the beach is continually changing.

Marine turtles
The isolated position of Piscinas makes it an ideal spot for loggerhead turtles to lay their eggs.

The Sardinian partridge favours sunny habitats. It was introduced from North Africa by the Romans.

Le Dune di Ingurtosu Hotel
This hotel overlooking the sea shore occupies an old restructured mine building *(see p176).*

The wild lily, though slim and delicate, manages to bloom and survive even in arid environments.

The sand, shaped by the wind, is an ever-changing landscape.

Tracks of wild animals can often be seen in the sand, particularly in the morning.

Mine railway
A section of the 19th-century narrow-gauge railway, once used to transport material from the mines to the sea, has been reopened near the beach.

Marram grass
This strongly rooted, perennial plant, *Ammophila arenaria*, is typical of sandy environments.

Wild rabbits are a common sight on the dunes. You may also come across other small animals such as foxes and lizards.

The sand dunes
Areas of the dunes are covered in thick maquis vegetation.

Exterior of San Nicola di Mira, at Gùspini, with its large rose window

❾ Gùspini

Road map: B5. 🏔 14,000. 🚌
ℹ️ Town Hall, Via Don Minzoni 10 (070 97 60). 🎉 15–31 Aug: Santa Maria. 🅦 comune.guspini.vs.it

Overlooking the flat and fertile Campidano plain, Gùspini is surrounded by olive groves and backed by the gradually rising foothills of Monte Arcuentu. The 17th-century church of **San Nicola di Mira**, in the main square, boasts a large rose window and is the hub of local life. The feast day of Santa Maria is celebrated with a procession and horse race.

The rose window of San Nicola di Mira

The **Montevecchio mine**, 8 km (5 miles) west, was one of the largest in Europe until the 1950s. Despite the state of abandon, the miners' houses, headquarters, church, school and hospital are worth a visit. There are guided tours of the mine and the office building as well as an exhibition on the life of the miners in the past.

🏛 **Montevecchio mine**
8 km (5 miles) W of Gùspini. **Tel** 070 97 31 73. **Open** days vary with season; check website. 🅿️ 🎟 every 30 mins from Piazzetta di Montevecchio. 🅦 minieramontevecchio.it

❿ Arbus

Road map: B5. 🏔 8,000. 🚌
ℹ️ Town Hall, Via XX Settembre (070 773 86 80). 🎉 13 Jun: Sant' Antonio; 21 Aug: Santo Lussorio Palio (horse race) 🅦 comune.arbus.ca.it

Granite houses characterize the village of Arbus, set on the slopes of Monte Linas. Arbus is known for the production of traditional knives with curved blades, *arrasoias*.

Southwest down the N126 for 7 km (4 miles), then due west across a winding mountain road, is the mining village of **Ingurtosu**, built by the French firm Pertusola. Once home to over 1,000 mine workers, the houses, office building and church are now abandoned. The pine forest surrounding the dilapidated buildings was planted by the mine workers.

A dirt road runs among the old mines, abandoned buildings and former dumping area as far as Naracauli, where there are ruins of a more modern mine complex built shortly after World War I. A train once transported the extracted lead and zinc to the sea, where it was loaded onto ships. Certain sections of the narrow-gauge track and some carriages can be seen on the Piscinas beach.

Stretching northwards from the dune beach of Piscinas is a maquis-covered coast aptly called the Costa Verde. A quiet, scenic road follows the coastline, offering spectacular views of the sea. The road goes as far as the resort of Marina di Arbus, with easy access to sandy beaches.

The large tanks at the Montevecchio mine

⓫ Temple of Antas

Road map B5. **Open** 9:30am–5:30pm daily 🚌 to Fluminimaggiore 🛈 Via Vittoria Emanuele (0781 58 09 90).

First discovered in 1966, the ancient Temple of Antas is believed to have been a sacred nuraghic site. It was adopted by the Carthaginians in the 4th century BC and dedicated to the deity Sid Addir Babài. A century later the Carthaginians restructured the building with an atrium and a central chamber. The temple was decorated with Egyptian and Ionic symbols.

In the 3rd century AD, the Romans rebuilt the temple using some of the existing material, such as the Ionic capitals of the columns. This temple was dedicated to the god and "creator of Sardinians", Sardus Pater. Although only six of the columns remain standing today, the temple's isolated position amid the wild maquis makes it an enchanting place to visit.

Environs
In the fertile valley of the River Mannu, 9 km (5 miles) north, is the small agricultural village of **Fluminimaggiore**, founded in the 18th century. Turning west towards the sea for 9 km (5 miles), the road proceeds to **Portixeddu beach**, protected by extensive sand dunes. The headland of Capo Pecora offers stunning views of the coast.

The old mining community of Buggerru, now a tourist resort

⓬ Buggerru

Road map B5. 🔺 1,500. 🚌.

Situated in a valley opening out onto the sea, Buggerru was founded in the mid-18th century in an area rich in mineral deposits. It soon became a flourishing mining town with a small theatre where opera singers used to perform, and the headquarters of the French *Société Anonyme des Mines de Malfidano*. In the lower part of the town, sculpture by Pinuccio Sciola *(see p66)* is dedicated to the miners who died in the strikes of 1904. The mines are now closed, but some of the abandoned tunnels and caves can still be seen.

Today, the town has been reclaimed as a harbour for pleasure boats, the only one between Carloforte and Oristano. The docks, where boats were once loaded with local minerals for export, now serve as a port for visitors to the wild western coast of the island and its long stretches of sandy, sheltered beaches. To the south is the long and secluded **Cala Domestica**, a rocky bay overlooked by a Spanish watchtower.

⓭ Iglesias

Road map B5. 🔺 30,000. 🚌 🚉 🚗 Easter Week 🌐 comune.iglesias.ca.it

Iglesias, or Villa Ecclesiae, was founded in the 13th century by Count Ugolino della Gherardesca (mentioned in Dante's *Inferno* XXXIII). The Pisans had conquered the area in 1257 and reopened mines abandoned in Roman times. Silver was extracted, and the city had the right to mint its own coins. In the

---

Temple of Antas

This plan shows how the later Roman temple incorporated the 3rd-century BC Carthaginian temple. The rectangular plan and six columns of the pronaos, the enclosed portico leading to the temple chamber, are still visible. An architrave above the entrance supported a triangular pediment and steps led up to the temple.

The columns, 8 m (26 ft) high, were made of smooth limestone blocks placed on bases about 1 m (3 ft) wide.

The capitals were in the Ionic style but are atypical, lacking the abacus and volutes.

Pronaos

Columns

Steps

The Roman temple was built over the Carthaginian temple.

The Easter procession during Holy Week at Iglesias

The Sulcis Mines

The history of Sardinia's mines is inextricably linked with the island's economic development. Ancient rock formations, particularly in the southwestern region of the island known as Sulcis, have left rich mineral deposits of silver, copper, lead, iron and zinc. Nuraghic people are known to have had metalworking skills and there is evidence of Phoenician and Roman mines. In the short-lived boom of 19th-century industrialization, the mines stood like citadels in a predominantly agricultural country. Today, the dream of prosperity through mining is vanishing, and all that remains is a rich heritage of mining architecture and culture.

Entrance to an abandoned mine

The area around Iglesias is the mining heart of Sardinia, and the landscape descending to the sea has been deeply scarred by mine working. At Monteponi the industrial plants, mine shafts and miners' houses look as though they were only recently abandoned, while at Masua, tunnels and railways are still visible. At Buggerru, the Malfidano mine, exploited for eight centuries, opens onto the sea front.

mid-19th century Iglesias grew into an important mining centre.

Today, the ruins of the mine buildings, most of which have been abandoned, create a striking contrast with the well-preserved historic centre. The elegant pedestrian shopping street, Corso Matteotti, leads to Piazza del Municipio and the Palazzo Vescovile (Bishop's Palace), built in 1785. On the west side is the 19th-century Palazzo del Comune (Town Hall) and opposite is the cathedral of **Santa Chiara**. Completed in the late 17th century, the cathedral has a Romanesque façade dating from 1288.

The narrow, winding streets around the cathedral are lined with two-storey buildings adorned with wrought-iron balconies. **San Francesco** on Via Don Minzoni was built between the 14th and 16th centuries and has side chapels dedicated to noble families. Half an hour's walk from Piazza Sella is the **Castello di Salvaterra**, built in 1284 as part of the city's medieval defensive walls. A part of these walls is also visible in Via Eleonora d'Arborea.

During Easter week, holy processions and performances of mystery plays take place in the town (see p30).

Environs

At Case Marganai, 10 km (6 miles) northeast of Iglesias, the **Linasia Botanical Gardens** extend over an area of 9 sq km

Romanesque portal of Santa Chiara, Iglesias

(3 sq miles) with several examples of plants from the maquis. The **Museo Casa Natura** here also has a collection of local plants and an exhibit of pieces from the local mine shafts. Guided tours of local mines are organized by the **Società Igea**. One tour takes in the lead and zinc Monteponi mine, with the elegant Bellavista building and Sella shaft. The Santa Barbara mine is also worth visiting; the shaft has unusual crenellated walls, which give it the appearance of a medieval castle.

🌼 Linasia Botanical Gardens
Località Marganai. **Tel** 0781 220 97. **Open** by appt only; phone Ente Foreste, 070 27 991. 🚿 🚻 **Museo Casa Natura**: **Tel** 0781 220 97. **Open** by appt; phone in advance.

⛏ Società Igea
Località Campo Pisano. **Tel** 0781 49 13 00 or 348 154 95 56. 🚿 🚻 phone in advance. 🌐 igeaspa.it

⓮ Costa di Masua

Road map B5. 🛈 (0781 311 70).

The corniche road between Fontanamare and Masua, 12 km (7 miles) north, follows a wild and splendid coastline. At Masua, the little beach of Porto Flavia is overlooked by pillars of eroded limestone and, offshore, the unmistakable profile of Pan di Zucchero ("sugarloaf") island. This sheer rock rises 132 m (433 ft) from the sea. At Nebida you can see the abandoned mines of the industrial archaeological area.

A panoramic path along the coast leads to the abandoned remains of La Marmora mine buildings and shafts.

The craggy limestone mass of Pan di Zucchero, jutting out from the sea

⑮ Island of San Pietro

Named after the apostle Peter, who is said to have taken refuge here during a storm, the island of San Pietro was virtually uninhabited until 1736, when Carlo Emanuele III offered it to a community of Ligurian coral fishermen whose ancestors had been exiled to the island of Tabarca, off the Tunisian coast. San Pietro's Ligurian origins can be seen in the architecture, dialect and cuisine, which also bears traces of North African influences. The rugged coast, inhabited by the rare Eleonora's falcon, has spectacular coves that can be reached only by sea. The island is covered in thick maquis vegetation.

VISITORS' CHECKLIST

Practical Information
Road map B6. 🚹 7,000. 🛈
Corso Tagliafico 1, Carloforte
(0781 85 40 09). In August book
a ferry. The Laguna and Sir
Lawrence motor boats at
Carloforte offer trips around the
island. 🎭 end Apr: Sagra del
Couscous; 29 Jun: San Pietro.

Transport
🚢 Saremar from Calasetta or
Portovesme. 🌐 saremar.it

Cala Fico
Walls of silver rock on one side and brown rock on the other enclose this sheltered inlet.

Cala Vinagra

Montagna di Ravenna

Capo Sandalo
The westernmost point of the island, dominated by a lighthouse, is frequently exposed to the mistral wind.

Monte di Gasparro

La Caletta

0 kilometres 2
0 miles 2

La Caletta
Protected from rough seas by Punta Spalmatore, the sheltered bay of La Caletta has a white, sandy beach.

Punta delle Colonne
The name, Cape of Columns, refers to the trachytic stacks that jut out from the sea.

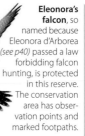

Eleonora's falcon, so named because Eleonora d'Arborea *(see p40)* passed a law forbidding falcon hunting, is protected in this reserve. The conservation area has observation points and marked footpaths.

Isola Piana

La Punta In September, for a couple of days only, local fishermen open their homes and feed visitors.

Carloforte
The only town on the island, Carloforte overlooks the port, with alleys and stairways descending to the water. The centre of social life is Piazza Carlo Emanuele III. The San Pietro feast day procession of boats is also worth watching.

Salt flats on the outskirts of Carloforte attract a large number of migratory birds.

Key

— Major road
═ Minor road
▨ Salt flat
— River

Carbonia's Piazza Roma, a typical example of Fascist architecture

⑯ Carbonia

Road map B6. 🚹 34,000. 🚌
🛈 Town Hall, Piazza Roma (0781 69 41). 🖥 **comune.carbonia.ci.it**

Carbonia, located in the mining region of Sulcis, was founded by Mussolini in 1936. The town has retained its Fascist town planning and architectural conception, with imposing buildings and broad streets that converge at the central Piazza Roma. The town's most important public buildings are found here, including the Town Hall, the Torre Civica tower and the parish church of San Ponziano.

Villa Sulcis, the former residence of the director of the mines, has become the **Museo Archeologico**. On display are earthenware and bronze statuettes and jewels from local *domus de janas*, and finds from the archaeological sites at Monte Sirai.

The **Museo Martel** has a collection of fossils dating back 600 million years.

Environs
West of Carbonia along the SS126, a signposted road leads to the imposing hill occupied by the Monte Sirai archaeological site. The stunning view alone is worth the visit, as you can see the islands of Sant'Antioco and San Pietro. The fortified **Parco Archeologico Monte Sirai** was built by the Phoenicians in 750 BC. The thick outer wall protected the acropolis and the surrounding garrison town, which could house 500 foot soldiers and 100 mounted soldiers. The ruins of this ancient military camp were discovered in 1963 and excavations are still under way.

The necropolis, northwest of the main citadel, is mainly Carthaginian, but there is a Phoenician section with common graves, as well as an area of Punic tombs.

🏛 **Museo Archeologico**
Villa Sulcis, Viale Arsia. **Tel** 0781 63 512. **Open** Apr–Sep: 10am–7pm Tue–Sun; Oct–Mar: 10am–3pm Wed–Sun.

🏛 **Museo Martel**
Grande Miniera di Serbariu. **Tel** 0781 66 21 99. **Open** Apr–Sep: 10am–2pm, 3–7pm Tue–Sun; Oct–Mar: 10am–3pm Wed–Sun.

🏛 **Parco Archeologico Monte Sirai**
3 km (2 miles) S of Carbonia. **Open** Apr–Sep: 10am–7pm Tue–Sun; Oct–Mar: 10am–3pm Wed–Sun.

Underground burial chambers in the necropolis of Monte Sirai

⑰ Calasetta

Road map B6. 🚹 2,800. 🚌 🛥
🛈 0781 885 34.

The second largest village on the island of Sant'Antioco *(see p76)* and a trading port for Carloforte, Calasetta was founded in 1769 to house the Ligurian fishermen arriving from the Tunisian island of Tabarca. The straight streets with their two-storey houses lead to the main square. Here, the parish church has a bell tower of Arab derivation. The road heading south along the western coast offers a panoramic view of alternating cliffs, coves and beaches.

Urns that held the ashes of babies in the Tophet outside Sant'Antioco

⑱ Sant'Antioco

Road map B6. 🗻 13,000. 🚌
🛈 Town Hall (0781 80 301); Pro Loco,
Piazza Repubblica 41 (0781
82 031). 🎭 2nd Mon after Easter:
Sant'Antioco; 29 Jun: San Pietro
🌐 comune.santantioco.ca.it

Sant'Antioco is the main town on
the island of the same name. The
island is connected to Sardinia
by a causeway and remains of a
Roman bridge are still visible
from the road. The *faraglioni*,
two large menhirs, stand on one
side. According to legend these
are the petrified figures of a nun
and a monk, turned to stone as
they tried to elope.

The town was founded by the
Phoenicians in the 8th century
BC and named Sulki. It soon
became a major port in the
Mediterranean, due to the
trade in minerals, including
gold, extracted from the area.
Ptolemy, the Greek astronomer,
gave it the name of *insula
plumbaria* (island of lead). The
Carthaginians used the port
during the second Punic War
(*see p38*), but this alliance was
harshly punished by the
victorious Romans. Under the
Roman Empire the town
flourished, until continuous
pirate raids during the Middle
Ages led to its gradual decline.

The picturesque town centre
climbs away from the sea and its
characteristic houses have small
wrought-iron balconies. The
main street, **Corso Vittorio
Emanuele**, is shaded by an
avenue of trees. Above the town
is the church of **Sant'Antioco**,
built in the 6th century with a
Greek cross plan and central
dome, but modified in the 11th
century. According to tradition
the remains of the island's
patron saint, Sant'Antioco, are
buried in the catacombs,
reached via the transept. The
body of the martyr is said to
have floated here after he was
killed by the Romans in Africa.
Some catacombs are open
to the public. The chambers
are less than 2 m (6 ft)
high and some are
decorated with frescoes.

The **Museo
Archeologico** contains
Phoenician and Roman
earthenware, jewels
and other objects found
in the area, including
urns from the nearby
Tophet necropolis.

The **Museo
Etnografico** is housed
in a former winemaking
plant. The large central hall
contains kitchen equipment
used to make cheese and
cultivate grapevines. The
weaving section has spindles
and looms on show, once used
for the processing of wool and
byssus, a fine filament taken
from the *Pinna nobilis,* the
largest bivalve mollusc in the
Mediterranean. Under the
arcade outside, original winemaking equipment and
implements used for raising
livestock are on display.

Dominating the town is the
red stone **Castello Sabaudo**,
rebuilt by the Aragonese in
the 16th century. Just outside
town, on a cliff overlooking
the sea, the bleak **Tophet** is
a Phoenician sanctuary and
necropolis. This burial ground
was used for the ashes of still-
born babies, or those who died
shortly after birth. Nearby is the
Carthaginian **Necropolis** with
about 40 underground family
tombs. This area was later used
by the Romans for the ashes of
their dead. The tombs occupy
the upper part of town and
were used as catacombs during
the Early Christian period.

Fresco in the catacombs of Sant'Antioco

🛈 **Sant'Antioco**
Via Necropoli.
Tel 0781 830 44. Catacombs:
Open 9:30am–noon, 3–5pm
Mon–Sat. 🎫 📷

Cala Domestica, north of Sant'Antioco (*see p72*)

🏛 Museo Archeologico
Piazza Sabatino Moscati.
Open 9am–7pm daily. 🐾 📷 ♿
🌐 **archeotur.it**

🏛 Museo Etnografico
Via Necropoli. **Open** 9:30am–1pm,
3–6pm daily (summer: 9am–8pm).
🐾 ♿ 🌐 **archeotur.it**

🏠 Tophet
Piazza Sabatini Moscati. 🛈 Archeotur
(0781 800 596). **Open** 9am–7pm
daily. 🐾

⑲ Tratalìas

Road map B6. 🚹 1,182. 🚌

This village in the Sulcis
region was the seat of the
diocese until 1413. The façade
of the Pisan Romanesque
cathedral of **Santa Maria**,
consecrated in 1213, is
divided horizontally by a row
of little arches surmounted by
a rose window. The tympanum
is curious, in that the last
section of a stairway juts out
from it.

The sides and apse
are decorated with
pilasters and
blind arches.
Inside, the three
naves
are separated
by large
octagonal
pillars. An altar-
piece from
1596 depicts St
John the Baptist and St John
the Evangelist with the
Madonna and Child.

Cathedral of Santa Maria, Tratalìas

⑳ Santadi

Road map C6. 🚹 4,100. 🚌
🛈 0781 94 201. 🎪 first Sun in Aug:
Matrimonio Mauritano.
🌐 **comune.santadi.ci.it**

Built on the banks of the River
Mannu, Santadi's old town sits
on the higher, north side. Some
traditional architecture made
from rough volcanic rock is still
visible in the medieval centre.
Evidence that the area has been
inhabited since the nuraghic
age can be seen in the copper,
bronze, gold and earthenware
objects found here, which are
now on display in the Museo
Archeologico in Cagliari *(see p62)*.
Local tools and furniture can be
seen at the **Museo Etnografico
Sa Domu Antiga**. The shop here
sells typical Sulcis handicrafts.

Environs
On a plateau southwest of the
town is the 7th-century BC
Phoenician fortress, **Pani
Loriga**. Continuing south
for 5 km (3 miles) are two
caves, **Grotta Is Zuddas**,
with splendid
formations of
stalagmites and
stalactites, and
Grotta Pirosu
(now closed)
where archaeo-
logical finds
such as a votive
lamp and a
Cypriot style tripod were found.
North of Villaperuccio, the
Montessu Necropolis has

*Domus de janas (tomb of giants) at the
necropolis at Montessu*

typical *domus de janas (see p37)*
tombs, some of which still have
traces of the original yellow and
red wall facing. Other tombs
were probably used for worship.

The August festival, Matrimonio Mauritano (Mauretanian
Wedding), is a ceremony that
may have started with the
North Africans who settled here
during the Roman era.

🏛 Museo Etnografico Sa
Domu Antiga
Via Mazzini 37. **Tel** 0781 94 10 10.
Open 9am–1pm, 5–7pm (3–5pm
winter) Tue–Sun.

🕳 Grotta Is Zuddas
Benatzu. 🛈 Cooperativa Monte
Meana (0781 95 57 41). **Open** Apr–
Jun. 11am–12.15pm, 3–6.30pm daily;
Jul–Sep: 10am–2.15pm, 2:30–6pm;
Oct & Mar: tours only, noon & 4pm
daily. 🐾 📷 compulsory.

🏠 Montessu Necropolis
Villa Peruccio, Località Montessu. 🛈
340 232 8331. **Open** 9am–8pm (to
3pm winter). 🐾 📷 🌐 **montessu.it**

Monte Arcosu

The mountains in the Sulcis region are covered with forests of
cork oak, holm oak, strawberry trees and heather, from which
the granite peaks seem to emerge. This area extends for about
7,000 hectares (17,300 acres), interrupted only by a rough road
that connects Santadi and Capoterra along the Mannu and
Gutturu Mannu river valleys. There are plans to make the area
into a National Park: the World Wide Fund for Nature (WWF)
has purchased 300 hectares (741 acres) of land on the slopes
of Monte Arcosu to protect the Sardinian deer, which roamed
the entire island until 1900, but is now restricted to a few isolated
areas. Other forest mammals include fallow deer, wild cats, boar
and martens. Among the birds found here are the golden eagle,

Stag in the Monte Arcosu reserve

peregrine falcon and goshawk. This nature reserve is open all year and visitors can stay overnight
in refuges. There are well-marked nature trails as well as unmarked wild walks, although an official
WWF guide is obligatory in some areas. The Cagliari-based Cooperativa Quadrifoglio (070 96 87 14)
has information regarding accommodation and trekking. To reach the reserve, take the road east
from Santadi along the Gutturu river.

The sheltered beach at Baia Chia

㉑ Baia Chia

Road map C6. **i** 070 923 50 15.

The Southern Coast (Costa del Sud) is an area of high sand dunes and white beaches that extend as far as the Capo Spartivento headland. Junipers grow in the sand and there is marshland frequented by egrets, purple herons, grebes and other migratory aquatic birds. There are plans to turn the area into the centre of a regional nature reserve.

Along the coastal road, the hamlet of Chia is a popular tourist destination set among orchards and fig trees. A rough road leads to the sheltered bay of Chia, flanked on one side by the 17th-century **Torre di Chia**, and on the other by red cliffs covered with maquis vegetation. At the foot of the

tower it is possible to visit the remains of Phoenician **Bithia**. This ancient city, mentioned in the writings of Ptolemy and Pliny the Elder, had been covered by the sea for centuries and has not yet been completely excavated.

Remains of a Punic and Roman necropolis are visible, as are the ruins of a temple probably dedicated to the god Bes. Earthenware pots and amphorae from the 7th century BC have been discovered in the sand, and traces of Roman wall paintings and mosaics decorate porticoed houses. Ancient Punic fortifications can be seen near the base of the watchtower and an elliptical cistern has also been found.

🏛 Bithia
Domus de Maria, Località Chia.
Open at all times.

Environs
Along the coast as far as the promontory of Capo Spartivento, where there are spectacular views, is a series of bays, dunes and pine forests that can be reached on foot.

The Roman theatre at Nora dating from the 2nd century AD

㉒ Nora

Road map C6. **i** 070 920 91 38.
Open 9am–sunset daily. 🎫 combined ticket with Museo Archeologico. 🖼
♿ 📧 🌐 coptur.net

Founded under Phoenician rule in the 9th–8th centuries BC, the ancient city of Nora was built on a spit of land jutting out to sea. The town became the island's main city, a role it continued to enjoy under the Romans.

Repeated Saracen raids and the lack of fertile land finally forced the inhabitants to abandon the city in the Middle Ages; the three ports were gradually covered up by the incoming sea, resulting in the legend of the submerged city.

The ruins extend to the headland of Capo di Pula, dominated by the Spanish **Torre del**

The promontory of Capo Spartivento overlooking the southern coastline

Coltelazzo. An impressive vestige of the Carthaginian city is the Temple of Tanit, goddess of fertility. Little else remains of the Punic period, although rich findings in the tombs testify to active trading.

Left of the entrance are the 2nd–3rd-century AD Terme di Levante, Roman baths decorated with mosaics. Nearby is a 2nd-century AD theatre, the only one in Sardinia, and the large rectangular Forum behind it. South of the theatre, the mosaics in the *frigidarium* and *caldarium* of the baths are decorated with white, black and ochre tesserae. Paved roads and the city's sewage system are also still visible.

Many finds, including Punic inscriptions in which the name of the island of Sardinia is first mentioned, are kept in Cagliari's Museo Archeologico Nazionale *(see p62).*

Some earthenware objects found at the site are on display in the small **Museo Archeologico Patroni**. The nearby Romanesque church of **Sant'Efisio**, built by French Victorine monks in the 11th century, is the site of an annual procession from Cagliari *(see p30).*

Ⅲ Museo Archeologico Patroni
Corso Vittorio Emanuele 67.
Tel 070 920 96 10.
Open Apr–Oct: 9am–7:30pm daily; Nov–Mar: 9am–dusk daily. 🗝 combined ticket with Nora. (no flash). 📷

The tower of Poetto, between Quartu Sant'Elena and Cagliari

㉓ Quartu Sant'Elena

Road map C6. 🏙 66,000. 🚌
🚉 Cagliari. ✈ Elmas. 🛈 070 860 11.
🎪 14 Sep: Sant'Elena

Situated on the outskirts of Cagliari, Quartu Sant'Elena has grown to become one of the island's largest cities. It lies at the edge of the salt flats and marsh of the same name which are a favourite breeding and nesting ground for flamingoes.

The medieval church of **Sant'Agata** stands in the town's main square, Piazza Azuni. From here Via Porcu leads to the **Casa Museo Sa Dom 'e Farra**, literally "the house of flour". This large country house, converted into a museum, features over 14,000 traditional farm and domestic tools and equipment collected over the years by Gianni Musiu, a former

Golden pen found at Nora

shepherd. Each of the museum's rooms is dedicated to different farm activities: displaying saddles and leather harnesses to wagons and blacksmiths' bellows. One of the more curious objects is the snow-cooled icebox. Gathered in the Barbagia region, the snow was taken to Cagliari on muleback and kept cold in large straw lined containers stored underground.

The farmstead consisted of the owner's home and living quarters for farm labourers. Other rooms around a large courtyard were used for various domestic and farm activities such as milling, bread-making and tool repair.

A bus ride southwest of Quartu Sant'Elena brings you to the beach resort of Poetto, a favourite with local people.

Ⅲ Casa Museo Sa Dom 'e Farra
Via Eligiu Porcu 143. **Tel** 070 81 23 40.
Closed for restoration.

Foresta dei Sette Fratelli

The Forest of the "Seven Brothers" was named after the seven peaks that can be seen from Cagliari and which tower over the holm oak forests and maquis. Run by Ente Foreste Sardegna (070 279 91), the forest covers an area of 4,000 hectares (9,800 acres), replanted with pine, eucalyptus and cypress trees, and reaching an altitude of 1,023 m (3,355 ft). It is also one of the few areas inhabited by the rare Sardinian deer, now almost extinct. The mountain has many mule trails, once used by coal merchants; one of these footpaths begins at the forest headquarters at Campu Omo on the SS125. To drive into the mountains take a right turn past the Arcu 'e Tidu pass on the SS125.

Densely wooded Foresta dei Sette Fratelli, which extends over seven hills

THE EASTERN COAST

Mile after mile of pastures and rocks characterize the interior of eastern Sardinia, falling away to inaccessible cliffs on the coast, refuge for the rare monk seal. The coastline of the Golfo di Orosei is now part of the Parco Nazionale del Gennargentu, a vast nature reserve founded to protect golden eagles and moufflon.

There are no towns of any great size along the eastern coast but there are some good seaside resorts around Arbatax and Villasimius. Except for a few stretches, the road runs inland, so that most of the beaches can be reached only after walking a long way or by driving on dirt roads. The largest towns are Orosei, Muravera and Dorgali, also situated in the interior at a certain distance from the coast. The historical reasons for this go back to the endemic malaria that afflicted the island until after World War II and, before that, the constant pirate raids which plagued the coasts for centuries. This is still unknown Sardinia, the interior the domain of shepherds and their flocks, and the southeast yet to be discovered by tourism. The region of Sarrabus used to be isolated because of the absence of negotiable roads. The only way of reaching it was via a narrow-gauge railway from Cagliari, which followed the contours of the valleys. It is still in operation, and offers a delightful opportunity to take a trip back into the past. Sarrabus today attracts visitors who prefer to stray from the beaten track. Further north, the Ogliastra region, with its sandy beaches which vary from pearly grey to a startling reddish colour, has rugged mountains and hills where time seems to have stood still, pastoral life has not been invaded by the 21st century and strong traditions survive. The Baronie region, in contrast, has the towns of Siniscola and Orosei, with good public transport systems and a fast modern motorway, making the area more accessible.

The alluvial plain around Posada, seen from the Castello della Fava

◄ Hikers in Su Gorroppu gorge in Gennargentu National Park, Nuoro

Exploring the Eastern Coast

Splendid natural scenery and prehistoric archaeological sites around Dorgali and Orroli are the main attractions of the eastern coast. The cliffs along the coast are steep, and the most secluded coves in the Golfo di Orosei (Cala Sisine, Cala Luna, Cala Goloritze) are most easily reached by boat. The alternative is a lengthy walk, best tackled in hiking boots. The countryside is marvellous however, and the trek rewarding. The main road winding through the region is the Orientale Sarda. There is a proposal – supported by the local people but vehemently opposed by environmentalists – to widen this road into a fast access motorway.

A glimpse of the Golfo di Orosei, near Baunei

0 kilometres   10
0 miles   10

Sights at a Glance

2 Arbatax
3 Santa Maria Navarrese
4 *Gennargentu National Park pp86–7*
5 Dorgali
7 Orosei
8 Galtellì
10 Siniscola
11 Posada
12 Lanusei
13 Jerzu
14 Gairo

15 Barì Sardo
16 Muravera
17 Villasimius
18 Orroli
19 Perdasdefogu

Tours

1 The Orientale Sarda Road
6 Codula di Luna
9 Monte Albo Tour
20 *A Trip on the Trenino Verde pp96–7*

Key

▬▬ Major road
▬ Secondary road
▭▭ Minor road
▬ Scenic route
⊶ Main railway
— Minor railway
△ Summit

For additional map symbols *see back flap*

Panoramic view of the foothills of Mount Gennargentu

Rocky outcrops of reddish granite at Arbatax

Getting Around

The Orientale Sarda road (SS125) was once famous for being winding and slow to drive. In 2007, works totalling nearly €50 million were completed. There is now a direct dual-carriageway link from Cagliari to Arbatax/Tortolì. There is also a north-south coach service. The Ogliastra plain (Tortolì and Arbatax) is connected to Cagliari by the Ferrovie Complementari della Sardegna narrow-gauge train; the trip takes about eight hours. It is slow, but the line goes through wonderful scenery.

Pisan tower at Orosei

One of the rocky coves on the eastern coast near Cala Luna

❶ The Orientale Sarda Road

Along the eastern peaks of the Gennargentu National Park *(see pp86–7)*, the SS125, or the "Orientale Sarda" route, connects Olbia to Cagliari. The most spectacular stretch is between Dorgali and Baunei, 63 km (39 miles) of winding road hewn out of the rock by Piedmontese coal merchants during the mid-1800s. These "foreigners" carved a road through the remote mountain valleys and felled trees that were sent to the mainland. The deforestation that resulted has proved irreversible.

② **Flumineddu River Valley**
This stretch of the SS125 road goes through rugged terrain with cliffs and a fine view of the Flumineddu river valley under the peaks of Monte Tiscali. There are many places where you can stop to enjoy the wonderful scenery.

③ **Genna Silana Pass**
This is the highest point of the tour at 1,017 m (3,336 ft). Stop here to get a dramatic view of the Gorroppu ravine. A footpath from Pischina Urtaddalà descends to the Flumineddu river bed.

④ **Urzulei**
Built on different levels on the slopes of Punta Is Gruttas, Urzulei was once an isolated town difficult to reach. The stone church of San Giorgio di Suelli dates from the 15th century.

Dorgali

Grotta Del Bue Marino

Golfo Di Orosei

Gennargentu National Park

Codula di Luna

Codula di Sisine

Flumineddu

(Orientale Sarda)

SS125

Key

━━ Major road
═══ Minor road
── River

⑤ **Baunei**
The white houses of this mountain village stand out under the limestone crags.

① Cala Gonone

A 400-m (1,300-ft) tunnel cut out of the limestone rock leads to the popular seaside resort of Cala Gonone. A winding road, with fabulous views of the sea, white rocks and the maquis, continues to the Grotta del Bue Marino where there have been sightings of the rare monk seal (see p23).

0 kilometres 4

0 miles 4

⑥ San Pietro

A rough track with precipitous hairpin bends climbs to a wooded plateau where wild pigs graze. At the end is the Golgo ravine, 295 m (967 ft) deep. A little further along is the 18th-century church of San Pietro. Shepherds still make offerings here and a rural festival takes place on 28–29 June.

The holiday resort of Cala Moresca, at Arbatax

② Arbatax

Road map D4. ⚠ 1,100. ✈ 🚍 🚌
ℹ Pro Loco (0782 69 12 76). 🎉 2nd Sun in Jul: Madonna di Stella Maris

The small town of Arbatax lies on the northern tip of the Bellavista promontory, a red porphyry cliff that plunges into the sea. The port, guarded by a Spanish tower, is the terminus for the narrow-gauge trains arriving from Cagliari. Ferries from Cagliari, Olbia and the Italian mainland also dock here.

This stretch of coast has clear, clean water and enticing coves such as **Cala Moresca**, south of Arbatax. Several tourist resorts now cover this small promontory, such as the popular *Vacanze Club* village, built to resemble a typical Mediterranean village. The solid wood doors and wrought-iron grilles on the windows were taken from the abandoned

The Aragonese tower at Santa Maria Navarrese

village of Gairo (see p93). Further to the south is Porto Frailis, also protected by a Spanish tower, and the long, sandy Orrì beach. From Arbatax footpaths lead up to the lighthouse high on the Bellavista promontory.

③ Santa Maria Navarrese

Road map D4. ⚠ 1,500. ✈ 🚍
ℹ 0782 61 08 23. 🎉 15 Aug: Festa dell'Assunta. 🌐 comunedibaunei.it

This seaside resort was named after the lovely country church around which it developed.

It is said that this three-aisle construction, with a semicircular apse, was built in the 11th century by the daughter of the king of Navarra after she had been saved from a shipwreck.

In the church courtyard is a gigantic wild olive tree that is reputed to be over a thousand years old.

The beautiful beach at Santa Maria Navarrese is bordered by a pine forest and protected by a Spanish watchtower. Opposite this is the huge Agugliastra (or Sa Pedra Longa) rock, a slim limestone pinnacle that rises up 128 m (420 ft) from the sea. Boat services from the little port of Santa Maria Navarrese will take visitors to the stack, as well as to Cala Luna, Cala Sisine and Cala Goloritzè, further up the coast.

The rocky Ogliastra island viewed from Capo Bellavista

For hotels and restaurants in this region see pp176–9 and pp186–9

❹ Gennargentu National Park

The park extends over 59,102 hectares (146,000 acres) of some of the wildest, most mountainous landscape in Sardinia, and includes the island's highest peak, Punta La Marmora. Established in 1989, most of the park lies in the province of Nuoro. There are 14 towns in this protected area, but few tarmac roads, and the steep-sided valleys and bare peaks give the area an isolated air. The unspoilt nature of the park makes it fascinating for walkers, geologists and naturalists alike. The climb up Punta La Marmora (1,834 m, 6,015 ft) is rewarding, and the limestone desert of Supramonte is one of Italy's spectacular sights. Monte Tiscali hides the prehistoric rock village of Tiscali *(see pp108–9)*, and the ravines of Su Gorroppu and the Su Gologone spring are unmissable. The coast to the east, home to the endangered monk seal, is one of Europe's loveliest. When walking, it is advisable to take an up-to-date map and plenty of water.

The Wild Cat
Larger than the domestic cat, the wild cat lives on Gennargentu and Supramonte.

The Mount Gennargentu Massif
In winter the barren peaks and the lower slopes, carpeted in oak and chestnut trees, are sometimes covered by snow.

The Highest Peak in Sardinia: Punta La Marmora

The massif of Gennargentu, whose name means "door of silver", reaches its peak in Punta La Marmora which, at 1,834 m (6,015 ft) above sea level, is the highest point on the island. The landscape here is quite barren and wild. The sky is populated by raptors circling around in search of prey and with a bit of luck you might be able to see, in the distance, small groups of moufflons, or mountain sheep.

Hikers on the top of Punta La Marmora

Refuge

Orgòs

Fonni

Baunei

SS128

Dèsulo

Aritzo

Flumendosa

Sev

0 kilometres 15

0 miles 15

The Crests of Supramonte
The peaks rise to the east of Gennargentu and their slopes descend towards the sea.

VISITORS' CHECKLIST

Practical Information
Road map D4. ℹ 0784 323 07 or 0784 23 88 78; Dorgali Pro Loco, Via La Marmora 108 (0784 962 43); Desulo Town Hall (0784 61 92 11); WWF Cagliari (070 67 03 08).
Ⓦ **wwf.it/sardegna**

Refuge

Dorgali

Codula de Luna

Urzulei

SS125

Baunei

Lago Alto Flumendosa

SS389

Arzana

The Monk Seal
The monk seal *(Monachus albiventer)*, once thought to be extinct, has been sighted again in the Golfo di Orosei. Tourism had been blamed for the fall in population.

Key

━━ Major road
═══ Minor road
━━ River

Tips for Drivers

Ascending Punta La Marmora
From Desulo, follow the road to Fonni for about 5 km (3 miles) until you come to the S'Arcu de Tascusí pass, then take the asphalt road on the right until you reach a fork. Follow the dirt road on the right for 100 m (328 ft) and then take the right-hand road leading to the Girgini holiday farm. Skirt around it by keeping to the left. In a little less than 4 km (2 miles), take the right-hand fork and continue for 5 km (3 miles) until you reach the control cabin for an aqueduct. Leave your car here and follow the road on the right on foot until you reach the end, then proceed up the valley floor on the left until you reach the crest. From here you can continue up to the summit (an hour and a half on foot).

Su Gorroppu
This wild gorge, with its steep sides, can only be scaled by expert climbers.

Displays of exhibits at the Museo Archeologico in Dorgali

⑤ Dorgali

Road map D3. 🏛 8,500. 🚹 Pro Loco
(0784 962 43). 🎭 16–17 Jan: Sant'
Antonio Abate 🕸 **dorgali.it**

The charming town of Dorgali
lies on a ridge that descends
from Monte Bardia and is 30 km
(19 miles) from Nuoro and a
little less than 10 km (6 miles)
from the sea at Cala Gonone.
Dorgali is predominantly an
agricultural centre, but it is also
important for locally produced

Santa Caterina parish church in the
centre of Dorgali

crafts such as leather, ceramics
and filigree jewellery, as well as
rug- and carpet-weaving.

In the old part of town the
buildings are made of dark
volcanic stone. These include
several churches: Madonna
d'Itria, San Lussorio and the
Maddalena. The central square,
Piazza Vittorio Emanuele, is
dominated by the façade of the
parish church, Santa Caterina,
home to a large carved altar.

Dorgali's **Museo Archeo-
logico** contains an important
collection of objects from
nuraghic sites, as well as finds
from sites dating back to Punic
and Roman times. Some of the
finest nuraghic pieces come
from the nearby site of **Serra
Òrrios**. The museum also
provides information on visits
to the rock village of Tiscali,
another major nuraghic site
(see pp108–9). The town is
known for its wine, and the

Nuraghic dwelling at Serra Òrrios

local wine-making cooperative
can be visited. The local dairy is
also of interest.

🏛 Museo Archeologico di Dorgali
Cooperativa Ghivina, Scuola Elemen-
tare, Via La Marmora. 🚹 338 834 16 18.
Open Sep–Jun: 9am–1pm, 3:30–6pm;
Jul & Aug: 9am–1pm, 4–7pm. 🚫 ♿

🔲 Serra Òrrios
🚹 338 834 16 18. **Open** daily
9am–1pm, afternoon hours vary.
🎥 compulsory, on the hour. 🚫

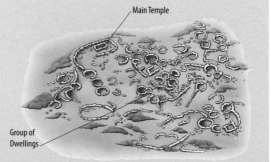

The Nuraghic Village of Serra Òrrios

At Serra Òrrios – about 10km
(6 miles) to the northwest of
Dorgali and 23 km (14 miles) east
of Nuoro – lies one of Sardinia's
best preserved nuraghic villages,
which dates from the 12th–
10th centuries BC. The 70 round
dwellings, each with a central
hearth, are arranged in at least
six groups around large central
spaces with a well. Small places
of worship have also been found
in the village.

Main Temple

Group of
Dwellings

❻ Codula di Luna

A four-hour walk down the "Valley of the Moon" will take hikers from the Supramonte to the sea. The path is straightforward but strenuous, with little shade. The track runs through aromatic maquis scrub, and passes shepherds' huts, as well as the entrances to enormous caves, many of which have not yet been fully explored. It is highly advised that you do not attempt this walk without a local guide.

The beautiful, secluded beach of Cala Luna, backed by a small lake

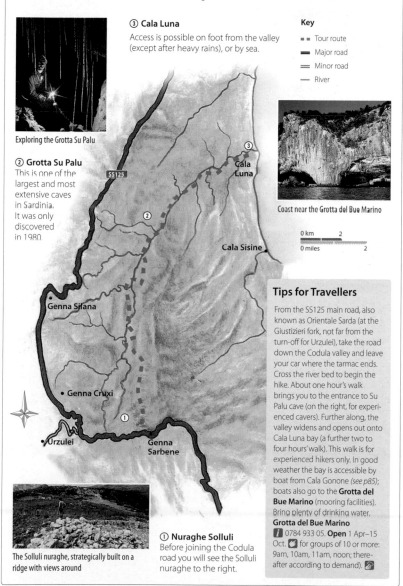

③ **Cala Luna**
Access is possible on foot from the valley (except after heavy rains), or by sea.

Key

- ▪ ▪ Tour route
- ▬ Major road
- ═ Minor road
- — River

Exploring the Grotta Su Palu

② **Grotta Su Palu**
This is one of the largest and most extensive caves in Sardinia. It was only discovered in 1980.

SS125

Cala Luna

Cala Sisine

Coast near the Grotta del Bue Marino

0 km   2
0 miles   2

Genna Silana

Genna Cruxi

Urzulei

Genna Sarbene

① **Nuraghe Solluli**
Before joining the Codula road you will see the Solluli nuraghe to the right.

The Solluli nuraghe, strategically built on a ridge with views around

Tips for Travellers

From the SS125 main road, also known as Orientale Sarda (at the Giustizieri fork, not far from the turn-off for Urzulei), take the road down the Codula valley and leave your car where the tarmac ends. Cross the river bed to begin the hike. About one hour's walk brings you to the entrance to Su Palu cave (on the right, for experienced cavers). Further along, the valley widens and opens out onto Cala Luna bay (a further two to four hours' walk). This walk is for experienced hikers only. In good weather the bay is accessible by boat from Cala Gonone (see p85); boats also go to the **Grotta del Bue Marino** (mooring facilities). Bring plenty of drinking water.
Grotta del Bue Marino
🛈 0784 933 05. **Open** 1 Apr–15 Oct. 📷 for groups of 10 or more: 9am, 10am, 11am, noon; thereafter according to demand). 🚶

The Chiesa delle Anime at Orosei

⑦ Orosei

Road map D3. 🏔 6,000. 🚌
ℹ Pro Loco (0784 99 83 67).
🎭 Easter Week, 26 Jul, San Giacomo.
🌐 orosei-proloco.com

The historic capital of the Baronia region is situated about 5 km (3 miles) inland, and has a bustling, well-kept historic centre with churches, archways and small, white-washed stone buildings over-looking flowered courtyards.

The town of Orosei was probably founded in the early Middle Ages and its golden age occurred under Pisan domination, when it was ruled by the barons of the Guiso family. Orosei developed into an important harbour with moorings alongside the Cedrino river. After yielding to Aragonese rule, the town began to decline as a result of malarial disease, repeated pirate raids and the gradual silting up of

The portal of
Santa Maria 'e Mare

the river. A labyrinth of alleys leads to the central Piazza del Popolo, where three churches stand. At the top of a flight of steps is **San Giacomo Maggiore** with an 18th-century façade and terracotta-tiled domes. Opposite is the **Chiesa del Rosario**, with a Baroque façade, and the **Chiesa delle Anime**, founded by the brotherhood of monks that participates in the Easter Week ceremonies.

Sant'Antonio Abate, once an isolated rural sanctuary, is now surrounded by the expanding town. Local handicrafts are on display in the Pisan tower inside the precincts of Sant'Antonio. The 17th-century Sanctuary of the Madonna del Rimedio, also once isolated, is now part of the outskirts and is surrounded by *cumbessias*, the houses used by pilgrims each September.

⑨ Monte Albo Tour

The massive white limestone ridge that gave this mountain its name (*albo* means white) extends like a bastion between the Barbagia and Baronia regions. There are magnificent panoramic views from the maquis-covered slopes of the mountain. The area is destined to become a reserve to protect 650 plant species as well as moufflons, wild boar and raptors. Part of this tour follows a narrow road along the base of the limestone cliffs.

The Annunziata Sanctuary, Lodè

② Lodè
This small town amid olive trees and maquis is the home of the Annunziata sanctuary, with its whitewashed, red-roofed *cumbessias*. On 22–23 May the sanctuary becomes a pilgrimage site.

③ Bitti
This lively town (*see p104*) lies in pretty countryside surrounded by clusters of oak and wild olive trees.

Key

━ Tour route
═ Other roads
— River

0 kilometres   4
0 miles   4

Environs

Near the mouth of the Cedrino river is **Santa Maria 'e Mare**, founded in the 13th century by Pisan merchants. The church is full of ex votos, and on the last Sunday in May it is the focus of a pilgrimage, when a statue of the Madonna is taken down the river on a boat, followed by a flotilla of boats.

At the mouth of the estuary the river divides into two. The northern part flows into an artificial canal, the southern half feeds the Su Petrosu marsh. This is where to find coots, moorhens, mallards and purple gallinules. The shallows are home to avocets, stilts, grey heron and egrets.

❽ Galtellì

Road map D3. 🏠 2,400. 🚌
ℹ 0784 90 150; Pro Loco, Via Garibaldi 2 (0784 904 /2). 📅 16–17 Jan, Sant'Antonio Abate; 2nd Sat in Aug, Festa dell'Immigrato/Turista.

Lying on the slopes of Monte Tuttavista, Galtellì was the most important town in the region during the Middle Ages. Until 1496 it was the regional bishopric, as can be seen in Romanesque San Pietro, the former cathedral built in the 12th century. After this era the town began to decline thanks to the ravages of malaria and frequent pirate raids, but traces of its glorious past have been preserved in the parish church of Santissimo Crocifisso.

The historic centre is pretty, with its whitewashed buildings and well-kept houses. In August, the town throws a party for all foreigners and tourists living or staying there.

Environs

One of the most interesting sights in this area is Monte Tuttavista. A dirt road and then a footpath take you to Sa Pedra Istampada ("the perforated rock"), a wind-sculpted arch 30 m (98 ft) high. There are splendid views from the summit.

Near the village of La Traversa, 12 km (8 miles) from Galtellì, is the Tomba di Giganti (giants' tomb) of **Sa Ena 'e Thomes**, a very impressive prehistoric monument with a 3-m (10-ft) stele hewn out of a single block of granite.

The Sa Ena 'e Thomes "giants' tomb" near La Traversa

---

① Sant'Anna
This pass is 624 m (2,050 ft) above sea level, and offers splendid scenic views. The road winds up among cliffs, euphorbia bushes and cluster pines.

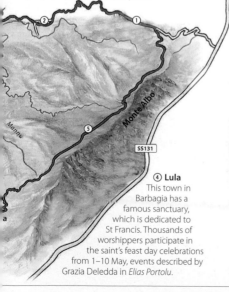

Tips for Drivers

Tour length: 76 km (47 miles). This tour takes about two hours by car, but allow half a day to include the stops.
Stopping-off points: the Sant'Anna roadman's house and the town of Bitti (see p104).

View of Monte Albo

④ Lula
This town in Barbagia has a famous sanctuary, which is dedicated to St Francis. Thousands of worshippers participate in the saint's feast day celebrations from 1–10 May, events described by Grazia Deledda in *Elias Portolu*.

⑤ The road leading up Monte Albo
The 20 km (12 miles) of this hillside road run along the northern slope of the mountain through pastures and maquis. On the right are steep limestone walls streaked with pink.

⑩ Siniscola

Road map D2. 🏔 11,000. 🚌
ℹ 0784 87 08 00. 🎿 18 Aug:
Sant'Elena. 🔲 **comune.siniscola.
nu.it**

Set at the foot of Monte Albo,
the once agricultural town of
Siniscola was an important
trading centre in the 14th
century under the principality of
Gallura *(see p40)*. Since then, the
town has grown in a haphazard
manner around the medieval
centre. On the lively main street,
Via Sassari, the 18th-century
parish church of **San Giovanni
Battista** is decorated with a
fresco cycle representing the
life of St John the Baptist. The
town is also well known for its
local pottery studios.

Environs
A straight road
northeast from
Siniscola leads to
La Caletta, a small
tourist port with a
wide sandy beach,
4 km (2 miles) long.
Heading south-
wards, the SS125
passes the fishing
village of **Santa
Lucia**. Probably
founded by
emigrants from
the island of
Ponza, the
village is guarded by a Spanish
watchtower. Today Santa Lucia
is a popular summer resort, with
a pine forest that extends
behind the beach. Continuing
southwards, a long walk along

The church at Santa Lucia

the shore will take you to the
white sand dunes and juniper
bushes of **Capo Comino** (also
accessible from the SS125).
   The headland of Capo
Comino consists of rounded
rocks and pebble beaches and
is overlooked by a lighthouse.
A two-hour walk along the
seashore and pine forest will
take you to **Berchida beach**,
where there is a huge rock
called *S'incollu de sa
Marchesa* (The
Marquise's Throat).
Eels and grey mullet
populate an area
of marshland here.
   An alternative
excursion is to take
the rough track
that turns right
from the SS125
after the
Berchida river.
Winding
through the maquis it leads
to a splendid white sand beach
and clear blue sea. On the way,
the road passes the remains of
the nuraghic settlement of
Conca Umosa.

Spanish tower at Santa Lucia

⑪ Posada

Road map D2. 🏔 2,600. 🚌
ℹ Via Giuseppe Garibaldi 4
(0784 87 05 00).

Perched on top of a limestone
bank covered with euphorbia
and lentiscus, this village is
dominated by the ruins of
Castello della Fava. The castle
was built in the 12th century
by the rulers of Gallura, who
were later conquered by the
princi-pality of Arborea before
passing under Aragonese
dominion *(see p40)*. In the
Carthaginian era this place was
known as the colony of Feronia.
   The town still retains its
medieval character, with
winding alleyways connected
by steep stairways, arches and
tiny squares. The castle has
had a face-lift, and wooden
steps lead to the top of its
square tower, where there is a
panoramic view of the sea, the
mouth of the Posada river and
the surrounding plain, covered
with fruit orchards.

Environs
Inland, 9 km (5 miles) west of
Posada, is the artificial lake of
Posada. The pine forests and fine
views make this a popular spot.

⑫ Lanusei

Road map D4. 🏔 5,800. ✈ 🚊 🚌
🚌 ℹ Via Roma 98 (0782 47 311). 🎿
22 Jul: Santa Maria Maddalena.

This large, austere-looking
town, situated on a hillside at
600 m (1,926 ft), overlooks the
plain that descends to the sea.

The white sand dunes at Capo Comino

The village of Posada and the Castello della Fava

It was once a health retreat due to its excellent climate, high altitude and the many walking trails in the forest that surrounds it. The town was built on various levels and still has some aristocratic buildings of interest.

⓭ Jerzu

Road map D4. 🏔 3,600. 🚌 ℹ 0782 700 23. 🎊 13 Jun: Sant'Antonio; 25 Jul: San Giacomo; 4 Aug: Sagra del Vino.

Tall, sharp pinnacles of rock, known locally as *tacchi* (high heels), are an impressive sight as they emerge from the maquis on the approach to Jerzu. This modern town is built on several levels up the hillside with houses of two storeys or more overlooking the main street. Steep side streets in the lower quarter lead to older houses that retain many of their original features.

Jerzu's economy is based mainly on viticulture and small vineyards cling to the steep slopes around the town. The area produces about 10,000 tonnes of grapes from which the local wine cooperative makes the good red wine Cannonau DOC, one of the most famous in Sardinia.

The most important holiday is the feast day of Sant'Antonio da Padova, on 13 June. One of the town's churches is dedicated to the saint.

Wine labels from Jerzu

Environs
At Ulassai, 7 km (4 miles) north-west of Jerzu, is the limestone **Grotta Su Màrmuri**. Steps descend to reveal spectacular pools and stalagmites. Wear warm clothes and sturdy shoes.

Grotta Su Màrmuri
ℹ Piazzale Grotta Su Marmuri (0782 798 59). **Open** Apr–Oct. compulsory: 11am, 2:30pm (& more in summer).

⓾ Gairo

Road map D4. 🏔 2,000. 🚌 🚇 ℹ 0782 76 00 00. 🎊 third Sun in Sep: Nostra Signora del Buoncammino.

Gairo Sant'Elena lies in the Pardu river valley, a deep ravine with limestone walls. The present-day village was built after 1951, when Gairo Vecchio had to be evacuated after excessive rain caused a series of landslides. All that remains of the abandoned village are gutted houses without doors and windows. The entire area has spectacular scenery.

Environs
On the coast, the bay of Gairo is protected by a headland covered with maquis. From here you can go to Coccorocci, the only beach with black sand in Sardinia. The coast road runs along the seashore, which is characterized by sandy inlets and cliffs of pink rock.

⓯ Barí Sardo

Road map D4. 🏔 4,500. 🚌 ℹ 0782 28 222. 🎊 29 Aug: San Giovanni Battista; 8 Sep: Nostra Signora di Monserrato.

This agricultural centre is set in fertile countryside filled with vineyards and orchards. The name of the town is derived from the Sardinian word for marshes, *abbari*. In the oldest part of town, around the district of San Leonardo to the south-west, original stone houses are still visible. Here, the parish church, **Beata Vergine del Monserrato**, has a Rococo bell tower dated 1813. The town is also known for its textiles: tapestries, rugs and linen cushions and bedcovers.

Environs
On the coast, east of Barí Sardo, **Torre di Barí** is a pleasant seaside resort that developed around the 17th-century Spanish tower built to defend the town from pirates. It has a sandy beach and small pine forest. During the festivities for San Giovanni Battista, known here as *Su Nenneri*, grain and vegetable seedlings are cast into the sea to encourage a good harvest.

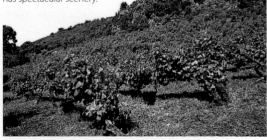

The vineyards at Jerzu produce Cannonau, Sardinia's best-known wine

The basalt rock promontory at Capo Ferrato, south of Muravera

⑯ Muravera

Road map D5. 🏘 4,500. 🚋 070 99 00 01. 🎭 14–15 Aug: l'Assunta.
Ⓦ comune.muravera.ca.it

Muravera lies at the mouth of the Flumendosa river, in the middle of an area of fruit orchards. It is a modern tourist town, catering to the resort complexes that have grown up along the coast. In ancient times this was the Phoenician city of Sarcapos. Today, the only building of any historical interest is the church of **San Nicola**, off the main street, which retains its original 15th-century chapels.

Environs
Muravera is an ideal starting point for trips along the coast and into the valleys of the interior. To the east, the beach around **Porto Corallo** is long and sandy, interrupted by small rocky headlands. Near this tourist port is another **Spanish tower** which, in 1812, was used as a stronghold in one of the rare victories of the Sardinians over the Muslim pirates.

Northwards, 11 km (7 miles) along the SS125, also known as the Orientale Sarda road (see p84), are the remains of the **Castello di Quirra** and the small Romanesque church of **San Nicola**, the only church in Sardinia built of brick.

To the south, the coast around **Capo Ferrato** is also beautiful, with basalt rocks, small white sandy coves and pine trees. Past the headland of Capo Ferrato is the **Costa Rei**, a stretch of straight coastline with beaches and tourist villages. The sea bed at the bay of **Cala Sinzias** further to the south consists of long slabs of rock, giving the water a strikingly clean and transparent look. Inland, the route towards Cagliari along the SS125 offers spectacular scenery, with red rock among myrtle, juniper and strawberry trees. A trip down the Flumendosa river valley, beyond San Vito, also offers spectacular scenery.

Castiadas is a hamlet behind the Costa Rei, set around a 19th-century prison amid vineyards and citrus trees. From the late 19th century to the 1950s the area was occupied by a prison farm, where prisoners worked on the land.

⑰ Villasimius

Road map D6. 🏘 3,000. 🚋
ℹ 070 793 02 71.
🎭 Jul: Madonna del Naufrago.
Ⓦ comune.villasimius.ca.it

With its hotels, residences and second homes, this modern town is the leading seaside resort on the south-eastern coast. Villasimius lies on the northern edge of a promontory that extends to **Capo Carbonara**. At the centre of the headland is the **Notteri marsh**, separated from the sea by Simìus beach, a long stretch of sand. In the winter the marsh is a popular stopping-off point for migratory flamingoes. On the very tip of the promontory the lighthouse offers a sweeping view of the coast and the tiny islands of **Serpentara** and **Cavoli** in the distance. The stretch of water between the two islands is shallow and has witnessed many shipwrecks over the years. Off the island of Cavoli,

The Town of the Launeddas

Northeast of Muravera is San Vito, an agricultural town that thrived in past centuries thanks to the silver mines on Monte Narba. In the centre of town, the parish church with its twin bell towers over the façade is worth a visit. San Vito is known for its tradition of craftmanship, in particular the flute-like instrument, the *launeddas*, which was originally played by shepherds (see p29). Luigi Lai, Sardinia's most famous player of this ancient instrument, lives here and makes the instrument himself. Other crafts at San Vito include fine embroidery and basketweaving with juniper twigs.

Luigi Lai, one of Sardinia's most famous *launeddas* players

The long beach separating the sea from Notteri marsh, south of Villasimius

at a depth of 10 m (33 ft), is the statue of the *Madonna dei Fondali* (Our Lady of the Sea Floor) by local sculptor Pinuccio Sciola. Excursions by glass-bottomed boat leave from the quay at Porto Giunco to view the submerged statue. This port is protected by the **Fortezza Vecchia**, a star-shaped fortress built in the 17th century. The sea around the headland is rich in fauna and flora and is popular with scuba divers.

⑱ Orroli

Road map C4. 🚂 3,300. 🚌
🅸 0782 84 70 06. 🎭 30 Jun: Santa Caterina 🔤 **comune.orroli.ca.it**

The town of Orroli lies in the rather barren Pranemuru plateau, at the edge of the Flumendosa valley. The area is dotted with archaeological sites, such as the necropolis of

Su Motti where *domus de janas* tombs are cut out of the rock.

Other archaeological sites in the area include the ruins of the **Arrubiu Nuraghe**, 3 km (1.8 miles) southeast of Orroli. This complicated, pentagonal site is larger than the one at Su Nuraxi *(see pp68–9)*. The complex, made of red stone, was built around a 14th century BC central tower which, according to experts, was 27 m (88 ft) high. Five towers, probably dating from the 7th century BC, connected by tall bastions, were built around the complex, and an outer defensive wall was added in the 6th century BC. The ruins of the nuraghic village, consisting of round and rectangular dwellings, lie around the nuraghe.

Another interesting site is the nearby **Su Putzu** nuraghe, which has numerous dwellings in excellent condition.

🏛 **Su Motti**
4 km (2 miles) SE of Orroli. **Tel** 0782 84 72 69. **Open** by appt for groups of 25 or more. 🅿 🔷

🏛 **Arrubiu Nuraghe**
Tel 0782 84 72 69. **Open** 9:30am–8:30pm (Oct–Apr: 9:30am–5pm). 🅿

The Arrubiu Nuraghe, one of several archaeological sites near Orroli

⑲ Perdasdefogu

Road map D4 & D5. 🚂 2,500. 🚌
🅸 0782 94 614. 🎭 12 Sep: San Salvatore.

An isolated mountain village in the lower Ogliastra area, Perdasdefogu lies at the foot of the striking *tacchi*, vertical limestone walls that tower over the maquis *(see p93)*. The road that meanders northeast towards Jerzu is one of the most scenic in Sardinia. It runs along a plateau at the base of these dolomitic walls, offering a spectacular view of the sea and Perda Liana peaks in the distance. Along the way is the rural church of **Sant' Antonio**, set in a meadow at the foot of Punta Coróngiu, one of the most impressive of the limestone *tacchi*.

View from the headland of Capo Carbonara, south of Villasimius

⑳ A Trip on the Trenino Verde

It takes just over five hours to travel 160 km (99 miles) on the narrow-gauge *trenino verde* (little green train), but the reward is a trip backwards in time through some of the wildest landscapes in Sardinia. The line passes through the softly rolling hills of Trexenta, carpeted with almond and olive trees, to the rugged mountains of Barbagia di Seui, where the train runs along the foot of a magnificent *tònnero*, with a broad view of its vertical limestone walls. This particular route – one of several across Sardinia – follows the craggy contours of the mountain and there are so many bends that it is easy to lose your sense of direction. The train makes two hairpin turns through the town of Lanusei in order to get over a steep slope. At peak service times it is possible to make the entire return journey in one day, but perhaps inadvisable: the hard seating makes such a long trip uncomfortable.

Lake Alto Flumendosa, on the southern side of Gennargentu

⑥ **Villanovatulo** This isolated shepherds' village has a view of the Flumendosa river basin. The walls of the houses have murals by Pinuccio Sciola.

The Trenino Verde
This picturesque train skirts the hillsides, well away from the road amid unspoilt scenery. As well as the timeless landscape, you can appreciate the atmosphere of a forgotten age.

VISITORS' CHECKLIST

Practical Information
ℹ️ Cagliari (070 57 93 03 46).
Trenino Verde: **Tel** 070 58 02 46.
🌐 treninoverde.com
Train timetable: mid-Jun–mid-Sep: from Arbatax, 8am and 2:50pm Wed–Mon; from Mandas, 8:40am and 3:30pm Wed–Mon; mid-Jul–Aug: from Mandas, 4:44pm daily. For other Trenino Verde routes, check the website. The train is also available for private hire all year round.

⑧ **Mandas** 69 km (43 miles) from Cagliari, Mandas is the leading agricultural town in the area. The church of San Giacomo, with statues of San Gioacchino and Sant' Anna, is worth a visit.

⑦ **Orroli** Surrounded by oak forests, the town of Orroli lies on a basalt tableland crossed by the Flumendosa river. Look out for the Arrubiu nuraghe *(see p95)*.

③ **Montarbu Forest** This is one of the best preserved forests in Sardinia, where moufflons live among ash, holm oak and yew trees. A striking feature here are the *tònneri*, massive vertical limestone walls.

② **Lanusei** This village lies on the slope of a hill commanding a fine view of the sea *(see p92)*.

① **Tortolí** The capital of the Ogliastra region is 3 km (2 miles) from the sea, on the edge of a large marsh which attracts thousands of migratory birds in winter. Watch out for the ruins of Castello di Medusa.

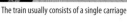

The train usually consists of a single carriage

⑤ **Sadali** Lying in the middle of a karstic plateau, Sadali boasts a 7-m (23-ft) waterfall fed by springs that flow into an underground chasm. There are numerous caves, such as Is Janas, 205 m (672 ft) long with an underground lake and impressive stalagmites and stalactites.

④ **Seui** The village of Seui, on the side of a steep valley, retains some traditional stone houses. The 17th-century Spanish prison is now occupied by the Civic Museum of Rural Culture with displays of traditional farm utensils and reconstructions of an 18th-century kitchen and bedroom.

| 0 kilometres | 4 |
| 0 miles | 4 |

Winding routes following the sheer slopes

Key

 Train route

▬ Major road

═ Minor road

— River

Tips for Travellers

Refreshments are not served on the train and the few stations en route are not equipped to offer restaurant facilities, so it is advisable to take along something to eat and drink. Going towards Mandas, the best views can be appreciated from the left-hand side of the train (and vice versa). The "normal" train, called *FL*, is superior to the AT (single-unit rail diesel car), which is noisier and less comfortable.

CENTRAL SARDINIA AND BARBAGIA

The central region of Sardinia is the area that most vividly reflects the ancient character of the island. Rugged mountains are marked by shepherds' trails and villages perch over steep valleys. The inhabitants of this isolated region are known as hardy and proud and have retained many aspects of their traditional way of life.

The name Barbagia derives from the Latin word *barbària*, used by the Romans to designate the inaccessible regions of the interior inhabited by "barbarians" (any culture that did not share the values and beliefs of the Roman civilization). Inhabited since prehistoric times and rich in archaeological sites, such as the nuraghic village of Tiscali *(see pp108–9)*, the heart of Sardinia resisted Roman invasions for many centuries and preserved its nuraghic religious rites up to the advent of Christianity.

Getting to know this rugged land requires some effort, since the roads are slow and winding, road signs are sometimes missing and many sights can be reached only via rough dirt tracks. The people, however, are often hospitable and tradition is still an essential part of local life. The churches and villages come to life during the colourful folk festivals, the patron saints' feast days and at religious festivities. At Mamoiada the *Mamuthones* lead the Mardi Gras processions wearing forbidding masks, cow bells and sheepskins *(see p106)*.

The mountainous landscape dominates central Sardinia. Trekkers can enjoy walks from the rocks of Supramonte di Oliena to the dense forests of holm oak on the slopes of Monte Novo San Giovanni *(see p111)* and the chestnut woods along the old railway near Belvì *(see p113)*.

The local cuisine is flavoured with herbs from the maquis, such as rosemary and thyme, while the handicrafts draw inspiration from pastoral life. Woven carpets, baskets and pottery with traditional motifs can be seen in Nuoro's Museo Etnografico *(see p103)*.

A shepherd and his flock in the high summer pastures at Pietrino

◄ One of the extraordinary murals that decorate the village of Orgòsolo

Exploring Central Sardinia and Barbagia

Nuoro is the capital of Sardinia's interior region: to the east lies the Supramonte mountain range, with Oliena, Orgòsolo, Urzulei, Baunei and Dorgali at its feet, while to the west the valleys descend towards Lake Omodeo and Macomer. In this landscape of hills and steep limestone walls (the *tònneri* formations) are some of the most important towns in the region: Mamoiada, Bitti and Sarule. To the south is the Gennargentu massif, carpeted with dense forests, on the slopes of which are typical mountain villages such as Gavoi and Fonni. Heading northeast and skirting the slopes of Monte Ortobene, which towers above the city of Nuoro, the road descends among almond trees and vineyards towards the Baronia region.

Barren slopes on the Gennargentu mountain range

Sights at a Glance

A mural painted on rocks near Orgòsolo

For additional map symbols *see back flap*

A dwelling in the nuraghic village of Tiscali

Getting Around

Public transport in the interior of Sardinia is slow and unreliable if it exists at all, and is not the best way to visit the area. If you have a car, the main roads are the SS131 from Siniscola to Nuoro up to Lake Omodeo; the SS125, the Orientale Sarda road, which skirts Supramonte and links Orosei to Arbatax, and the SS389, which also goes to Arbatax from Nuoro, passing Gennargentu on the east. For sights such as Tiscali and Punta La Marmora, you have to hike up fairly steep footpaths.

A pleasant alternative mode of transport is to travel on the little narrow-gauge train that runs between Mandas and Sòrgono on the Cagliari-Sòrgono line (see p113).

Key

━━━ Major road
━ ━ Secondary road
⋯⋯ Minor road
━━━ Scenic route
── Minor railway
△ Summit

0 kilometres   10
0 miles   10

❶ Nuoro

Nùgoro, as the locals still call their city, is one of Sardinia's most important centres. The city began to expand in the 14th century, but by the 18th century there was social unrest and riots erupted. In 1746 the Piedmontese prefect, De Viry, described the city as "a hotbed of bandits and murderers". A decree in 1868 that put an end to the common use of farmland culminated in a popular rebellion known as *Su Connottu*. At the beginning of the 20th century Nuoro became the heart of the island's cultural life, producing political and social writers such as Grazia Deledda. The city became the provincial capital in 1926, and today it is the commercial heart of Barbagia.

Santa Maria della Neve, Nuoro's imposing Neo-Classical cathedral

The huge granite blocks in Piazza Sebastiano Satta

Exploring Nuoro

The city is set in spectacular surroundings on a granite plateau beneath Monte Ortobene. Its isolated position and limited exposure to tourism have helped to preserve local culture, traditions and costumes.

The modern city retains many picturesque streets and buildings in the old centre. Corso Garibaldi, once known as Bia Maiore, leads up to the quarter of San Pietro and the city's Neo-Classical cathedral, **Santa Maria della Neve** (1836). Near Corso Garibaldi is the whitewashed Piazza Sebastiano Satta, paved in 1976 with large granite blocks.

Nuoro is the birthplace of some of Sardinia's most notable men and women of letters, who at the end of the 19th century injected new life into the island's culture. Apart from Grazia Deledda, other native literary figures are politician and essayist Attilio Deffenu (1893–1918) and poet Sebastiano Satta (1867–1914).

🏛 Museo Nazionale Archeologico

Via Manno 1. **Tel** 0784 316 88. **Open** 9am–1pm Tue–Sat (also 3–5:30pm Tue & Thu). 🔖

This museum combines the collections of fossils and fossil plants of the *Gruppo Speleologico Nuorese*, with archaeological finds excavated over many years in the area.

Exhibits range from Neolithic to medieval objects, including the skeletons of an ancient hare, *Prolagus sardus*, and a collection of cave finds. Also of interest are nuraghic bronze statuettes. Finds from the Roman era include belt buckles and other everyday household objects.

🏛 Museo Deleddiano

Via Grazia Deledda 28. **Tel** 0784 25 80 88. **Open** 9am–1pm, 3–5pm Tue–Sun (mid-Jun–Sep: 9am–8pm). 🔖 🖂

Grazia Deledda's birthplace retains the atmosphere of a mid-19th-century Sardinian home. The house has been arranged according to her own description, set out in her novel *Cosima*, with objects marking the stages of her career. The courtyard leads to what was the kitchen garden (now the venue for cultural events), while the upper floors are given over to displays of the covers of her books, programmes for her plays, and a copy of the diploma for the Nobel Prize for Literature.

Grazia Deledda (1871–1936)

Grazia Deledda won the Nobel Prize for Literature in 1926 in recognition of her perceptive portrayal of the power and passions in the primitive communities around her. Born in Nuoro in 1871, she has become a symbol of Sardinian culture and an example of the island's prolific artistic production. The eventful and difficult years of her early career are described in the autobiographical novel *Cosima* (1937). Her world of fiction revolves around Barbagia, with its mysteries and strong sense of identity. Among her best-known novels are *Elias Portolu* (1900), *Cenere* (1903), and *Canne al Vento* (1913). She died in Rome in 1936.

The author Grazia Deledda

The whitewashed Museo Etnografico in Nuoro

VISITORS' CHECKLIST

Practical Information
Road map D3. 38,000.
0784 23 88 78. 19 Mar: San
Giuseppe; 6 Aug: San Salvatore;
last Sun in Aug: Processione del
Redentore **provincia.nuoro.it**

Museo Etnografico

Via Antonio Mereu 56. **Tel** 0784 25 70
35. **Open** mid-Mar–Sep: 9am–1pm,
3–6pm Tue–Sun; Oct–mid-Mar:
10am–1pm, 3–7pm Tue–Sun.
isresardegna.it

The Museum of Sardinian life
and popular traditions was
designed in the
1960s by architect
Antonio Simon
Mossa. The aim of
the project was
to recreate a
typical Sardinian
village, with
courtyards, alleys
and stairways, as a setting for
artifacts, objects and costumes
representing Sardinian daily life.

Chest and cover in the Museo
Etnografico

On display in this popular
ethnographic museum are
traditional pieces of furniture,
such as a 19th-century chest
and cover and silver jewellery
used to adorn aprons or hand-
kerchiefs. Characteristic costumes worn daily or on special
occasions by women are also
on show, as are different types
of traditional bread moulds,
looms and hand-woven carpets.
One room is dedicated to
carnival masks and costumes.

The museum also has a library
specializing in anthropological
literature, an auditorium and an
exhibition centre. Every other
October, the museum features a
festival of ethnographic and
anthropological films.

Environs

Monte Ortobene

East of Nuoro.
Nuoro was founded on the
granite slopes of this mountain
and the inhabitants have always
held it in high regard. To reach
its wooded areas, take the
SS129 Orosei road
east out of the city.
The road passes
the church of
**Nostra Signora
della Solitudine**,
where Grazia
Deledda is buried.
At the summit is a
statue of the Redentore (Christ
the Redeemer) that overlooks
the city below and next to it is
the church of **Nostra Signora
di Montenero**. On the last
Sunday in August this church
is the focus of the solemn
procession known as the

Processione del Redentore, in
which representatives from
almost every town in Sardinia
take part (*see p32*).

Traditional costume from Dèsulo, Museo
delle Tradizioni Sarde

Necropoli di Sas Concas

SS128. **Tel** 0784 23 88 78. **Open** daily.

To visit this necropolis, take the
SS131 15 km (9 miles) west out
of Nuoro and then the SS128
south for 3 km (2 miles) towards
Oniferi. The complex consists of
a series of *domus de janas*, some
decorated with bas reliefs, such
as the *Tomba dell'Emiciclos*
(Tomb of the Hemicycle). The
area is unattended, so a torch
for the tombs may be useful.

The Sagra del Redentore procession on Monte Ortobene

Su Tempiesu well-temple near Bitti, a relic of Sardinia's nuraghic civilization

❷ Bitti

Road map D3. 👥 3,800. ℹ️ Town Hall, Piazza G Asproni (0784 41 51 24). 🎉 23 Apr: San Giorgio

This picturesque pastoral village has become known thanks to the *Tenores de Bitti* musical group, whose interpretations of traditional Sardinian close-harmony songs have won them acclaim throughout Europe *(see pp20–21)*. Experts say the local dialect is the one that most resembles Latin.

The 19th-century church of **San Giorgio Martire** stands in the central Piazza Giorgio Asproni. In the nearby parish home is a fine small collection of local archaeological finds.

Environs

Not far from Bitti on the road to Orune (watch out for the signs, which can be difficult to follow) is the **Su Tempiesu** well-temple. This consists of several chambers made of large square basalt stones, and houses the sacred well. The well water was used in nuraghic rituals. A little way east of Bitti are five churches, Santo Stefano, Santa Maria, Santa Lucia, San Giorgio and *Babbu Mannu* (Holy Ghost). These become lively during religious festivities.

❸ Bono

Road map C3. 👥 4,100. ℹ️ Town Hall, Corso Angioj 2 (079 79 169). 🎉 31 Aug: San Raimondo Nonnato

Set at the foot of the Gocèano mountain range, Bono is an ideal starting point for trips to the wooded Monte Rasu and the Foresta di Burgos. In the centre of town is the parish church of **San Michele Arcangelo**, which has been rebuilt several times over the years. Inside is a curious clock driven by the weight of four cannonballs, shot at the town during the 1796 siege, when the government troops were driven out by the city's inhabitants. This episode is reenacted every year during the traditional festival held on 31 August. On this day the largest pumpkin from the local kitchen gardens is awarded to the person who comes in last in the festival horse race as a facetious sign of recognition of the "valour" of the routed army. Until recently, this pumpkin was rolled down the mountain to the valley to symbolize the government troops escaping from the local inhabitants.

In early September Bono plays host to the colourful *Fiera dei Prodotti Tipici Artigiani del Gocèano*, a fair featuring typical handicrafts from the Gocèano region.

Environs

From the Uccaidu pass, northwest of Bono, you can hike up the ridge to the summit of Monte Rasu at an altitude of 1,258 m (4,125 ft). From here there are magnificent sweeping views of the Foresta di Burgos and surrounding mountain range as well as most of Sardinia.

The countryside between Bono and Burgos

❹ Burgos

Road map C3. 👥 1,100. ℹ️ 079 79 31 34.

The hamlet of Burgos lies below a cone-shaped peak in the Gocèano mountains. The town was founded in 1353 by Mariano d'Arborea and is

The village of Burgos, dominated by the 12th-century castle

Small Giara horses in the Foresta di Burgos

dominated by the ruins of **Burgos Castle**, built in 1127. The castle was the scene of many battles between the Sardinian principalities and mainland colonists during the Middle Ages. It was from here that in 1478 Artaldo di Alagon's troops marched from the castle to the battle of Macomer, marking the start of Aragonese dominion. Inside the outer defensive walls, further fortifications surround a restored tower. The entrance to the tower was once through a wooden stairway that could be raised in case of a siege.

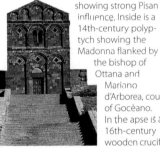

San Nicola, near Ottana

Environs
The **Foresta di Burgos**, 5 km (3 miles) northwest of Burgos, is a well-kept forested area with holm oak and cork oak trees, cedars, conifers and some chestnut trees. The area is also known for the small Sardinian Giara horses that graze in fenced-off pastures.

❺ Ottana

Road map C3. 🏠 2,700. ℹ️ Town Hall (0784 75 623). 🎭 Carnevale

Ottana lies in the valley of the river Tirso, not far from the slopes of the Barbagia di Ollolai region. In the Middle Ages the town was an important religious centre. On the southern outskirts of town is the church of **San Nicola**, once the cathedral of the regional diocese. It was built in 1150 in austere Romanesque style, with black and purple trachyte ashlars showing strong Pisan influence. Inside is a 14th-century polyptych showing the Madonna flanked by the bishop of Ottana and Mariano d'Arborea, count of Gocèano. In the apse is a 16th-century wooden crucifix. Almost abandoned in the 16th century due to an outbreak of malaria, Ottana was chosen in the 1970s as an industrial development site, promoted by ENI, the National Hydrocarbon Corporation. The industries have not produced the expected profits, however, and the ecological problems are so serious that the entire project is to be abandoned.

Carnival is a popular festival in Ottana, when locals dress in sheepskin and bells and wear bull-like masks (see p33).

Asphodel, used in traditional basket-weaving at Ollolai

❻ Ollolai

Road map C3. 🏠 1,800. ℹ️ Town Hall (0784 51 051). 🎭 24 Aug: San Bartolomeo

Ollolai was once the medieval administrative centre of the Barbagia di Ollolai region, an area that included the northern part of Barbagia and still retains the name today. The town's decline began in 1490 after a terrible fire destroyed most of it and today it is a small hamlet.

Some original houses decorated with dark stone doorways are visible in the old centre and there are still a few craftsmen who weave the traditional asphodel baskets in their courtyards.

Environs
A short distance west of Ollolai is the church of **San Basilio**. A traditional rural religious festival is held here on 1 September. A rough road climbs up to S'Asisorgiu peak to an altitude of 1,127 m (3,700 ft). From here there are fabulous views of the surrounding mountain range and the summit is popularly known as "Sardinia's window".

Typical masked figures dressed for the Carnival at Ottana

Sarule seen from the nearby hills

● Sarule

Road map C3. 🏔 1,840. 🛈 Town Hall (0784 760 17). 🎪 8 Sep: Madonna di Gonare.

Sarule is a village of medieval origin which has preserved its tradition of carpet-weaving. Along the main street you can still see the workshops where these vividly coloured carpets with stylized figures are woven on antique vertical looms and then sold on the premises.

Perched on a spur overlooking the village is the sanctuary of **Nostra Signora di Gonare**, one of the most sacred shrines in Sardinia. The church was built in the 13th century for the ruler of the principality, Gonario II di Torres, and by the 16th century it had already become a famous pilgrimage site. The sanctuary was enlarged in the 17th century with a dark stone exterior and austere buttresses.

To reach the sanctuary, a rough road heads east from Sarule and climbs up Monte Gonare for 4 km (2.5 miles). This granite rock mountain is interspersed with layers of limestone and outcrops of schist covered in vegetation. The mountain slopes are populated by many species of birds, including partridges, turtle doves, woodpeckers, shrikes and various birds of prey.

The forest has holm oaks and maples, while in the spring the undergrowth is enlivened by brightly coloured cyclamen, peonies and morning glory. The road ends at an open space with pilgrims' houses *(cumbessias)*, and a winding footpath up the bluff through the holm oak forest leads to the sanctuary. From here there are marvellous views of Monte Ortobene towering over Nuoro, Monte Corrasi near Oliena, and the Gennargentu mountains in the distance.

From 5–8 September a lively festival takes place at the sanctuary for the Madonna di Gonare, to which pilgrims travel on foot from all of the neighbouring villages. As well as religious festivities, a horse race is held, and the square resounds with poetry readings and sacred songs sung in traditional dialect.

The sanctuary of Nostra Signora di Gonare at Sarule

● Mamoiada

Road map D3. 🏔 2,700. 🛈 Town Hall (0784 560 23). 🎪 17 Jan, Carnival Sun & Shrove Tue: Mamuthones procession.

Some old buildings, possibly of Aragonese origin, are still visible among the modern houses that line the main street of Mamoiada. In 1770 the town was mentioned by the Savoyard viceroy, Des Hayes, as a place of some interest with numerous vineyards and an exceptional number of sheep. Flocks are still taken every summer to the slopes of Barbagia di Ollolai to graze. Mamoiada is best known for the dark, forbidding masks of the *Mamuthones*, who appear in the village streets

---

Traditional Festivals in the Barbagia

S'Incontru, the procession held in the streets of Oliena on Easter Day, commemorates the resurrection of Christ and his subsequent encounter with the Virgin Mary. On this occasion, and during the festivities in honour of San Lussorio on 21 August, you can admire the colourful traditional costumes and watch the impressive procession of horsemen through the streets of the town.

The carnival *Mamuthones* at Mamoiada

At Mamoiada the lively celebrations on the night of Sant'Antonio Abate (17 January), Shrove Tuesday and the last night of Carnival, all revolve around the figures of the *Mamuthones* and *Issohadores*. The former wear tragic masks and shepherds' garb, with a set of cow bells tied on their backs. The bells jangle in time with their rhythmical steps as they go through the village to the main square, where there is music and dancing all evening. The *Issohadores*, with their red waistcoats, are more colourful: they "capture" spectators and drag them inside the circles of the traditional round dance.

The *S'Incontru* procession

A typical street in the town of Oliena

on the feast days of Sant'Antonio Abate (17 January), the Sunday of Carnival and in particular on Shrove Tuesday, during the Barbagia's most famous Carnival celebrations (*see p33*).

Environs
About 5 km (3 miles) south-west of Mamoiada, along a secondary road towards Gavoi, is the **Santuario di San Cosimo**. This typical rural church has a central structure surrounded by *cumbessias*, lodgings for pilgrims to the sanctuary. The present-day church dates from the 17th century and its main feature is the single nave. At the end of the nave, restoration has brought to light an Aragonese niche with columns and an architrave made of volcanic rock.

A further 6 km (4 miles) to the south is the **Santuario della Madonna d'Itria**, an imposing church with *cumbessias*. Here, on the last Sunday of July, there is a horse race around the church, known as *Sa Carrela*.

❾ Oliena

Road map D3. 🏔 8,000. 🚹 Town Hall (0784 28 02 00). 🎭 Easter am: S'Incontru; 21 Aug: San Lussorio.

The approach to Oliena towards evening, along the northern road from Nuoro, is an unforget-table sight. The lights of the town shine at the foot of the steep white mass of Supramonte, which rises eastwards towards the Golfo di Orosei. The country-side is covered in vineyards, which yield the famous Sardinian wine Cannonau.

Some original houses, built around courtyards with external stairways and pergolas and brightly coloured rooms, are still visible along the narrow streets and alleyways. There are also several religious buildings, such as the church of **Santa Croce**, said to be the oldest in the town. Rebuilt in the 17th century, it has a bell tower decorated with an unusual trident motif.

The **Jesuit College** on Corso Vittorio Emanuele II is a reminder of the arrival of this religious order in Oliena. From the beginning of the 17th century onwards, the Jesuits encouraged the town's economy by promoting wine making and the breeding of silkworms. Next door to the Jesuit college, the church of **Sant'Ignazio di Loyola** has wooden statues of Sant'Ignazio and San Francesco Saverio, as well as an altarpiece depicting San Cristoforo.

Oliena, known for its good wine, is also famous for its jewellery, cakes and the traditional costumes worn by the women: a black shawl, interwoven with silk and gold, and a light blue blouse. There are two important festivals at Oliena that end with impressive processions: *San Lussorio* in August and *S'Incontru* on Easter morning.

Environs
South of Oliena, it is possible to take various hiking tours on the rugged and spectacular rocks of the **Supramonte di Oliena**. Starting from the Monte Maccione refuge, you can cross the chain and descend into the Lanaittu valley floor.

The **Su Gologone** natural springs are 8 km (5 miles) east of Oliena. The waters, which have cut channels through the mountain rock, are refreshingly cool in summer and turn into an extremely cold, rushing torrent in winter. Su Gologone is the largest spring in Sardinia, with an average production of 300 litres (66 gallons) per second. It lies in a pleasant wooded area ideal for picnics in the shade.

For many years speleologists have been exploring the depths of the underground cave of **Grotta Sa Oche**, in the Supramonte mountains. Every year divers penetrate further underground into the Supramonte mountains to study the various aspects of this natural phenomenon.

The Su Gologone natural spring at the foot of Supramonte

⑩ Tiscali

A little over a century ago some woodcutters, travelling over the mountain range that dominates the Lanaittu valley, discovered a nuraghic settlement hidden in the depths of an enormous chasm in Monte Tiscali. The village of Tiscali, which had been inhabited up to the time of the Roman invasion, consists of a number of round dwellings with juniper wood architraves around the doors and roofs. Years of neglect have led to the partial deterioration of the site, but it is still one of the most exciting nuraghic finds in Sardinia, in particular because of its unique position. The climb to Tiscali can be hazardous and tiring, and is over rocky ground.

The Path to the Village
Red arrows on the rocks indicate the way to the village.

Dwellings
Round nuraghic dwellings are still visible among the crumbling rocks and ruins.

KEY

① **The chasm** had no natural springs, so the inhabitants collected water that dripped down the walls of the rock.

② **The roofs** were made of juniper wood.

③ **The walls** of the dwellings were made of limestone blocks.

Bronze Model
Cagliari's Museo Archeologico (see p62) has a model of the dwellings.

View of Monte di Tiscali
Hidden inside this 518-m (1,700-ft) high mountain, the nuraghic village of Tiscali was discovered in the 19th century. Archaeological excavations did not begin until many years later.

Entrance to the Chasm
The difficult terrain and steep walls were the best defence for the inhabitants of Tiscali.

Tips for Drivers

From Oliena take the road east towards Dorgali. After about 5 km (3 miles), take the right-hand turn for Su Gologone. Just after the hotel of the same name *(see p177)*, take the dirt road to the right that goes to the Lanaittu plain. Proceed along the floor of the valley (keeping to the left) until the road becomes too difficult for vehicles. Clear red arrows on the rocks and trees indicate the footpath to the chasm of Tiscali. The walk will take you about 3–4 hours and can be extremely difficult. It is highly advisable to go with a tour guide.
It is possible to make other trips in this area, and again it is recommended you go with a guide. Places to head for include the Gole di Su Gorroppu ravines, parts of the caves of Su Bentu, Sa Oche or S'Elicas Artas, or the climb down to the Codula di Luna valley *(see p89)*.

The Nuraghic Village of Tiscali

This reconstruction of the nuraghic village shows how the settlement would have looked. A crater opening allows natural light in and steps from the entrance made the descent easy.

Murals in Sardinia

Sardinian murals began to appear on walls at Orgòsolo in the 1960s and soon became a feature of many of the island's villages and towns. The most famous of these is San Sperate *(see p66)*, the home town of the artist Pinuccio Sciola. The themes of this particular artistic genre are satirical, political or social. The styles vary greatly but are always characterized by bright colours. Even in the open country you may come across faces, shapes, hands and penetrating stares painted onto the boulders, rocks or cliffs. The *Associazione Italiana Paesi Dipinti* (Italian Association of Painted Towns) was founded to preserve and publicize the towns with these murals and also to encourage creativity and cultural exchange between different regions.

Mural at Orgòsolo

Mural on a wall at San Sperate

A mural painted on rock near Orgòsolo

⑪ Orgòsolo

Road map D3. 👥 4,800. 🛈 Town Hall (0784 40 09 01). 🎪 first Sun of Jun: Sant'Anania; 15 Aug: Festa dell'Assunta.
🌐 comune.orgosolo.nu.it

This characteristic village in the interior of the island has been compared to an eagle's nest and a fortress, perched precariously on the mountainside. The villagers are known as rugged and hardy shepherds, proud of their lifestyle and traditions. Rampant banditry in the 1960s was documented in Vittorio De Seta's film *Bandits at Orgòsolo*, in which the hard life of the shepherds and their mistrust of the government is narrated with cool detachment. The passion of the locals for social and political issues is also visible in the hundreds of murals painted on the walls of houses and on the rocks around Orgòsolo. The images describe the harsh life of the shepherds, their struggles to keep their land and Sardinian traditions, as well as injustices committed in other parts of the world.

Simple low stone houses line the steep and narrow streets of the town and some original features are still visible on a few isolated houses. On Corso Repubblica, the church of **San**

Pietro retains its 15th-century bell tower. Traditional dress, a brightly coloured apron embroidered with geometric patterns and a saffron-yellow headscarf, is still worn by some local women.

In summer two popular local festivals draw large crowds: the Assumption Day Festival on 15 August and Sant'Anania's feast day on the first Sunday of June.

Environs

Just outside Orgòsolo is the 17th-century church of **Sant'Anania**. The church was built where the saint's relics are said to have been found. Orgòsolo is an ideal starting point for excursions up to the surrounding Supramonte mountains, where open pastures are interspersed with dense forests of oak. A road leads to the **Funtana Bona**, 18 km (11 miles) south of Orgòsolo. These natural springs emerge at an altitude of 1,082 m (3,550 ft), at the foot of the limestone peak of **Monte Novo San Giovanni**, 1,316 m (4,316 ft) high. From here it is also possible to reach the shady **Foresta di Montes**, a forest of holm oak that stretches out to the south.

Sculpted detail on San Gavino, Gavoi

⑫ Gavoi

Road map C3. 👥 3,100. 🛈 Town Hall (0784 52 90 80). 🎪 last Sun of Jul: rural festival at Sanctuary of the Madonna d'Itria; second Sun after Easter: Sant'Antioco's feast day.

For many centuries this village was famous in Sardinia for the production of harnesses and bridles. Today its most characteristic product is cheese, including *fiore sardo* pecorino, made from sheep's milk *(see p183)*. The centre of town is dominated by the pink façade of the 14th-century church of **San Gavino**, which overlooks the square of the same name. Some of Gavoi's oldest and most characteristic streets begin here.

A stroll down these narrow alleys will reveal historic buildings with dark stone façades and balconies overflowing with flowers, such as the two-storey building on Via San Gavino.

In the little church of **Sant' Antioco**, in the upper part of town, dozens of ex votos in gold and silver filigree are pinned to the wall. There is also a fine statue of the saint, whose feast day is celebrated the second Sunday after Easter.

View of the Lago di Gusana seen from Gavoi

⓭ Fonni

Road map D3. 🏔 4,600. ℹ️ Town Hall (0784 591 31). 📅 first Sun & Mon in Jun: Madonna dei Martiri. 🌐 **comune-fonni.it**

Fonni is one of the highest towns in Sardinia, lying at an altitude of 1,000 m (3,280 ft). Its economy relies on tradition and tourism, offering locally made produce, such as traditional sweets, as well as fabrics and rugs known for their fine workmanship. Although the modern building has slightly diminished its charm, at first sight the town gives the impression of sprouting from the mountainside.

On the edge of town is the Franciscan **Madonna dei Martiri** complex, which dates from the 17th century. Inside is a curious statue of the Virgin Mary made from pieces of ancient Roman sculptures.

The town's major festival is held in mid-June to celebrate the return of the shepherds and their flocks from the winter pastures.

On the road towards Gavoi, 4 km (2 miles) west of Fonni, is the **Lago di Gusana**, a large artificial lake. Its tranquil shores, surrounded by holm oaks, make it a popular spot.

⓮ Teti

Road map C4. 🏔 900. ℹ️ Town Hall (0784 680 23). 📅 third Sun in Sep. San Sebastiano. 🌐 **comune.teti.nu.it**

Perched on the rocky mountains that dominate Lago di Cucchinadorza, the village of Teti distinguishes itself by its small museum, the **Museo Archeologico Comprensoriale**. Run by a team of enterprising young local people, the museum illustrates with clarity and detail the history of the area's ancient nuraghic settlements (in particular the village of S'Urbale and the sacred precinct of Abini). The display cases contain pieces found during excavations, including everyday objects used by the nuraghic people. One hall features a reconstruction of a round dwelling dating from about 1000 BC. Inside are spinning tools, pots, small axes and granite mills. In the middle of the house is the area used as a fireplace.

The halls of the lower floor are used for temporary exhibitions on local culture and traditions, such as traditional costumes and handicrafts.

Bronze statuettes found at Teti, Cagliari Museo Archeologico

Environs

About one kilometre (half a mile) southwest of Teti is the entrance to the nuraghic archaeological site of **S'Urbale**. The village was inhabited from 1200 to 900 BC, and the ruins of many prehistoric dwellings are still visible. The ancient nuraghic village of **Abini** is found 10 km (6 miles) to the north of Teti.

🏛 **Museo Archeologico Comprensoriale**
Via Roma. **Tel** 0784 681 20. **Open** 9am–12:30pm, 3–6pm (to 5:30pm Oct–May) Tue–Sun. 🌳 📷 ♿

Foresta di Montes

At the foot of the rocky bluffs of Monte Novo San Giovanni and Monte Fumai is the largest holm oak forest in Europe. Although many trees were destroyed in the past by fires – often started by shepherds in order to acquire more grazing land – the vast forest is once again increasing in size thanks to replanting, and today it attracts visitors from all over the island. Even in the

Monte Novo San Giovanni

heat of the summer, a walk through this area and the plateau around the River Olai is very enjoyable, as the dense forest offers shade from the sun and there is a chance to see sheep and pigs, as well as asphodels in bloom. The many footpaths around the Funtana Bona forest headquarters offer opportunities for hiking and mountain-biking.

The rural Sanctuary of San Mauro, near Sòrgono

⑮ Sòrgono

Road map C4. 🏠 2,100. 𝒊 Town Hall (0784). 🚌 26 May: San Mauro feast day.

Situated in a densely cultivated area of orchards and vineyards, famous for producing Cannonau wine *(see p184)*, Sòrgono has been an important town since Roman times. Today it is the administrative centre of the Mandrolisai area.

Two rather dilapidated sites in the town are worth a visit; the 17th-century **Casa Carta**, featuring a typical Aragonese window, and a medieval fountain of Pisan origin.

Just west of town is one of the most interesting and oldest rural sanctuaries in Sardinia, the **Santuario di San Mauro**. This imposing church is surrounded by the traditional *cumbessias*, the houses used by the pilgrims during their stay at the sanctuary. The building is a mixture of local architectural features and the characteristic Gothic-Aragonese style. A fine stairway flanked by two stone lions leads to the grey trachyte façade, which boasts a beautiful carved Gothic rose window. Numerous inscriptions are recorded on the stones of the church, some many centuries old and others more recent, carved by pilgrims to commemorate their visits to the sanctuary.

The interior of San Mauro has a single vault and is interrupted only by an arch that leads into the presbytery. Here there are a Baroque altar and some statues. Various buildings were added to the original church to accommodate pilgrims and

offer them adequate dining facilities, in particular during the San Mauro feast day. One of Sardinia's most important livestock and horse fairs used to be held on this day in the grounds of the sanctuary.

Not far from the church are two further sites worth visiting: the **Tomba di Giganti di Funtana Morta** (Tomb of the Giants) and, on a hilltop overlooking the church, the **Talei Nuraghe**, built with large granite stones and partly into the surrounding rock.

The Pisan fountain at Sòrgono, a relic from the Middle Ages

⑯ Làconi

Road map C4. 🏠 2,500. 𝒊 Town Hall (0782 86 62 00).

The town of Làconi is built around a rocky spur of the Sarcidano mountain range

and boasts beautiful panoramic views. Làconi also features the ruins of **Castello Aymerich** in the park above the town. Only a single tower from the original fortress, built in 1053, remains. The rest of the castle includes later additions such as the 15th-century hall and the 17th-century portico. The magnificent park around the castle includes a botanical garden and waterfall, and today it is a popular destination for walks and picnics.

Once the seat of the local noble overlords, Làconi has preserved the Neo-Classical **Palazzo Aymerich**, built in the first half of the 1800s by architect Gaetano Cima from Cagliari. Within the palace is the **Menhir Museum**, a collection of 40 pre-nuraghic megalithic monuments.

Near the 16th-century parish church is the birth-place and small museum of **Sant' Ignazio da Làconi**, a miracle worker who lived here in the second half of the 18th century. There is also a monument in his honour in the square.

Environs
The area around Làconi has many prehistoric remains. Among these are several anthropomorphic menhirs, single stones on which ancient sculptors carved human features. These can be seen at Perda Iddocca and Genna 'e Aidu, but it is advisable to be accompanied by a local guide.

The ruins of Castello Aymerich at Làconi

⑰ The Cagliari–Sòrgono Railway

Compared to travelling by car, the train line between Cagliari and Sòrgono offers a slow but picturesque approach to the foothills of the Gennargentu mountain range. In the first stretch, up to Mandas, the train goes over the rolling hills of Trexenta. It then climbs up to the road house at Ortuabis, an area of thick vegetation with a backdrop of mountain peaks, and on beyond Belvì through a wood of dense tree heathers. At Mandas, you will need to break your journey to pick up the little *trenino verde* service *(see also pp100–1)* up to Sògorno. This part of the rail route offers both spectacular scenery and an insight into travel from another age. DH Lawrence described the trip in his book *Sea and Sardinia* (1921).

Lush scenery and waterfalls characterize the stretch between Làconi and Meana.

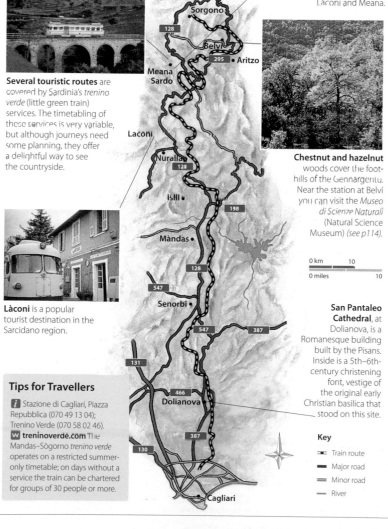

Several touristic routes are covered by Sardinia's *trenino verde* (little green train) services. The timetabling of these services is very variable, but although journeys need some planning, they offer a delightful way to see the countryside.

Chestnut and hazelnut woods cover the foothills of the Gennargentu. Near the station at Belvì you can visit the *Museo di Scienze Naturali* (Natural Science Museum) *(see p114).*

0 km   10
0 miles   10

Làconi is a popular tourist destination in the Sarcidano region.

San Pantaleo Cathedral, at Dolianova, is a Romanesque building built by the Pisans. Inside is a 5th–6th-century christening font, vestige of the original early Christian basilica that stood on this site.

Tips for Travellers

ℹ Stazione di Cagliari, Piazza Repubblica (070 49 13 04); Trenino Verde (070 58 02 46).
🆆 **treninoverde.com** The Mandas–Sògorno *trenino verde* operates on a restricted summer-only timetable; on days without a service the train can be chartered for groups of 30 people or more.

Key

🚂 Train route
▬ Major road
═ Minor road
— River

Canoeing on the Flumendosa river near Aritzo

⑱ Aritzo

Road map C4. ⛰ 1,700. 🅘 Town Hall (0784 62 72 23). 🎭 second Sun in Aug: Sant'Isidoro; first weekend Nov: chestnut festival.

The small town of Aritzo was once famous for selling snow, at a very high price, packed in straw-lined boxes and transported throughout the island during the hot summer months. Under Aragonese rule, the town had the privilege of being governed by its own inhabitants, locally elected.

There are still many traces of the old town. Some houses retain typical stone façades and long, wooden balconies. Among the most important buildings are the **Casa degli Arangino** (in Neo-Gothic style) and the impressive 17th-century stone **Aritzo prison** on Via Maggiore.

The market for snow no longer exists, but the town has continued its tradition of making wooden furniture, such as hand-carved wedding chests. These are sold from the craftsmen's workshops.

The good climate, the high altitude and panoramic views make Aritzo a pleasant tourist destination in the summer. Rodeos are a popular attraction outside town and interesting walking tours and horseback

rides take place towards the Gennargentu massif and the upper Flumendosa river valley. Here canoeing on the river is a popular activity.

Environs

Just north of Aritzo is the **Tacco di Texile**, a vertical limestone pinnacle, 975 m (3,200 ft) high, in the shape of a mushroom. From here there are spectacular views of the mountains of the Barbagia region.

During the Middle Ages, the humble saint Efisio lived in this area. For many years he preached to the local inhabitants and eventually converted them to Christianity.

Wedding chest made by Aritzo craftsmen

⑲ Belvì

Road map C4. ⛰ 810. 🅘 Town Hall (0784 62 92 16). 🎭 28 Aug: Sant'Agostino feast day.
🌐 comune.belvi.nu.it

The village of Belvì lies in a dominating position overlooking the Iscra river valley, which is full of fields of hazelnut trees and orchards.

In the past it must have been an important economic and trading centre, as the surrounding mountain region, Barbagia di Belvì, has also adopted the name.

The railway which connects Mandas and Sòrgono runs along the stretch of road near the village. The route goes through magnificent scenery as well as tackling a thousand tortuous bends and high viaducts (see p113).

In the village, several old houses are still visible. One of these, on the main street, Via Roma, houses the private **Museo di Scienze Naturali** (Natural Science Museum). Founded in 1980 by a group of enthusiasts (including a German naturalist who lived in Belvì for almost ten years), the museum has palaeontology and mineralogy departments, as well as occasional exhibitions of its collection of typical Sardinian fauna and insects.

🏛 **Museo di Scienze Naturali**
Via San Sebastiano. **Tel** 339 753 1025. **Open** by appt only. 🚫 🎫

The rodeo held near Aritzo

Overlooking Dèsulo

⑳ Dèsulo

Road map C4. 🏔 3,200. **ℹ** Town Hall (0784 61 92 11). 🎭 second Sun of Pentecost, Corpus Domini.

Perched at an altitude of 895 m (2,900 ft) on the slopes of Gennargentu, the village of Dèsulo was not converted to Christianity or ruled by outsiders until the 7th century. Unfortunately, unregulated building development has had a devastating impact on the village and has almost eliminated the traditional schist houses. It is still quite common, however, to see villagers in traditional dress.

The local economy is based on sheep-raising and the ancient tradition of cultivating the chestnut groves and mountain pastures. In the past the inhabitants, skilled in wood-carving, used to travel to the various markets and fairs throughout Sardinia to sell their hand-made spoons, cutting boards and other wooden objects, as well as locally grown chestnuts.

The parish church of **Sant' Antonio Abate**, and other churches such as the **Madonna del Carmelo** and **San Sebastiano**, are worth a visit for a series of colourful wooden statues sculpted in the mid-1600s. But the main reason to visit this village is its natural scenery and the splendid views of the highest peak on the

island. There are plans to give the area National Park status, incorporating it into the Gennargentu National Park. Dèsulo is a favourite destination for hikers keen to climb up Gennargentu and Punta La Marmora *(see p86)*. As groups of walkers become more common, a number of hotels and hostels catering for this form of tourism have been built.

㉑ Tonara

Road map C4. 🏔 2,600. **ℹ** Town Hall (0784 63 823). 🎭 second Sun in Aug: Sagra del Torrone.
W comunetonara.gov.it

In the past the economy of Tonara was based largely on the chestnut and hazelnut groves that surround the town, and on other products typical of a mountain environment. Since tourism discovered this side of the mountain, the local production of cow bells, *torrone* (nougat) and hand woven rugs has become famous. During the local festivals in the town square, blacksmiths forge the celebrated Tonara bells by hammering the metal

Chestnuts

on specially shaped stone moulds. The inhabitants will be more than willing to tell you how to arrange to see craftsmen at work and purchase traditional rugs. The atmosphere of a typical mountain village can still be seen in the shepherds' houses, which have not changed in over a century.

Tonara is another popular starting point for excursions to the Gennargentu massif. One of the most interesting is the tour to **Punta Mungianeddu** (1,467 m, 4,800 ft). A road climbs through holm oak and chestnut woods to reach the summit, from which there are magnificent views.

Stone used as a mould for making cow bells at Tonara

Sardinian Nougat

Nougat (*torrone* in Italian) is one of the most common sweets in the culture and tradition of central Sardinia. Every local fair or festival will have stalls selling the delicious, hard nougat made in Tonara, Dèsulo or one of the other mountain villages. The main ingredients are almonds, walnuts, hazelnuts, various qualities of honey and egg whites (in some cases the yolk is also used). Cooking – during which the mixture has to be stirred continuously – takes more than five hours. The different styles of nougat are created by variations in the type of honey, the flavour of the nuts or number of eggs used. There are many nougat confectioners and, no matter how big or small the premises, visitors are always welcome to watch the preparation and choose a favourite flavour. Blocks of nougat are cut for you while you wait. One excellent outlet is Signora Anna Peddes in Tonara, at No. 6 Via Roma; she makes particularly delicious and fragrant nougat.

The Nougat Festival at Tonara

THE WESTERN COAST

Each year thousands of flamingoes choose the marshes and wetlands of western Sardinia as their favoured place for over-wintering, creating clouds of pink against the vegetation of the maquis. The coastline is vulnerable to the cool mistral, and years of strong winds have sculpted massive dunes along the shore.

The natural harbours and fertile land in this part of Sardinia have attracted foreign ships for centuries. The Phoenicians discovered the safe harbours of Sulki and Tharros as well as the great commercial potential of the obsidian from the slopes of Monte Arci. The Romans and Spaniards also left their mark at Bosa, the latter transforming Alghero into a Catalonian town.

The area around Oristano is one of the largest wetland areas in Europe. As well as freshwater pools and marshy lakes, there are saltwater lagoons, sandbanks and sand dunes. A combination of the waters of the Tirso river and the mistral is responsible for this particular ecosystem. Over the course of centuries massive dunes have formed at the river mouth, whipped up by the violent winds from the west, effectively blocking the flow of water out to sea. At

the beginning of the 20th century, this marshland was infested with malaria-transmitting mosquitoes but, thanks to land reclamation in the 1930s and the Rockefeller-funded anti-malaria campaign, the soil can now be cultivated without risk. Today this is one of the most fertile areas in Sardinia, producing spring vegetables for sale to mainland Italy, as well as olives and citrus fruits. Vineyards cover the land around Oristano and near the beaches in the Sinis region, yielding quantities of white Vernaccia wine. The coastline is lovely – small beaches and seaside resorts nestle against sand dunes shaded by thick pine forests. Some beaches are made of grains of translucent quartz, which suits wild lilies. Some stretches of cliff, wild and rocky, can only be reached by boat or after a lengthy trek.

The historic town of Bosa seen from the Temo river

◄ Flamingoes flocking in the shallow lagoons around Oristano

Exploring the Western Coast

The western coast of Sardinia offers a wide variety of activities – whether you prefer to explore the towns and countryside, or relax on a beach at places like Is Arutas near San Salvatore or Bosa Marina. There are extensive nature reserves teeming with wildlife, and fortified cities with Romanesque cathedrals. One of Sardinia's best-known wines, Vernaccia, is made in this region, from the vineyards north of Oristano. At Tharros you can explore the ruins of a Phoenician coastal town, founded in the 8th century BC. The relatively short distances between sights and the flattish terrain, especially in the Sinis and Campidano di Oristano regions, make this area ideal for cycling tours. Walkers may prefer the hiking trails and riders can choose from the bridle paths that converge on the coast near Arborea. At the headland of Capo Caccia you can explore caves and grottoes, some of which extend for kilometres under the cliff.

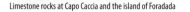

Limestone rocks at Capo Caccia and the island of Foradada

Archaeological excavations at Tharros

For additional map symbols *see back flap*

View from Capo Falcone towards the island of Asinara

Sights at a Glance

Traditional fisherman's house, San Giovanni di Sinis

0 kilometres 10

0 miles 10

Key

— Major road
— Secondary road
··· Minor road
— Scenic route
— Main railway
— Minor railway
△ Summit

Getting Around

The coastal road is quite good but not especially fast; the same is true of the roads connecting the villages and those used for mountain tours. The SS131, known as the Carlo Felice road, goes from Oristano to Sassari. There are good railway connections from Oristano to Cagliari, Olbia and Porto Torres, the main ports for ferry connections.

❶ Street-by-Street: Alghero

In the early 12th century, the aristocratic Doria family from Genoa decided to establish two strongholds in Sardinia, which became Castelgenovese (now Castelsardo) and Alghero. Because of the abundant quantities of algae off the coast, the latter city was named Alquerium – *s'Alighera* in Sardinian dialect and *l'Alquer* in Catalan. After a very short period of Pisan rule, Alghero was conquered by the Aragonese in 1353, and has always been the most Spanish city on the island. The old centre lies within the ancient fortified quarter and the local economy is based on tourism and handicrafts – particularly jewellery and other items made of coral.

★ San Francesco
Parts of this jewel of Catalan architecture date back to the first half of the 14th century. The lovely cloister becomes an open-air concert venue in summer.

Sign in Catalan
The street signs in Alghero are still written in Catalan.

Porta Terra tower

The Maddalena tower and ramparts

PIAZZA CIVICA

MAGELLANO

BASTIONI

VIA ROMA

MAR

BASTIONI

Alghero Marina
Via Garibaldi starts at the marina and runs alongside Alghero's long, sandy beach towards the lido and Fertilia.

★ Duomo Doors
Built in the mid-1500s, the carved doorway, together with the bell tower, is the oldest part of Alghero's cathedral.

Torre di Sant'Erasmo

Torre della Polveriera

Key
— Suggested route

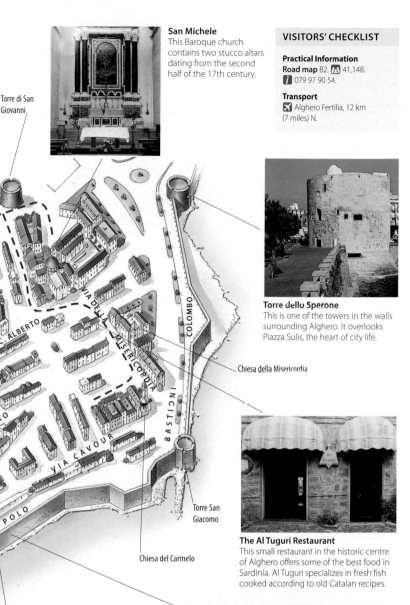

San Michele
This Baroque church contains two stucco altars dating from the second half of the 17th century.

Torre di San Giovanni

VISITORS' CHECKLIST

Practical Information
Road map B2. 41,148.
079 97 90 54.

Transport
Alghero Fertilia, 12 km (7 miles) N.

Torre dello Sperone
This is one of the towers in the walls surrounding Alghero. It overlooks Piazza Sulis, the heart of city life.

Chiesa della Misericordia

The Al Tuguri Restaurant
This small restaurant in the historic centre of Alghero offers some of the best food in Sardinia. Al Tuguri specializes in fresh fish cooked according to old Catalan recipes.

Torre San Giacomo

Chiesa del Carmelo

Via Carlo Alberto is the central shopping street in the city. In the summer months craftsmen set out their coral jewellery to tempt visitors to buy.

0 metres   50
0 yards   50

★ Ramparts
Positioned between the old city and the sea, the ramparts are now popular places for strolling, especially on warm evenings.

Exploring Alghero

Despite the considerable damage wrought by Allied bombardments in World War II, the heart of the old city is, for the most part, intact and can easily be explored on foot. The main roads from Bosa (to the south) and Sassari (to the northwest) lead to the city walls, and the best way to explore is to leave your car outside and walk around the narrow, high-sided streets of the old city. Strongly influenced by Spanish culture, Alghero remains the most Spanish city in Sardinia. The Alghero dialect is closely related to that of Catalonia, so much so that since 1970, street signs have been printed in Italian and Catalan, and you are likely to hear as much Catalan spoken on the streets as Italian.

The old town, Alghero

🏛 Porta a Terra
Piazza Porta a Terra.

This 14th-century city gate now has a rather stranded air, as most of the associated fortifications were demolished to make room for present-day Via Sassari. The gate was once known as Torre degli Ebrei (dels Hebreus in Catalan), or Tower of the Jews, because of the contribution made by the Jewish community to Catalan king Pietro III's conquest of the city. The tower was originally one of two gates. A drawbridge linked Porta a Terra and the large Gothic arch which is now a war memorial. The ground floor, covered by a stone vault, is now used as a small exhibition centre.

A window at
Palazzo d'Albis

🏛 Torre di San Giacomo
Situated in front of the 17th-century church of Carmen, on the waterfront, is the restored Torre di San Giacomo. It differs from the other towers in Alghero with its unique octagonal form. It is also known as the Torre dei Cani (the Dogs' Tower) reflecting its earlier use as an enclosure for the stray dogs of the town.

🏛 Bastione and Forte de la Magdalena
Around sunset locals and tourists alike enjoy the pleasant stroll along the seafront. Starting from the south, Lungomare Dante is followed by Lungomare Cristoforo Colombo and Lungomare Marco Polo, which has a series of ramparts with towers (the Torre di San Giacomo, the Mirador rampart, the Torre de la Polvorera, the Torre de Castilla), leading to the port. Not far from the steps which run from the seafront to the old Porta a Mare city gate, is Forte de la Magdalena, the city's most important Spanish fortification. On its walls a plaque commemorates Giuseppe Garibaldi's landing here on 14 August 1855.

🏛 Palazzo d'Albis
Piazza Civica (Plaça de la Dressana).

This 16th-century palace with twin lancet windows is also known as Palazzo de Ferrera. It is a rare example of Catalan civic architecture, and is famous for having hosted Charles V in October 1541. The emperor stopped at Alghero with his fleet on the way to Algiers, and was very flattering in his reactions to the city. According to tradition, the emperor spoke to the populace from the balcony of Palazzo d'Albis, and had the following to say about the city: "Bonita, por mi fé, y bien assentada". ("Beautiful, by my faith, and quite solid") and told the inhabitants "Estade todos caballeros" ("You are all gentlemen"). The monarch's sojourn ended with a massive requisition of cattle, which he needed for the Spanish troops. The animals were then slaughtered after an impromptu bullfight, held by the palazzo in Piazza Civica.

⛪ Cattedrale di Santa Maria
Piazza Duomo. **Tel** 079 97 92 22. **Open** 6:30am–noon, 5–8pm.

The doorway of Alghero's Neoclassical Cathedral opens out onto the small Piazzetta Duomo. The cathedral, dedicated to Santa Maria, was first built in the 14th century. In the mid-1500s the building was restructured in the Catalan-inspired late Gothic style. The unusual octagonal bell tower dates from the same period.

The 15th-century Torre di San Giacomo

View of the harbour and broad seafront in Alghero

In the interior there is a striking difference between the layout of the central part, which is late Renaissance, and that of the 16th-century Gothic presbytery. Items of Catalan jewellery are on display in the sacristy.

Displays of coral jewellery

Via Principe Umberto

This narrow street, which begins at the Cathedral, was one of the main arteries in the old walled city. Of interest are the Casa Doria (16th century), Palazzo della Curia and, in Piazza Vittorio Emanuele II, the 19th-century Savoyard Teatro Civico.

San Francesco and Cloister

Via Carlo Alberto. **Tel** 079 97 92 58. **Open** 9:30am–noon, 4:30–6:30pm. San Francesco may very well be the most important Catalan monument in the whole of Sardinia. Built at the end of the 1300s and then partially rebuilt when some of the structure collapsed, the church displays different stylistic influences. The bell tower is Gothic, with a

hexagonal body set on a square base. The cupola, dressed with multicoloured tiles, has become the symbol of Alghero.

The two-aisle, white sandstone interior still has Baroque altars made of carved wood and, under the star-spangled Gothic vault of the presbytery, there is an 18th-century altar. The sculptures include a *Dead Christ* and *Christ at the Column*.

The cloister, accessible from the sacristy, is well worth a visit. It is an eclectic sandstone construction, built in different periods. The lower part dates from the 14th century, while the upper part was added in the 1700s. The 22 columns are in two sections, with round or polygonal bases and sculpted capitals. During the summer music season, the Estate Musicale Internazionale di Alghero, concerts and other cultural events are held in these lovely surroundings. In other seasons of the year events and art exhibitions are held in the old refectory.

The Beaches

The port of Alghero has never been an important trading place, partly because of its position and the low-lying coast. There is no heavy industry here and, as a result, the sea is not polluted. A series of resorts can be found just outside the old town. The best-known beach is the Bombarde, a strip of pure white sand bordered by crystal-clear sea, 8 km (5 miles) northwest of the city. Another good beach nearby is the Lazzaretto, which

owes its name to the hospital for the poor which was there during the period of the black plague. When the weather is clear, the impressive vertical profile of Capo Caccia stands out on the horizon.

Environs

To the north is the coastal town of **Fertilia**, a small yacht harbour built during the Fascist era as the centre of the land reclamation programme. Nearby you can still see the 13 arches of the Roman bridge at the ancient city of Carbia. At one time the bridge connected Carbia to Portus Nympharum, now Porto Conte bay. A few minutes away stands the site of **Palmavera Nuraghe**. This prehistoric complex contains two towers and a courtyard surrounded by a barbican.

East of Alghero are the **Necropolis Anghelu Ruju**, the largest pre-nuraghic burial place of its kind in Sardinia, and the Sella & Mosca vineyard and museum *(see p191)*.

Entranceway to the prehistoric site of Palmavera Nuraghe

❷ Porto Torres

Road map B2. 🚹 22,000. ℹ️ 079 50 08 711.

The chief port in northern Sardinia lies in the Golfo dell'Asinara. Porto Torres was known to the Romans as Turris Libisonis, and was once a prosperous colony. Trade with the city of Kàralis (today's Cagliari) was carried out along the main road on the island. Relations with Rome were very close, as can be seen from the ancient mosaics at the Foro delle Corporazioni in Ostia Antica.

After a lengthy period of decline that began in the Middle Ages, Porto Torres began to recover in the 19th century, when it became the port for Sassari, and again in the 20th century with the development of local industries.

The basilica of **San Gavino** is one of the most important Romanesque churches in Sardinia, built in the Pisan style in 1111. Noteworthy elements are the portal in the northern façade, with its 15th-century bas relief, and the other Gothic doorway, which shows Catalan influences.

Inside there is a crypt, with access to an area of late Roman-Early Christian ruins, as well as the 18th-century statues of the martyrs Gavino, Proto and Gianuario, and a medieval inscription celebrating emperor Constantine.

The **Terme Centrali** archaeological area presents a reasonably faithful picture of an ancient Roman quarter, and the **Antiquarium Turritano** contains finds from the excavations here. Not far away, the 135-m (440-ft), seven-arched **Ponte Romano** (Roman bridge) crosses the Mannu river.

Environs

A short distance from here lies one of the most interesting sites in ancient Sardinia, the pre-

The Romanesque basilica of San Gavino, in Porto Torres

nuraghic **Santuario di Monte d'Accoddi**. From Porto Torres, head towards Sassari along the SS131; a short distance after the Sorso junction (at kilometre marker 222.3) a signposted road leads to the archaeological site. The sanctuary dates from the Copper Age (2450–1850 BC) and provides the only example of a megalithic altar in the entire western Mediterranean. The shape is that of a truncated pyramid with a trapezoid base, supported by walls of stone blocks. On the southern side, a ramp leads to the top, about 10 m (33 ft) high, while the base is about 30 m by 38 m (98 ft by 124 ft).

Gold bracelet from the Porto Torres excavations

Around the altar you can see foundations for houses, some sacrificial stone slabs and fallen menhirs. A group of *domus de janas* (rock-cut tombs) was once part of this complex. The material found at this site,

including ceramics, is on display at the Museo Nazionale in Sassari *(see p167)*.

🏛️ **Antiquarium Turritano**
Tel 079 51 44 33. **Open** 9am–8pm Tue–Sun. ♿ 🅿️ ⭐

🏛️ **Santuario di Monte d'Accoddi**
Open Apr–Oct: 9am–6pm Tue–Sat (to 7pm Jul & Aug), 9am–2pm Sun; Nov–Mar: 9am–2pm Tue–Sun. **Tel** 334 807 44 49. ♿ 🅿️ 📷

❸ Stintino

Road map B2. 🚹 1,200. ℹ️ Town Hall (079 52 30 53). 🎣 end Aug: Vela Latina; 8 Sep: Santissima Maria Immacolata 🌐 comune.stintino.ss.it

The road to Capo Falcone, the northwestern tip of Sardinia, passes by the large wind turbines at the Alta Nurra ecological energy plant. Beyond this is the pleasant fishing village of Stintino (named from the Sardinian word *s'isthintinu*, or narrow passageway, the traditional name for the inlet where the village lies). Now a holiday town, Stintino was once important for its tuna fishing grounds, off the island of Asinara. In the summer the two ports, Portu Mannu and Portu Minori, have facilities for aquatic sports of all kinds. The long, sandy beach is the most accessible in the area and very popular.

North of Stintino, the road skirts the coastline as far as **Capo Falcone**. The place is still "defended" by a tower on its highest point and by the two Spanish fortifications at Pelosa and Isola Piana, in the inlet of Fornelli, opposite the island of Asinara.

Portu Mannu, one of the two harbours in Stintino

The barren cliffs on the island of Asinara

❹ Parco Nazionale dell'Asinara

Road map B1. 🛈 079 50 33 88.
🚌 📷 compulsory.
🌐 **parcoasinara.org**

This rugged island, once home to the Fornelli maximum-security prison, became a National Park in 1997. Asinara is less than 18 km (11 miles) long and 7 km (4 miles) wide and ends at the headland of Scomunica. The island's ecosystem is unique in the entire western Mediterranean and includes rare or endangered animal species.

In fact, the pristine coastline and lack of traffic on its 51 sq km (19 sq miles) make Asinara an ideal refuge for raptors, various species of sea birds, moufflons and wild boar. There is also a rare species of small endemic albino donkey, after which the island must have been named (*asino* meaning donkey). The rocky, volcanic terrain supports a holm oak forest, and the typical low-level maquis brush shields numbers of rare plants.

As a protected area, the island cannot be visited unaccompanied. Day boat trips start at Stintino and Porto Torres. Tours are by bus, on foot or, for the most comprehensive, by offroad vehicle.

Albino donkey from Asinara

❺ Argentiera

Road map B2.

Many places in Sardinia still carry reminders of the island's former mining industries. At Argentiera, not far from the modern town of Palmadula, the ancient Romans, and the Pisans in the Middle Ages, dedicated themselves to mining the precious metal that gave its name to the area (*argento* means silver).

In the 19th century, mining complexes, with wooden and masonry buildings, were constructed along the coast, so that the mined silver could then be transported by sea to other destinations, where it could be processed and eventually sold. A number of ambitious restoration and restructuring projects, many of which are yet to be completed, have changed the face of the town, but it still remains one of the most fascinating examples of industrial archaeology in Sardinia.

In the summer, the tranquil bay at Argentiera, with its crystal-clear water, is a great favourite with visitors.

The old mine buildings at Argentiera

❻ Capo Caccia

Towering above the sea, the Capo Caccia promontory, with a lighthouse perched on the outermost point, offers wonderful views of Alghero. Wild pigeons, swifts, peregrine falcons and herring gulls nest in the crevices and gullies of the precipitous cliffs. On the western side of the headland – opposite the barren profile of the island of Foradada – 656 steep steps (known as the Escala del Cabirol, or Roe-deer's Staircase) take you down the cliff to the fascinating caves of the Grotta di Nettuno (Neptune's Grotto). The cave can also be reached in about three hours by boat from Alghero.

Griffon vulture
Only a few of these rare creatures survive in Sardinia.

Herring gulls
These birds nest in cliff crevices and ravines.

Peregrine falcons
These raptors prefer calm, open spaces with rocky cliffs – Capo Caccia is a favoured ground.

KEY

① Torre Pegna

② Torre del Tramariglo

③ Cala d'Inferno

④ Isola Foradada

⑤ Lago La Marmora

⑥ Punta del Bollo

⑦ Punta del Quadro

Capo Caccia
In the past this promontory was frequented by travellers and prominent naturalists such as Alberto La Marmora. The name Capo Caccia derives from the *caccia*, or wild pigeon hunting, that was once popular here.

Grotta Verde
The name of this large cave, Green Grotto, derives from the colour of the moss and other plants that cover the stalagmites and stalactites. On the shores of a small lake at the far end of the gallery, ancient graffiti have been discovered.

Escala del Cabirol
From the ridge of land separating the headland from the lighthouse point, the Escala del Cabirol steps wind down to the entrance of the Grotta di Nettuno.

Grotta di Nettuno
Neptune's Grotto, one of the most picturesque caves in Sardinia, was first explored in the 1700s. The grotto extends for 2,500 m (8,200 ft), while the guided tour covers 200 m (650 ft).

Romanesque Santo Stefano, at
Monteleone Rocca Doria

⑦ Monteleone Rocca Doria

Road map B3. 🏛 140.
ℹ 079 92 51 17.

Situated on the top of the Su
Monte cliff (420 m, 1,380 ft), the
little village of Monteleone Rocca
Doria has a sweeping view of
Lake Temo and the Nurra plain.
Today it is tranquil, although
inhabitants look back proudly
on a noble, warlike past. In the
13th century the Doria family
from Genoa built a fortress here
which was totally destroyed in
1436 after a three-year siege by
troops from Aragon, Sassari,
Bosa and Alghero.

Many inhabitants departed
to found the town of Villanova
Monteleone, but a few people
remained behind. Monteleone
was not included in development programmes and, at one
point, locals tried to improve
their lot by putting the village
up for sale. In the centre of
Monteleone is the 13th-century
Romanesque parish church,
Santo Stefano.

⑧ Bosa

See pp130–31.

⑨ Macomer

Road map C3. 🏛 12,000. ℹ Town
Hall (0785 79 08 51). 🎪 17 Jan:
Sant'Antonio Abate.

Built on a platform of volcanic
rock, Macomer is one of the
most important commercial
centres in the interior of
Sardinia. Macomer developed

around key communication
routes – the Carlo Felice road
(the N131 that runs through
most of the island) and the
railway – and owes its
prosperity to agriculture,
livestock raising, dairy products
and light industry, while
retaining traces of its past. The
parish church of **San Pantaleo**
is an example of 17th-century
Spanish Gothic. On the evening
of 17 January the traditional *Sa
Tuva* celebration is held in
honour of Sant'Antonio Abate.
The event takes place in the
large square in front of Santa
Croce, and a huge bonfire lights
up the entire quarter.

San Pantaleo, in Macomer

Environs
Not far from the town centre,
near the Carlo Felice road, a
short walk will take you to the
impressive **Santa Barbara
Nuraghe**. Its sheer size means
that it dominates a series of
smaller towers and ramparts.

⑩ Sedilo

Road map C3. 🏛 2,700. ℹ 0785 56
00 01. 🎪 5–8 Jul: S'Ardia at Santu
Antine sanctuary.

The rocky terrain in the
Abbasanta plateau gave the
people of Sedilo the raw
material to build their houses.
There are still a few originals
remaining, representing a style
that has virtually disappeared.
The main sight of interest is the
church of **San Giovanni Battista**
in the centre of town. However,
Sedilo's most notable claim to
fame is the **Sanctuary of Santu
Antine**, otherwise known as
San Costantino, or Constantine,
after the early champion of
Christianity who is much
revered in Sardinia. The church,
with the typical *cumbessias*
houses for pilgrims, stands on a
cliff overlooking Lake Omodeo.
Within the precinct there are
numerous nuraghic sculptures
on display, including the
so-called *Perda Fitta*, a monolith
which, according to legend, is
actually the body of a woman
who was turned into stone
because she was disrespectful
towards the patron saint.

The open space opposite
the sanctuary is the setting for
the annual *S'Ardia* competition.
This horse race ends the July
festivities commemorating
Constantine the Great's victory
over Maxentius in the battle
of the Milvian Bridge in
AD 312. The inside walls of
Santu Antine are covered
with quantities of ex votos.

The S'Ardia horse race run around the Santu Antine sanctuary, Sedilo

The Losa nuraghe near Abbasanta

⑪ Ghilarza

Road map C3. 👥 4,700.
ℹ️ Town Hall (0785 56 10).

An unfinished Aragonese tower stands in the centre of Ghilarza, but the place is known principally as the town in which the famous Italian political thinker and writer Antonio Gramsci spent his childhood years. A small door on Corso Umberto leads to the **Casa di Gramsci**, now occupied by a research and study centre. There is also an exhibition of historical material relating to the Communist leader, who died in prison during the Fascist era. On the second floor is the small bedroom that was Gramsci's from 1898 to 1908.

Environs
A short distance from Ghilarza, on the road to Nuoro, is the beautiful church of **San Pietro di Zuri**, which was relocated, along with the village of the same name, after the artificial lake Omodeo was created in 1923.
The original church dates from 1291. The building was commissioned by Mariano d'Arborea, and carried out by architect Anselmo da Como. The architecture is prevalently Romanesque, with some interesting details which anticipate the transition towards the Gothic style.

🏛️ **Casa di Gramsci**
Corso Umberto 36. **Tel** 0785 541 64.
Open May–Sep: 10am–1pm, 4–7pm Mon, Wed–Sun (daily in Aug); Oct–Apr: 10am–1pm, 3:30–6:30pm Fri–Sun.

⑫ Abbasanta

Road map C3. 👥 2,700.
ℹ️ Town Hall (0785 56 16).

This village, the centre of which still has some old traditional houses made of dark local basalt stone, revolves around the parish church of Santa Cristina, with its impressive Renaissance-inspired architecture. Situated in the middle of a highly developed agricultural region, Abbasanta owes its importance to its strategic position near main artery routes, both ancient and modern.
In the vicinity are two of the most important archaeological sites in the whole of Sardinia: the **Losa Nuraghe** and the **Santa Cristina** nuraghic complex near Paulilàtino *(see p141)*. In order to reach the Losa Nuraghe, take the Carlo Felice road towards Cagliari until you reach kilometre marker 123

(indicated on a road sign). Here, a turning to the right leads to the entrance to the archaeological site, which is fenced off. Together with the monuments at Barùmini *(see pp68–9)* and Torralba *(see pp28–9)*, this nuraghic complex is one of the most important remaining from the immediate pre-Punic period.
In the middle of this vast structure is a keep thousands of years old, dating from the second millennium BC, while the ramparts were built some centuries later. The outer defensive walls were the last to be built, and date from the 7th century BC.
Inside the nuraghe there are three roofed chambers with a great many niches, which were probably used for storage. A spiral staircase leads to the upper floor, which features a terrace above.
All around the main structure are the foundations of a series of later buildings, dating from the Bronze Age to the Middle Ages.
A small **Antiquarium** stands about 100 m (328 ft) from the nuraghi themselves. It houses an interesting exhibition of plans and illustrations of a number of nuraghic monuments in this part of Sardinia.

🏛️ **Losa Nuraghe**
SS Carlo Felice 123.5 km. **Tel** 0785 52 302. **Open** 9am–1 hour before sunset daily. 🅿️ 🎟️ 📷 🏛️

Antonio Gramsci

Antonio Gramsci was born at Àles in 1891 to a humble family. After completing his studies at Turin, he entered politics full-time. He was one of the co-founders of the radical weekly *L'Ordine Nuovo* and in 1921 helped to found the Italian Communist Party, later becoming its Secretary-General. He was elected to parliament but was arrested by the Fascists in 1926 and given a 20-year prison sentence. He did not see freedom again, dying in prison in 1937. The complete edition of his writings, *Quaderni del Carcere* (Prison Notebooks) was not published until 1976. *Lettere dal Carcere* (Letters from Prison) are a moving statement of his sufferings as a prisoner.

The young Gramsci

❽ Bosa

Dominated by the Castello dei Malaspina, the pastel-coloured houses of Bosa lie on the right bank of the Temo river, the only navigable river in Sardinia. The town was originally founded by the Phoenicians on the opposite bank of the river. In the Middle Ages, under threat from constant pirate raids, the townspeople sought the protection of the Malaspina family on the slopes of the hill of Serravalle. Bosa was granted the status of royal city under Spanish rule and always maintained a close relationship with the Iberian peninsula. This fascinating town is famous for its artisan traditions of gold-filigree jewellery and lace-making. In the Sa Costa medieval quarter, a labyrinth of cobblestone alleys and steps, you can still see women sitting outside their homes making lace. Environmentalists say the nearby seaside is the cleanest in Italy.

Interior of the Cathedral in Bosa, with Baroque ornamentation

🏛 Cathedral

Piazza Duomo. **Tel** 0785 37 32 86.
Open 9–11:30am, 3–5pm daily (3:30–6:30pm in summer).

Dedicated to the Virgin Mary, the Cathedral was rebuilt in the 19th century in the majestic late Baroque Piedmontese style. In the interior is a statue of the *Madonna and Child*, of the Catalan school, sculpted in the 16th century. On either side of the main altar are two marble lions killing dragons. The side altars are made of multi-coloured marble.

🏛 Corso Vittorio Emanuele II

The main street in Bosa, paved with stone, runs parallel to the river. It is lined with aristocratic buildings and goldsmiths' workshops where filigree and coral jewellery are made.

🏛 Casa Deriu

Corso Vittorio Emanuele II 59.
Tel 0785 37 70 43. **Open** Jul: 10:30am–1pm Mon, 10:30am–1pm, 5–8pm Tue–Sun; Aug: 10:30am–1pm, 5–8pm, 10pm–midnight daily; Sep–Jun: 10am–1pm, 3–5pm daily (to 6pm Sat & Sun). 🖼

Casa Deriu is a typical 19th-century Bosa building which has been transformed into an exhibition centre. The first floor features traditional local products such as cakes,

Detail of the architrave of San Pietro

wine and bread, as well as a display of old black-and-white photographs. On the second floor is a fine reconstruction of the elegant Deriu apartment, with its olive wood parquet, frescoed vaulted ceiling, majolica tiles from Ravenna and locally made lace curtains.

The top floor houses the Pinacoteca Civica (municipal art gallery), featuring the collection of Melkiorre Melis, a local artist and one of the leading promoters of 20th-century applied arts in Sardinia.

The works on display span a 70-year period of graphic art, oil painting, ceramics and posters. There are also Arab-influenced works of Melis, executed while he headed the Muslim School of Arts and Crafts in Tripoli.

🏛 Castello Malaspina

Via Ultima Costa 14. **Tel** 333 544 56 75.
Open 15–31 Mar & 1–15 Nov: 10am–1pm daily; Apr–Jun: 10am–7pm daily; Jul–Aug: 10am–7:30pm daily; Sep: 10am–6pm daily; Oct: 10am–5pm daily; 16 Nov–14 Mar: by appt only. 🖼 🖼

Built in 1112 by the Malaspina dello Spino Secco family, this castle is still impressive, even though only its towers and outer walls have survived. It was enlarged in the 1300s, when the main tower, built of light ochre trachyte, was added. Inside the walls the only building standing is the church of **Nostra Signora**

View of Bosa from the Temo river, with fishing boats

For hotels and restaurants in this region see pp176–9 and pp186–9

Aerial view of Bosa Marina with its Aragonese tower

di Regnos Altos, built in the 14th century. Restoration carried out in 1974–5 brought to light a cycle of Catalan school frescoes, one of the few left in Sardinia. From the ramparts there are splendid views of the church of San Pietro, the lower Temo river valley and the red roofs of the Sa Costa quarter. You can walk down to the centre of town by following the steps skirting the walls that once defended Bosa to the east.

Sas Conzas

The buildings on the left bank of the Temo river were once used as tanneries. Abandoned years ago after a crisis in the leather goods market, the buildings are currently being restored. Two of the buildings now house a tannery museum and a small restaurant. The Sas Conzas quarter can best be admired from the palm-lined

street on the other side of the river, Lungotemo De Gasperi, where the fishermen of Bosa moor their boats.

🏛 San Pietro

Tel 333 544 56 75. **Open** Apr–Sep: 9:30am–12:30pm, 3.30–6pm (4–7pm in Aug) Tue-Fri, 9:30am–12:30pm Sat, 3:30–6pm Sun, Oct–Mar: by appt.
🎫 📷

About 1 km (half a mile) east of the left bank of the Temo stands the church of San Pietro, built in red trachyte stone, one of the most interesting of Sardinia's Romanesque churches. It was built in different periods, beginning in the second half of the 11th century, while the bell tower, apse and side walls were added the following century. The façade combines elements of Romanesque with touches

of French Gothic, imported by the Cistercian monks. On the architrave of the doorway is a singular *Madonna and Child with Saints Peter, Paul and Constantine.*

Bosa coat of arms

Environs:
Bosa Marina, just over 2 km (1 mile) from the centre of town, has a lovely secluded beach with dark sand. Isola Rossa is linked to the mainland by a long jetty. The Aragonese tower is open in July and August and hosts temporary exhibitions.

The coastline between Bosa and Alghero is spectacular. Part of the Trenino Verde route *(see pp96–7)* goes from Bosa Marina to Macomer, skirting the Pedras Nieddas (black stones) before going up the Rio Abba Mala valley to Modolo, Tres-nuraghes and Sindia.

The Castello Malaspina in Bosa

VISITORS' CHECKLIST

Practical Information
Road map B3. 🚹 7,786.
🎉 Easter Week: Settimana Santa Bosana; 29 Jun: boat procession on river; first Sun of Aug: Santa Stella Maris; second Sun of Sep: Sagra di Nostra Signora di Regnos Altos.
🌐 comune.bosa.or.it

Transport
🚉 🚌

The paired horse race held during Carnevale at Santu Lussurgiu

⓭ Santu Lussurgiu

Road map B3. 🏔 2,900. 🚉 🚌 ℹ Town Hall (0783 55 19). 🎭 Carnevale: horse race in town centre; 2–3 Jun: Horse Fair; 21 Aug: San Lussorio.
Ⓦ comunesantulussurgiu.it

The village of Santu Lussurgiu lies at 500 m (1,640 ft) above sea level on the eastern slope of the extinct volcanic mountain, Mount Montiferru, laid out like an amphitheatre on the edge of a volcanic crater, and surrounded by olive groves.

The historic centre is fascinating, with its steep, narrow streets and tiny squares surrounded by beautiful tall stone houses painted in bright colours. Some have decorated architraves and wrought-iron balconies. On Via Roma, an elegant 11-room 18th-century building houses the **Museo della Tecnologia Contadina**, (Museum of Rural Culture), founded by the local Centro di Cultura Popolare. The "Su Mastru Salis" collection is the work of Maestro Salis, the museum curator, who in over 20 years has collected more than 2,000 objects related to the culture and traditions of Santu Lussurgiu.

A guided visit to this interesting museum is like making a trip backwards in time. Room after room contains fascinating displays of everyday objects used by the farmers, shepherds and coal merchants who worked at the foot of Mount Montiferru. Some of the most interesting exhibits are in the sections given over to spinning and weaving, cooking and crafts. The room devoted to winemaking is also interesting. Equipment includes a fulling-mill, the implement used to soften and felt fabric. Over 40 of them were once in use in the Santu Lussurgiu area.

In the upper part of town is the 15th-century church of **Santa Maria degli Angeli**, which has a fine 18th-century carved wooden altar.

There are still several craftsmen in Santu Lussurgiu who specialize in making knives and fittings for horse-riding (bridles, bits, saddles and leather riding boots).

At Carnevale the street in front of the museum is turned into a track for a breakneck horse race between pairs of riders dressed as knights.

Environs

A few kilometres from Santu Lussurgiu there is a forest of pine, holm oak and oak near the village of **San Leonardo de Siete Fuentes**, which is famous

Local crafts on display in the Museum of Rural Culture

Flamingoes in the Sale Porcus Reserve

The Sale Porcus marsh is one of the largest reserves on the Sinis peninsula, its many white sand dunes covered with maquis vegetation. In winter and spring over 10,000 flamingoes and thousands of cranes, wild geese, cormorants and mallards make their home here, making the area look like a colourful East African lake. In summer, drought reduces the water level, transforming the lake into a white area with a thick, hard salty crust that you can walk across. One of the least intrusive ways to explore this natural oasis is by horse. For more details on environmentally friendly visits to the reserve, contact Engea Sardegna, the regional chapter of an association of horse-back guides.

🏛 **Oasi Sale Porcus**
Open daily. **Tel** 0783 39 10 97.
Ⓦ sitogea.net

Flamingoes in the Sale Porcus reserve

One of the seven springs at San Leonardo de Siete Fuentes

for its seven springs of radio-active, diuretic water that flow out of seven fountains at a constant temperature of 11°C (52°F). The streams meander through a wood popular for family outings. In the centre of town is the small church of San Leonardo, which once belonged to the Knights of Malta. It was constructed with dark trachyte stone in the 12th century, and acquired its present Romanesque-Gothic appearance the following century. The single-nave interior bears the insignias of the Knights of Malta. Opposite the church stands a small public library.

In early June, San Leonardo plays host to an important saddle-horse fair packed with horse races and other events.

Museo della Tecnologia Contadina
Via D Meloni 1. **Tel** 0783 55 06 17.
Open by appt only.

⑭ Cuglieri

Road map B3. 3,400. Via Carlo Alberto 33 (0785 36 82 00). Good Friday: procession and 'Iscravamentu; 5 Aug: Madonna della Neve.
comune.cuglieri.or.it

The agricultural town of Cuglieri lies 500 m (1,640 ft) above sea level on the western slopes of Mount Montiferru, with a panoramic view of the sea. It is dominated by the striking church of **Santa Maria della Neve**, which has an 18th-century façade and twin bell towers. The walk up to the church is lovely, winding through alleyways and stepped streets lined with tall stone houses.

Santa Maria della Neve, in Cuglieri

The square in front of Santa Maria offers a fine view of the town and the coast between Santa Caterina di Pittinuri and Porto Alabe.

Environs
The coast is 15 km (9 miles) away on main road 292. **Santa Caterina di Pittinuri** is a seaside town set around a white-stone inlet enclosed by a limestone cliff, where the Spanish Torre del Pozzo tower stands. This stretch of coast is scenic, with rocky headlands and white sand and pebble beaches. The most famous sight is **S'Archittu**, a large natural bridge created by coastal erosion. A dirt road off main road 292, between Santa Caterina di Pittinuri and S'Archittu, goes to the ruins of the Punic-Roman city of **Cornus**, the setting for the last battle between the Romans and Sardinian Carthaginians headed by Amsicora (215 BC).

In the 9th century the city was abandoned because of repeated Saracen raids and the inhabitants founded a new city, Curulis Nova, present-day Cuglieri, on the nearby mountainside. The dirt road peters out just before the Early Christian town of Columbaris, while the acropolis of Cornus is visible on the hill to the southwest. Although the archaeological site may seem abandoned, it still has some sarcophagi and the remains of a three-nave basilica. It seems likely that all of these date back to the 6th century.

The cliff with the famous S'Archittu di Santa Caterina natural bridge at Pittinuri, near Cuglieri

Aerial view of the Cabras marsh area

⓯ Cabras

Road map B4. 🏛 10,000. 🚌 ℹ️
Town Hall (0783 3971). 🎉 first Sun in
Sep: Festa di San Salvatore.
🌐 **comunedicabras.it**

The town of Cabras, not far from
Oristano, is characterized by its
old, one-storey houses. It stands
on the edge of the largest
freshwater lake and marsh in
Sardinia (2,000 hectares, 5,000
acres), and is connected to the
sea via a series of canals. The
presence of both fresh and salt
water attracts coots, marsh
harriers, peregrine falcons and
purple gallinules.

In the past, local fishermen
used long, pointed boats, called
is fassonis, made of dried rushes
and other marsh plants using
a technique similar to that
known to the Phoenicians.
Another Phoenician survival is
the marinading technique
called sa merca, in which fresh
fish is wrapped in plant leaves
from the lake and left to soak in
salt water.

Environs
At the northern end of the
Golfo di Oristano is the **Laguna
di Mistras**. Separated from the
sea by sandbars, in wetlands
of international scientific
importance, this lagoon makes
an ideal habitat for flamingoes,
cormorants, grey herons and
ospreys. In a modern complex
by the lagoon, the **Museo Civico
di Cabras** displays finds from
Tharros (see pp136–7) and other
local archaeological sites, and
explores the ethnographic and
ecological makeup of the area.

🏛 Museo Civico di Cabras
Via Tharros. **Tel** 0783 29 06 36 **Open**
9am–1pm, 4–8pm (winter 3–7pm)
daily. 🎫 (ticket also valid for Tharros).

⓰ San Salvatore

Road map B4. ℹ️ Cabras. 🎉 end of
Aug–first Sun in Sep: Corsa degli Scalzi
di San Salvatore.

Typical white houses for
pilgrims, or cumbessias,
surround the country church
of San Salvatore. They are
occupied for nine days each
year in late August and early
September, for the novena
of the saint's feast day. In the
1960s the church's central
square was used as a location
for "spaghetti westerns".

San Salvatore was built in the
17th century on the site of a
nuraghic sanctuary for the
worship of sacred waters. In the
6th century the site was transformed into an underground
church. In the left-hand nave
stairs lead to the hypogeum,
which has six chambers: two
rectangular ones flanking a
corridor leading to a circular
atrium with a well, around
which three further chambers
lie. The hypogeum was partly
hewn out of the rock; the

The annual Corsa degli Scalzi (barefoot race) at San Salvatore

Marsh samphire, a typical plant growing in the Cabras marshes

vaulted ceilings are made of sandstone and brick. On the walls are graffiti of animals (elephants, panthers and peacocks) and heroes and gods (Hercules fighting the Nemean lion, Mars and Venus with a small winged cupid). There are even Arabic writings about Allah and Mohammed, and numerous depictions of ships, which experts believe are ex votos.

The Latin letters RVF, interlaced as in a monogram and repeated several times, seem to derive from the Phoenician language and are said to stand for "cure, save, give health".

On the first Saturday in September, the feast day of San Salvatore is celebrated. The event is marked with a barefoot (*scalzi*) race in memory of local youths, who, in the Middle Ages, left the village to escape from the Saracens but returned to save the statue of the saint.

Just east of the sanctuary are the ruins of the Domu 'e Cubas Roman baths.

⑰ San Giovanni di Sinis

Road map B4. 40. *i* Cabras.

At the edge of the Sinis peninsula is a bathing resort once famous for its fishermen's huts made of wood and reeds (*see p119*). Today only a few survive; the largest group lies east of the motorway, not far from the archaeological site of Tharros (*see pp136–7*).

As visitors enter the small village of San Giovanni di Sinis they will see the early Christian church of **San Giovanni** which, together with San Saturnino in Cagliari, is the oldest in Sardinia. It was built in the 5th century, though much of the present-day church was the result of 9th- and 10th-century rebuilding. The three-nave interior is barrel-vaulted.

Environs

Near San Giovanni di Sinis is the WWF **Torre 'e Seu** reserve, where some of the last dwarf palms in the area survive. A dirt road at the northern end of San Giovanni di Sinis leads to the reserve. At the gate there is a path to the sea and the Torre 'e Seu Spanish tower.

The Vernaccia Wine of Sardinia

The countryside north of Oristano is one of the most fertile areas in Sardinia, carpeted with olive trees and grapevines. The Vernaccia made in Oristano is perhaps Sardinia's most famous white wine and is produced in the towns of San Vero Milis, Cabras, Zeddiani, Narbolia, Riola and Baratili. The wine is full-bodied and strong, with 15 degrees of alcohol, and is aged for at least three years in large oak barrels. You can take a tour of the wine-producing area, and pause for a wine-tasting at the Cantina Sociale della Vernaccia, where the entrance is framed by an impressive 18th-century gate.

Vernaccia grapes

🏛 **Cantina Sociale della Vernaccia**
Località Il Rimedio 149. **Tel** 0783 33 155. **Open** 10am–noon Mon–Fri. 🅿 🚫 book in advance. 🆆 **vinovernaccia.com**

The 18th-century gate, Cantina Sociale

Wine barrels in the Cantina Sociale della Vernaccia

Rows of Vernaccia vines

⓲ Tharros

The city of Tharros was founded by the Phoenicians around the end of the 8th century BC, on a spit of land called Capo San Marco, which offered safe anchorage for cargo-laden ships. By the 6th and 5th centuries BC, Tharros had become a flourishing port and this prosperity continued under the Romans, from 238 BC on. With sea on two sides, this is one of the most intriguing ancient sites in the Mediterranean. Only a third of the area has been unearthed so far. Most of the visible remains date back to the Punic-Roman era, but there is also evidence of previous civilizations: the nuraghic village (late Bronze Age) and the Tophet (Phoenician) located on the hill, Su Murru Mannu.

7th–6th century BC necklace
Made of gold and cornelian, this necklace was found in the southern necropolis.

Capo San Marco
At the southern tip of the Sinis peninsula, Capo San Marco still has the remains of nuraghe Baboe Cabitza, dating back to the late Bronze Age. During this time, the whole peninsula was likely subject to intense settlement.

Remains of the Fortifications
At the foot of San Giovanni is a quadrangular base of squared sandstone blocks thought to date back to the 3rd century BC.

KEY

① **San Giovanni Spanish tower**

② **Deep tombs** were installed by the fortifications north of the city during Roman times.

③ **Tophet**

④ **Sanctuary of Demeter**

⑤ **The Castellum Acquae** is an imposing rectangular building, the function of which is still in doubt. The archaeologist G Pesce thought that this was the cistern feeding the city's water system.

⑥ and ⑦ **Baths**

Distinctive Residence
The presence of a courtyard of basalt millstones in this house has led archaeologists to believe that this was an area dedicated to working wheat, or possibly even a bakery.

Drainage System
A drain ran along the middle of the paved road. The system was linked to the rows of houses on either side of the street.

VISITORS' CHECKLIST

Practical Information
Road map B4.
San Giovanni di Sinis.
Cooperativa Penisola Sinis
(0783 37 00 19). **Open** 9am–7pm summer, 9am–5pm winter.

Head of Goddess
Found in the Punic necropolis, this 5th-century BC head is now in Cagliari's archaeological museum (*see p62*).

★ Corinthian Columns
These reconstructed columns are part of the process of re-erecting monuments that occupied Tharros between the 1st and 3rd centuries AD. One of the columns has an original Corinthian capital.

★ Cistern
This quadrangular cistern (3rd–4th centuries AD) on the southern side of the temple is made of large blocks of sandstone and adorned with Doric half-columns.

⑲ Oristano

Placed at the northern border of the Campidano region, between the mouth of the Tirso river and the Santa Giusta marshlands, Oristano is the largest town in western Sardinia. It was founded in 1070, after the powerful and prosperous city of Tharros was abandoned, the inhabitants defeated by constant pirate raids. The period between 1100 and 1400 saw the rise of the city under enlightened rulers such as Mariano IV and his daughter Eleonora, who controlled most of Sardinia. Oristano became the provincial capital only in 1974. The town stands in the middle of a fertile plain with a network of pools, well-stocked with fish. The historic centre, once protected by the city walls, is small and mostly a pedestrian-only zone.

The Cathedral of Oristano with its octagonal campanile

🏛 Cattedrale

Piazza Mannu. **Tel** 0783 786 84. **Open** 7am–noon, 4–6:30pm daily. &

Dedicated to the Blessed Virgin Mary, the Cathedral was built in 1228 by Lombard architects and masons for Mariano di Torres. It was totally rebuilt in the 17th century in the Baroque style and now displays a mixture of influences. The remaining original elements are the octagonal bell tower with its onion dome and brightly coloured majolica tiles, the bronze doors and the Cappella del Rimedio, which has a fine marble balustrade decorated with Pisan bas relief sculpture depicting Daniel in the lions' den. The Renaissance choir behind the main altar is another important work. The rich and varied Tesoro del Duomo, the cathedral treasury, is housed in the chapterhouse, and silverwork, vestments and illuminated manuscripts can be seen upon request. On Piazza del Duomo are the Palazzo Arcivescovile (arch-bishop's palace) and the Seminario Tridentino.

🗼 Torre di Mariano II

Piazza Roma.

Also called Torre di San Cristoforo or Porta Manna, this sandstone tower at the northern end of the former city walls was built in 1291 by the ruler of the Arborea principality, Mariano II. This and the Portixedda tower, just opposite, are the sole surviving remains of the old city walls. At the top of the tower is a large bell made in 1430. The Torre di Mariano is open on its inner façades and looks over Piazza Roma, the heart of city life, with its fashionable shops and outdoor cafés.

🏛 Corso Umberto

This pedestrian street, also known as Via Dritta, is the most elegant in Oristano with impressive buildings such as Palazzo Siviera, once the residence of the Marquise d'Acrisia, which has a dome on top, and Palazzo

---

The Knights of the Star

The Sa Sartiglia procession and tournament is centuries-old and is held on the last Sunday of Carnival and on Shrove Tuesday. It was probably introduced in 1350 by Mariano II to celebrate his wedding. On 2 February the procession leader, *su Componidori*, is chosen. On the day of the event he is dressed by a group of girls. A white shirt is sewn on him, his face is wrapped in fasciae and covered with a woman's mask, and a bride's veil and black hat are placed on his head. He then leads a procession of knights, trumpeters and drummers through the city to the tournament grounds by the Arcivescovado and the Cathedral. At a given signal the tournament begins. The leader has to run his sword into the hole in the middle of a star hanging from a string, and pick it up. If he succeeds, this signals a prosperous year.

The Sa Sartiglia tournament at Oristano

Falchi, built in the 1920s. Oristano's smartest shops are found here and it is the most popular street for the traditional evening stroll.

🏛 Piazza Eleonora D'Arborea

This long, irregular, tree-lined square is named after the ruler who established the famous Carta de Logu body of laws in 1392. A 19th-century statue of Eleonora stands in the middle of the square. This piazza also boasts noble buildings such as Palazzo Corrias and the Palazzo Comunale, the town hall, once the Scolopi monastery. The octagonal church of San Vincenzo was part of the monastery.

Eleonora d'Arborea

⛪ San Francesco

Piazza Mannu. **Tel** 0783 782 75.
Open 9:30–11:30am, 5–6:30pm.
This Neo-Classical church was built over the remains of a Gothic church which was completely destroyed in the early 19th century. The façade has six columns with Ionic capitals. In the interior is one of the most interesting statues in Sardinia: a crucifix executed by

an unknown late 14th-century Catalan artist. Another important work, by Pietro Cavaro, depicts *The Stigmata of San Francesco*.

⛪ Santa Chiara

Via Garibaldi. **Tel** 0783 780 93.
Open for Mass only (6pm daily).
The Gothic church of Santa Chiara was built in the 14th century. The façade displays sandstone ashlars, a severe rose window and small bell gable. The interior has wooden Gothic corbels with carved animal figures.

🏛 Antiquarium Arborense

Palazzo Parpaglia, Via Parpaglia 37.
Tel 0783 79 12 62. **Open** mid-Jun–mid-Sep: 9am–2:30pm, 3:30–9pm daily; mid-Sep–mid-Jun 9am–8pm daily .
🅿 📷 ♿ 🏛 w antiquarium
arborense.it

Housed in the Neo-Classical Palazzo Parpaglia, this interesting museum features archaeological finds from Tharros, an art gallery and a section given over to medieval Oristano. The gallery has interesting altarpieces in Catalan style: the San Martino *retablo* (15th century) attributed

to the workshop of the Catalan artist Ramon de Mur; the *Retablo di Cristo* (1533), by followers of Pietro Cavaro, of which only nine panels remain; and the *Retablo della Madonna dei Consiglieri* (1565) by the Cagliari artist Antioco Mainas, representing the councillors of Oristano kneeling before the Virgin Mary.

The archaeological collection contains over 2,000 Neolithic obsidian scrapers, bone hair slides, small amphoras from Greece and Etruria, and Roman glass objects and oil lamps. These all belong to the Collezione Archeologica Efisio Pischedda. Among the most notable objects in the collection are a terracotta mask used to ward off evil spirits, scarabs made out of green jasper, and carved gemstones from the Roman period.

Oristano

① Cattedrale
② Torre di Mariano II
③ Corso Umberto
④ Piazza Eleonora
⑤ San Francesco
⑥ Santa Chiara
⑦ Antiquarium Arborense

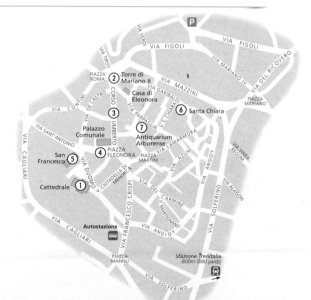

0 metres 300
0 yards 300

Fishermen using *fassonis*, traditional sedge boats, on the Santa Giusta lake

⓴ Santa Giusta

Road map B4. 🗚 4,700.
ℹ Via Amsicora 17 (0783 35 45 00).
🎉 14 May: Sagra di Santa Giusta.

This agricultural town, built on the banks of the Santa Giusta lake and marsh, was built over the ruins of the Roman city of Ottona. The cathedral of **Santa Giusta**, a jewel of Pisan Romanesque architecture blended with Arab and Lombard elements, stands on the rise as you enter the town. The cathedral was built in the first half of the 12th century and has a narrow façade, with a triplelancet window.

The columns in the interior are in various styles, and originally came from the nearby Roman cities of Neapolis, Tharros and Othoca. From the sacristy there is a lovely view of the lake, one of the best fishing areas in Sardinia, where you can still see the long *is fassonis* sedge boats of Phoenician derivation. On the feast day of Santa Giusta in May, a lively regatta is held here. The local gastronomic speciality is *bottarga* (salted mullet roe).

Soapstone scarab found in Santa Giusta digs

🏛 Santa Giusta
Via Manzoni. **Tel** 0783 35 92 05. **Open** 9am–noon, 3–7pm (2–6pm winter).

㉑ Arborea

Road map B4. 🗚 3,900. ℹ Town Hall (0783 80 331). 🎉 Good Friday: living representation of the Passion of Christ. 🌐 **comune.arborea.or.it**

Arborea was founded in 1930 during the Fascist period and was initially named

Cathedral of Santa Giusta, a masterpiece of Romanesque architecture

Mussolinia. The town was built on a regular grid plan typical of modern cities. All the civic buildings (school, parish church, hotel and town hall) are found in Piazza Maria Ausiliatrice, from which the main streets radiate. The avenues are lined with trees and the two-storey Neo-Gothic houses are surrounded by gardens. The **Museo della Bonifica** is dedicated to the land reclamation scheme of the 1920s and 1930s, and also contains finds from excavations in the area, including the Roman necropolis of S'Ungroni, north of Arborea, discovered during the land reclamation.

About 9 km (6 miles) to the southwest is the pretty fishing village of Marceddi, on the edge of the marsh of the same name, dominated by the 16thcentury Torrevecchia.

🏛 Museo della Bonifica
Corso Italia 44. **Tel** 0783 80 20 05 or 347 434 2502. **Open** 9:30am–noon, 4:30–7pm Tue–Fri, 5–7:30pm Sat & Sun. 🔋

㉒ Fordongianus

Road map C4. 🗚 1,200. ℹ Via Traiano 7 (0783 601 23). 🎉 21 Apr & 21 Aug: Festa di San Lussorio.

Ancient Forum Traiani was once the largest Roman city in the interior. Located in the Tirso river valley, it was fortified against the local Barbagia people. Today the centre consists of houses in red and grey stone. One of the best preserved is Casa Madeddu, a typical old "Aragonese house" of the early 1600s with Catalan-style doorways and windows. On the same street is the 16th century parish church of San Pietro Apostolo, in red trachyte, which has been almost entirely rebuilt. The **Roman Baths** lie on the banks of the river, with a fine portico and several rooms with mosaic pavements. The rectangular pool still contains warm water from the hot springs.

A short distance south of Fordongianus stands the rural church of San Lussorio, built by Victorine monks around AD 1100, over an early Christian crypt.

🏛 Roman Baths

Via Terme. **Tel** 0783 60 157 **Open** 9:30am–1pm, 3–5pm (summer 3:30–8pm) daily.

Earrings found at the Forum Traiani

㉓ Paulilàtino

Road map C4. 🗻 2,500. ℹ Viale della Libertà 33 (0785 556 23). 🎉 second Sun in May: Sagra di Santa Cristina.

This rural village at the edge of the Abbasanta basalt plateau is surrounded by olive groves and cork oak woods. The houses are built of dark stone and have Aragonese doorways and small wrought-iron balconies. The same stone was used to build the church of San Teodoro in the 17th century. This Aragonese Gothic church has a stained-glass rose window and a bell tower with an onion dome. **Palazzo Atzori** houses a museum of folk culture with domestic tools and objects on display.

🏛 Palazzo Atzori

Via Nazionale 127. **Tel** 0785 554 38. **Open** summer: 9:30am–1pm, 4–6:30pm, winter: 9:30am–1pm, 3–5:30pm. **Closed** Mon.

Environs

About 4 km (3 miles) from town, a turning off state road 131 takes you to the nuraghic village of **Santa Cristina**. A stone wall

encloses the archaeological area, where there is a well temple dedicated to the local mother-goddess dating from the 1st millennium BC. The well is in a good state of preservation, and a broad stone stairway leads to its vaulted underground chamber. Nearby is an enclosure that was probably used for general assemblies. The sacred nature of this site has been maintained over the centuries with the construction of a church dedicated to Santa Cristina. Worshippers continue to flock to the church, which is surrounded by *muristenes*, houses intended for those who come here for novena on the saint's feast day.

To the right of the church, among the olive trees, another archaeological zone includes a well-preserved nuraghe and two rectangular nuraghic-age stone dwellings. The best preserved of these is 14 m (46 ft) long and 2 m (6 ft) high.

🏛 Santa Cristina

Km 114,300, SS131 Cagliari-Sassari. ℹ Cooperativa Archeotour (0785 554 38). **Open** 8:30am–dusk.

Steps leading to the temple of Santa Cristina at Paulilàtino

Panoramic view of Àles at the foot of Monte Arci

㉔ Àles

Road map C4. 🗻 1,700. ℹ Town Hall (0783 91 131). 🎉 first Sun in Aug: Santa Madonna della Neve. 🌐 comune.ales.or.it

Àles, the main village in the Marmilla area, lies on the eastern slope of Monte Arci. In the upper part stands the cathedral of San Pietro, built in 1686 by Genoan architect Domenico Spotorno, who used the ruins of the 12th-century church on this site as material for his construction.

Twin bell towers with ceramic domes rise above the elegant façade, while in the Baroque interior, the sacristy has lovely carved furniture and a rare 14th-century crucifix. The Archivio Capitolare contains elegant gold jewellery.

In the same square stand the Palazzo Vescovile and the seminary and oratory of the Madonna del Rosario.

Àles is also the birthplace of Antonio Gramsci (1891–1937) *(see p129)*. The house is marked with a plaque.

Environs

Àles is a good starting point for a hike to the top of Trebina Longa and Trebina Lada, the highest peaks on **Monte Arci**, the remnants of an ancient crater. Along the way you are likely to spot pieces of obsidian, the hard black volcanic glass which was cut into thin slices and used to make arrowheads, spears and scrapers. The obsidian of Monte Arci was in great demand, and not only supplied the whole of Sardinia, but was also sold throughout the Mediterranean in the 4th–3rd millennia BC.

THE NORTH AND THE COSTA SMERALDA

Northeastern Sardinia's beauty is familiar from the classic images of a rugged coastline, beautiful inlets, sparkling turquoise sea and beaches of brilliant white sand. To the north, the islands crowded in the Straits of Bonifacio, a stone's throw from Corsica, have great appeal for those in search of unspoilt calm.

The most well-known development in the northeast is the famous Costa Smeralda, founded by a consortium of financiers including the Aga Khan in 1962. In the space of 40 years, few areas in Sardinia have undergone such profound changes as the northeastern coastline. Villas and residential hotels have sprung up almost everywhere, and small harbours have been equipped as marinas. The surroundings are undeniably beautiful, with spectacular scenery at headlands such as Capo d'Orso and Capo Testa. The perfume of the Mediterranean maquis still manages to reach the beaches of pure white sand, and there are still unspoilt areas that have resisted the encroachment of holiday homes. Tourism brings its own problems however, and there is increasing recognition of the need for stricter controls on building, if the growing influx of visitors is not to damage the island's unique environment.

In the interior, the Gallura region displays quite a different character, with extensive forests of cork oak trees and rough, rocky terrain. Granite outcrops create enchanting landscapes like the Valle della Luna near Aggius (see p156). This part of Sardinia is characterized by its wholesome cooking, the continuing practice of traditional handicrafts and frequent reminders of its long history. As well as prehistoric nuraghe, an exceptional series of Romanesque churches survives in the Logudoro area (see pp160–1), culminating in the black and white striped stone church of Santissima Trinità di Saccargia (see pp162–3)

The shore of San Teodoro, ideal for bathing and sunbathing

◄ The beautiful, crystal-clear waters off the Costa Smeralda

Exploring the North and the Costa Smeralda

The port and airport in Olbia handle most of the visitors headed not only for the Costa Smeralda holiday villages, but the rest of Sardinia as well. The appeal of the northern part of Sardinia is the beautiful long coastline, with magnificent beaches and wind-eroded cliffs. From Olbia the road winds northwards to Santa Teresa di Gallura, then turns westwards, beyond the Castelsardo headland, until it reaches Porto Torres. In the interior, Tempio Pausania, capital of the Gallura region, makes an excellent starting point for local tours.

The bear-like cliff at Capo d'Orso

Sights at a Glance

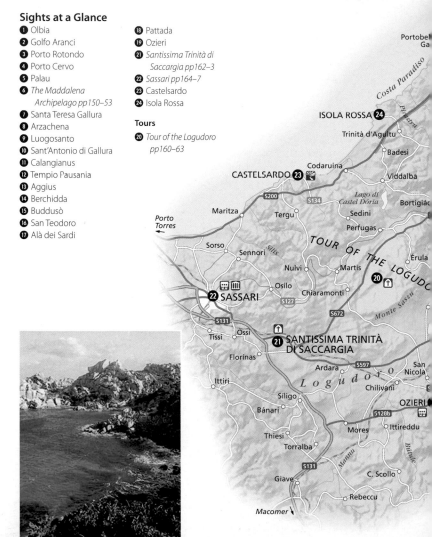

A stretch of coast at Capo Testa

For additional map symbols *see back flap*

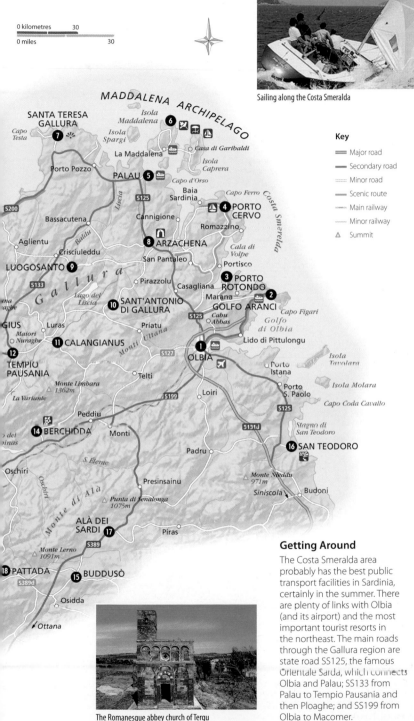

0 kilometres   30

0 miles   30

Sailing along the Costa Smeralda

Key

━━ Major road

━━ Secondary road

═══ Minor road

━━ Scenic route

╌╌ Main railway

── Minor railway

△ Summit

The Romanesque abbey church of Tergu

Getting Around

The Costa Smeralda area probably has the best public transport facilities in Sardinia, certainly in the summer. There are plenty of links with Olbia (and its airport) and the most important tourist resorts in the northeast. The main roads through the Gallura region are state road SS125, the famous Orientale Sarda, which connects Olbia and Palau; SS133 from Palau to Tempio Pausania and then Ploaghe; and SS199 from Olbia to Macomer.

The ruins at Cabu Abbas, a nuraghic site just outside Olbia

❶ Olbia

Road map D1 & 2. 📶 43,000. ✈
🚌 🚉 ⛴ *i* 0789 52 206.
📅 15–20 May: San Simplicio.
🖥 olbiaturismo.it

Olbia is only 200 km (125 miles) from the port of Civitavecchia on the mainland of Italy, and has always been the main arrival point on the island, rather than the capital Cagliari. The building of the airport just outside Olbia, to serve the Costa Smeralda, has confirmed this role.

Olbia is a modern city and usually considered as a stopoff on the way to the coast. Of interest in the town are a Roman cistern in Piazza Margherita, proof of ancient Roman occupation, and the Romanesque **San Simplicio.** This church was built from the 11th century onwards and enlarged in the 13th century.

Environs

There are two interesting prehistoric sites near Olbia: the **Cabu Abbas** nuraghic complex (4 km, 2 miles to the northeast) and the **Sa Testa** holy well.

To reach Cabu Abbas from the old port of Olbia, go along Corso Umberto and then Via d'Annunzio. Once past the railway you will see the country church of Santa Maria Cabu Abbas. From here a dirt path winds up towards the top of the mountain, another 15 minutes on foot. The site offers a great view of the island of Tavolara. There is a central well with a tower where remains of sacrifices – burnt bones and pieces of pottery – were found in 1937. This large megalithic zone extends for about 200 m (656 ft).

To reach the Sa Testa holy well, take road SP82 to Golfo Aranci as far as the Pozzo Sacro hotel. This site consists of a wide paved courtyard, from which 17 covered steps lead down to a well chamber.

❷ Golfo Aranci

Road map D1. 📶 2,100. 🚌 ⛴
📅 15 Aug: Assunta.
🖥 golfoaranci.com

The name "Aranci" means oranges, but you will not see orange groves here. Golfo Aranci owes its name to a mistaken interpretation of the local place-name *di li ranci,* meaning "some crabs". Formerly a part of Olbia, the village of Golfo Aranci became an independent town in 1979. Since 1882 increasing numbers of ferries from the mainland have used Golfo Aranci as a stopping place. Corsica Sardinia Ferries *(see p205)* has a direct service from here to Livorno.

Luxury sailing craft moored at the Porto Rotondo Yacht Club

❸ Porto Rotondo

Road map D1. *i* 0789 34 105.

Porto Rotondo is not so much a town as a large, well-planned tourist village which grew from nothing during the Costa Smeralda boom. The buildings, placed around the inevitable yacht marina, were designed to fit in as much as possible with the natural surroundings. The result is certainly pleasant, and Porto Rotondo has been a great success as a tourist resort, despite its perhaps slightly artificial air.

Mussel beds at sunset in the Bay of Olbia

Aerial view of Porto Rotondo

The Porto Rotondo quay and Piazzetta San Marco are lined with famous designer shops, and throughout the summer the cafés and restaurants are crowded with visitors, lunching, dining, meeting friends, or just watching the world go by. Out of season Porto Rotondo is quiet and even deserted.

The church of San Lorenzo, designed by Andrea Cascella, holds pretty wooden statues by Mario Ceroli depicting Biblical figures.

Just outside Porto Rotondo is the attractive headland called Punta della Volpe, which separates the Golfo di Marinella from the Golfo di Cugnana.

Architecture on the Costa Smeralda

In the early 1960s, a stretch of coastline in northeastern Sardinia was transformed into the most exclusive tourist resort in the Mediterranean, the Costa Smeralda, or Emerald Coast. Back in 1962 the beaches were the preserve of grazing cattle, then taken to overwinter on the islands of Mortorio, Soffi and Li Milani. The Consorzio Costa Smeralda was formed to transform the area. The group initially consisted of the landowners, but expanded to include property owners. Building regulations were established and an architectural committee was founded to supervise any new building in the area. The prominent architects Luigi Vietti, Jacques Couelle, Giancarlo and Michele Busiri Vici, Antonio Simon, Raimond Martin and Leopoldo Mastrella were appointed to design the resorts. The area has since changed beyond recognition. Luxury hotels, sumptuous villas and huge holiday villages have gone up, together with sporting facilities: the famous Yacht Club and one of the most attractive golf courses in the Mediterranean, as well as small villages such as Porto Cervo.

The Neo-Mediterranean style is a combination of the various elements frequently seen in Mediterranean architecture.

In planning Porto Rotondo, the architects decided that only native plants should be used, so trees such as pine, poplar and eucalyptus are banned because they would not blend in with the local strawberry trees, myrtle, lentiscus, oleanders and mimosa.

The materials used must be traditional local stone, pebbles, curved tiles and brick.

An aerial view of Porto Cervo

❹ Porto Cervo

Road map D1. **ℹ** 0789 89 20 19.

The heart of the Costa Smeralda and a paradise for European VIPs, Porto Cervo is centred around two yacht harbours with some of the most spectacular private craft in the world. In summer there is a series of top sporting events, including regattas and golf tournaments *(see p200 and p203)*. The traditional evening stroll along the quay is almost obligatory, with fashionable designer shops on one side, and luxury yachts on the other. The church of Stella Maris has a canvas attributed to the painter El Greco.

Environs
There are plenty of good beaches around Porto Cervo, such as Liscia Ruja to the south, framed by the sheltered Cala di Volpe.

❺ Palau

Road map D1. **⚐** 3,300. **ℹ** 0789 70 70 25. **w** palauturismo.com

The logical departure point for a trip to the Maddalena archipelago, Palau also owes its success to the appeal of the narrow-gauge Sassari-Tempio-Palau railway, part of the Trenino Verde *(see pp96–7)*. Life here is rather frenetic in the summer and revolves around the ferry boat wharf and the yacht harbour. From Palau you can travel to some of the most fascinating and famous places on the coast, such as the jagged Capo d'Orso (Bear Cape)

promontory, which ends in a large, bear-shaped rock, sculpted by the wind.

To get to Punta Sardegna, take the road that goes up to Monte Altura and then go on foot to the beach of Cala Trana, on the tip of the headland. There is an extraordinary view of the coast and the islands, which is particularly lovely in the early morning and at sunset, despite

the fact that 21st-century construction work is slowly but surely spoiling the unique beauty of this part of Sardinia.

❻ The Maddalena Archipelago

See pp150–51.

❼ Santa Teresa Gallura

Road map C1. **⚐** 4,200. **ℹ** 0789 75 41 27. **⚑** 15–18 Oct: Festival.
w santateresagalluraturismo.com

The area around Santa Teresa was inhabited in Roman times and was also important to the Pisans, who used the local granite for building. The present-day town was built from scratch during the Savoyard period. It has a regular grid plan with streets intersecting at right angles, in

Sunset at Palau, departure point for the Maddalena Archipelago

The Aga Khan and the Costa Smeralda

The Consorzio Costa Smeralda group of foreign investors was founded in 1962 with Prince Karim Aga Khan IV at its head. The Harvard-educated prince, rich and charismatic, was then in his mid-twenties. He is reputed to have spent more than 1,000 million dollars in creating an opulent jet-set playground, complete with yachting marinas, luxury hotels, villas and elegant restaurants along the Gallura coastline, all designed to harmonize with the rugged Sardinian landscape. The project has proved very successful: Porto Cervo and the nearby villages quickly became popular holiday spots, especially for the wealthy and famous of the international jet set, who can be seen on the quays of Porto Cervo in the summer.

Aga Khan IV

Overlooking Santa Teresa Gallura

the middle of which is a small square and the church of San Vittorio. The local economy is based on fishing (including coral fishing) and tourism.

On the rocky headland stands the Torre Longosardo, a tower built in the 16th century during the Aragonese period; it affords a magnificent view of Porto Longone bay and, in the distance, the white cliffs circling the city of Bonifacio in Corsica, which is located only 12 km (7.5 miles) away.

To the left the coast falls away to the beach of Rena Bianca, which ends not far from the Isola Monica, a tiny island which has the remains of an abandoned quarry.

The Capo Testa lighthouse

Environs
About 5 km (3 miles) away is **Capo Testa**, a rocky promontory connected to the mainland by a thin sandbar. The headland can be reached via a very pretty route around the bays of Colba and Santa Reparata. A walk through the ancient and modern quarries – which supplied the Romans with the granite for the columns in the Pantheon – accompanied by the sweet fragrance of the maquis will take you to the Capo Testa lighthouse.

❽ Arzachena

Road map: D1. 🚗 12,000.
ℹ️ 0789 84 40 55.

As recently as the 1960s, this was a peaceful shepherds' village. Today it is the centre of one of the most famous tourist resorts in the world, the Costa Smeralda, and has undergone considerable change. Towering above the houses is a curious rock formed by wind erosion, called the Fungo (mushroom), and there are many traces of prehistoric settlements in the vicinity. Must-sees include the **Albucciu Nuraghe**, the **Tomba di Giganti Coddu Vecchju** and the **Li Muri Necropolis**.

🏛 Albucciu Nuraghe
GeSeCo Srl **Tel** 0789 81 391. **Open** summer: 9am–8pm daily; winter: 10am–6pm daily. 🚗 💻 📷
🌐 **gesecoarzachena.it**

From Arzachena, take the road to Olbia and after about 600 m (650 yds), at the end of town, follow the turn-off and then take the footpath on the right. Once at the nuraghe, go up

the ladder to the upper level, to visit the side section.

The stone brackets that once supported the original wooden structure are still intact.

🏛 Tomba di Giganti Coddu Vecchju
For contact details & opening hours see Albucciu Nuraghe. 🚗 💻 📷

To get to the Giants' Tomb, take state road SS427 towards Calangianus and, after about 3 km (2 miles), take the turning to the right signposted Luogosanto. After about 1,800 m (1 mile) you join the Capichera road; another 500 m (550 yds) on there is a path leading to the tomb, which lies to the right. In the middle of the funerary monument there is a stele 4 m (13 ft) high, surrounded by a semicircular wall of stone slabs set into the earth.

🏛 Li Muri Necropolis
For contact details & opening hours see Albucciu Nuraghe. 🚗 (book ahead for a trek combining archaeology and nature).

Once outside Arzachena, follow signs for Calangianus (SS427) and then the right-hand turning for Luogosanto. Continue for 4.5 km (3 miles) and take another turning to the right (a dirt road), which goes to the necropolis of Li Muri.

This site includes a number of ancient tombs: burial chambers surrounded by concentric circles of stones. These funerary circles constitute the most important monumental complex left from the era archaeologists now refer to as the Arzachena Culture.

The mistral whipping up the surf off Capo Testa

❻ The Maddalena Archipelago

Seven islands (Maddalena, Caprera and Santo Stefano to the southeast, Spargi, Budelli, Razzoli and Santa Maria to the northwest) make up the Arcipelago della Maddalena. Beyond lie the Straits of Bonifacio, which became a marine reserve of international status at the beginning of 1997. Rugged, jagged coasts, rocks hewn by wind and water erosion, and tenacious maquis vegetation characterize this group of islands, known during the Roman period as *Cuniculariae*, or "rabbit islands". In the 18th century Maddalena was used as a military base – a convenient landing place, it lay in a strategically important position. A tour of the island would be incomplete without a visit to Caprera, to see the places where the Italian hero Giuseppe Garibaldi lived and is buried.

Razzoli   Sant
Mar

Budelli

Budelli
Cactus grows on the shores of this island, popular with divers.

Spargi

La Maddal

Spargi
Uninhabited, like Budelli, Razzoli and Santa Maria, this island has marvellously clear water and secluded beaches, making it an ideal site for swimmers, snorkellers and scuba divers.

KEY

① **A scenic route** of just over 20 km (12 miles) runs around the island, providing magnificent views of the archipelago, Corsica and the four Corsican islands of Lavezzi.

② **Guardia Vecchia** is the highest mountain on the island. The Savoy rulers chose it as the site for the fort of San Vittorio, which is now occupied by a lighthouse.

③ **The bridge over Passo della Moneta** was constructed in 1891 to link the islands of Maddalena and Caprera.

④ **Monte Teialone** is the highest point on Caprera.

Regattas
The west wind, an almost constant presence in the Maddalena archipelago, makes this a popular place for yachting competitions.

★ La Maddalena

This is the most important town in the archipelago. Town life centres around Piazza Umberto I and Piazza Garibaldi. There is a wide choice of boat trips to the nearby islands from the harbour.

★ Tomb of Garibaldi

The "hero of two worlds" was buried here on 2 June 1882.

Santo Stefano

Caprera

Caprera

The island of Caprera extends over nearly 1,600 hectares (3,950 acres).

Bird Life

The many rock formations in this archipelago are frequently visited by sea birds such as cormorants, to the delight of bird-watchers.

Exploring the Maddalena Archipelago

The small Maddalena Archipelago is a favourite with sailing fanatics, fans of underwater fishing and with people who appreciate tranquillity and unspoilt surroundings. Except for the two largest islands, the archipelago is uninhabited and, together with the many other small islands, make perfect summer destinations for boat trips, sunbathing and swimming in solitude.

The Sardinia Regional Naval headquarters at La Maddalena

La Maddalena

Road map D1. 12,000. 0/89 /3 63 21. from Palau. 20–22 Jul: Santa Maria Maddalena.

The town that is now the capital of the island was founded in 1770 and replaced a small village built on the shores of the Cala Gavetta bay. After the unsuccessful invasion on the part of the French in 1793, British admiral Horatio Nelson stopped at La Maddalena in 1804 and in 1887 the entire Maddalena Archipelago was turned into a naval base by the Savoy rulers. On Via Amendola, which runs along the seafront, a series of 19th-century buildings bears witness to the rapid development of the town in this period. In Piazza Garibaldi, the Municipio (town hall) has on display a French bomb dating from France's attempt to conquer Sardinia in 1793.

In the evening, particularly in summer, the residents of the island can be found taking a leisurely stroll around Via Garibaldi. Not far away is the church of Santa Maria Maddalena, which has two candelabra and a silver cross given by Admiral Nelson to the island's inhabitants. La Maddalena is still the headquarters of the Sardinia Regional Navy.

The Scenic Route

The road around the island is about 20 km (12 miles) long and goes through the Cala Spalmatore, Stagno Torto and Baia Trínita bays.

On your way from La Maddalena, you will see the church of the Trinità, then the turn-off for Monte Guardia Vecchia, on the summit of which is the Savoyard fort of San Vittorio, and lastly the island of Giardinelli, which is connected to La Maddalena by a narrow strip of land. Further north are Porto Massimo, the inlets of Abbatoggia and Cala d'Inferno, and the other large fortification on the island, Forte dei Colmi. In the first stretch of this tour is the **Museo Archeologico Navale "Nino Lamboglia"**, the maritime museum with finds from the "ship of Spargi", an ancient Roman cargo vessel discovered in the 1950s.

Museo Archeologico Navale "Nino Lamboglia"

Località Mongiardino. **Closed** until further notice. **Tel** 0789 79 06 60/33.

Caprera

Road map D1. 0789 73 63 21. This small island has 34 km (21 miles) of coastline, and is connected to the island of Maddalena by the 600 m (1,968 ft) Passo della Moneta bridge. Walkers will enjoy the climb up the steps to the top of Monte Teialone (212 m, 695 ft).

The island of Caprera became the property of Giuseppe Garibaldi in 1856 (see pp44–5). His estate is now part of the **Compendio Garibaldino** museum area. A visit here includes a fascinating tour of the stables, moorings and the Casa Bianca (white house) where Garibaldi lived. The stable still has a period steam engine used for threshing, while the Casa Bianca contains mementos of Garibaldi's adventurous life, including weapons, flags, portraits, the hero's clothes (including his famous red shirt) and a model of the Battle of Solferino.

Garibaldi and Caprera

The legendary Italian revolutionary and hero Giuseppe Garibaldi escaped to the island of Caprera in 1849, after the fall of the Roman Republic. He returned in 1855 after the death of his wife Anita and decided to buy most of the island. The rest of the land was then given to him by some English friends. Garibaldi, who went on to play a key role in the unification of Italy, settled on Caprera permanently in 1857, and died here in 1882.

Giuseppe Garibaldi wearing the famous red shirt

The famous pink sand beach at Budelli

Garibaldi's favourite room was the salon, and he asked to be taken there before he died. The calendar and clocks in the room have not been changed since that day, and still show the exact time of his death: 6:20pm on 2 June 1882.

Caprera also has a famous sailing school, the Centro Velico Caprera *(see p201)*.

🏛 Compendio Garibaldino
Tel 0789 72 71 62. **Open** 9am–1:30pm, 2–8pm Tue–Sun. **Closed** 1 Jan, 25 Dec. 📷 🐕 ♿ 🔤 compendiogaribaldino.it

Santo Stefano
Road map D1. 🛈 0789 73 63 21. The small island of Santo Stefano lies about halfway between Palau and the island of Maddalena and can be reached via the boats that depart at regular intervals from La Maddalena harbour. Dominating the scene is the Santo Stefano (or San Giorgio) fortress, also known as Napoleon's fort, built at the end of the 18th century.

There is a tourist village on the beach of Pesce, on the western coast.

Spargi
Road map D1. 🚢 from La Maddalena. 🛈 0789 73 63 21. Spargi is little more than 2 km (1 mile) in diameter and is completely uninhabited. The terrain is fairly barren and the coast steep and inaccessible, but there is a lovely beach for bathing, although keep in mind that it has no facilities. An ancient Roman ship was found opposite the Cala Corsara cove on the southern coast; its cargo is now in the Museo Archeologico Navale "Nino Lamboglia" at La Maddalena. Tourist boats make regular stops at Cala Corsara.

Budelli
Road map D1. 🛈 0789 73 63 21. This beautiful uninhabited island is remarkable for its unique beach of rose-coloured sand. Even though there are no facilities, Budelli is popular with visitors because of its beautifully unspoiled natural setting. It was also used in a film by the director Michelangelo Antonioni.

The clear, unpolluted water is also ideal for scuba diving, either to observe marine life or for underwater fishing.

Sailing In Northern Sardinia

The Straits of Bonifacio are dotted with small islands and rocks with lighthouses which create natural buoys, making the area ideal for yacht and dinghy racing. The wind is pretty constant, and in summer the west wind blows steadily at 40 km per hour (24 mph).

The Costa Smeralda Yacht Club at Porto Cervo, founded by the Aga Khan, is the main sailing facility in this area. This world-famous club organizes several major sailing races and other competitions. The most well-known are the Sardinia Cup, an international deep-sea championship held in even-numbered years, and the Settimana delle Bocche, a summer race for speedboats from all over Italy.

In the odd-numbered years the old harbour at Porto Cervo provides space for 50 or so vintage boats, from the *gozzo* with its characteristic lateen sail to 30-m (98-ft) schooners. This popular event, which has been held since 1982, is usually followed by the world yacht championship for boats in the Maxi class. Other important races, such as the European and world championships of various yacht categories, also take place here. The Costa Smeralda Yacht Club represented Italy in the 1983 America's Cup with the yacht *Azzurra* and in 1987 the club organized regattas to select the Italian representative in the America's Cup in Perth, Australia.

Yachts racing in the Straits of Bonifacio

San Trano, a 12th-century hermitage near Luogosanto

⑨ Luogosanto

Road map C1. 🏔 1,900. **ℹ** Town Hall (079 65 790). 🎉 first Sun in Aug: San Quirico's feast day.

The small village of Luogosanto is surrounded by maquis, and is well known for the production of bitter honey, often served with *seadas (see p183)*. The village is typical of the Gallura region, backed by greenery and wind-eroded pinkish-grey rocks. Every seven years a colourful and solemn ceremony celebrates the opening of the Porta Santa (holy door) of the church of Nostra Signora di Luogosanto.

San Quirico's feast day ends with a dinner for all of the villagers. The traditional dish *carr'e cogghju*, made with pork and cabbage, is served.

About 1 km (half a mile) to the east of Luogosanto is the **San Trano hermitage**, perched at 410 m (1,345 ft), dominating the landscape towards the north of the town. This small church was built in the 12th century in memory of the hermit saints San Nicola and San Trano, who, according to the legend, lived in the small cave to the rear of the altar.

Nearby is the Filetta spring, the waters of which are famous throughout the island. Squares, steps and street lamps have been set around the spring.

⑩ Sant'Antonio di Gallura

Road map D1. 🏔 1,700. 🚌 **ℹ** Town Hall (079 66 90 13). 🎉 last weekend in Sep: Sant'Antonio.

This village has always been an important farming and sheep-raising centre. In the heart of town, situated on a rocky spur, is a small, archaeological park, known for its intricate landscape of windsculpted rocks. This same site was inhabited in prehistoric times. During the first week of September, the feast days of Sant'Antonio, San Michele and Sant'Isidoro are celebrated with a procession. Decorated oxen and tractors follow the statues of the saints through the streets.

Environs
2 km (1 mile) away is the artificial lake of Liscia, capable of holding 150,000,000 cubic m (5 billion cubic ft) of water.

⑪ Calangianus

Road map C2. 🏔 4,800. 🚌 **ℹ** Town Hall (079 66 00 00). 🎉 third Sun in Sep: Sant'Isidoro's feast day.

In the forests around the town of Calangianus you can see evidence of cork harvesting everywhere: the barked cork oaks have that characteristic reddish colour that will remain until the bark grows again, while the cork strips themselves are heaped up in large piles to dry.

Calangianus is the cork production centre of the Gallura region and there are numbers of workshops and factories for processing the material. There is also an important trade school whose curriculum focuses on the cultivation of cork oaks and making the

The artificial lake of Liscia near Calangianus

maximum use of cork bark. In September every year Calangianus hosts an exhibition and trade fair of cork oaks and their many by-products, both on an industrial and domestic scale.

In the centre of the old town, in a small, isolated square, is the small parish church of Santa Giusta, which was built in the 17th century.

Cork items produced in the Gallura region

Environs

Near the village of **Luras** (northwest of Calangianus), a series of prehistoric dolmens is open to visitors. To reach the site, go through the village in the direction of Luogosanto and then turn right just before the end of town. At the point where the paved road ends, take the dirt road on the right, which takes you to the **Ladas Dolmen**, the most impressive of them all. It has a rectangular plan, is roofed with two granite slabs, and is 6 m (19 ft) long and 2.20 m (7 ft) wide.

🕛 Tempio Pausania

Road map C2. 🏛 14,000. 🚍
ℹ️ Pro Loco (079 639 00 80).
🎭 Shrove Tuesday: Carnival.

The capital of Gallura, Tempio Pausania consists of a large number of modern buildings which tend to obscure the charming old town. Investigate further and discover two- and three-storey buildings with dark granite stone walls and characteristic balconies.

Detail of Santa Croce

A short walk from the central Piazza Gallura, site of the town hall and other public buildings, is the **Cathedral** – founded in the 15th century but rebuilt in the 1800s. Also nearby are the Oratorio del Rosario and the small **Santa Croce** church.

Not far from town are the **Rinaggiu springs**, whose mineral water is famous for its beneficial qualities. As well as the traditional festivals, an international folklore festival is held here in July (see p31).

Environs

A short distance away, on state road SS133, is the turning for the **Maiori Nuraghe**, one of the best preserved megalithic structures in the area. By heading south from the town on state road 392 for 17 km (10 miles) you will pass close to the summit of **Monte Limbara** (1,359 m, 4,459 ft), which can be reached in a few minutes on foot from the paved road. Along the way you will see the Curadoreddu road house (about 6 km, 4 miles, from Tempio Pausania); here, a turning to the left will take you to an abandoned fish farm, from which you can admire an impressive view of mountain rock pools and waterfalls. Water flows from one great mass of rocks to the other, creating cascades and hollows. The spectacle is at its most striking during the winter months.

The bed of the mountain stream near Curadoreddu

Cork and the Handicrafts of Gallura

Cork is obtained from the stripped bark of cork oak trees (Quercus suber) and has always been a fundamental part of the Gallura regional economy. The material is used for everyday purposes as well as local handicrafts. Among kitchen utensils in use are cork spoons and ladles (such as the s'uppu, a small ladle used to collect water), buckets and different containers for water and wine, and large serving dishes – called agiones in dialect – for roasts and other dishes. Today the Tempio Pausania region produces 90 per cent of the bottle stoppers used in Italy, although the cork is also used as a building and insulating material.

Strips of cork bark ready for processing

Cork is very versatile, thanks to its lightness, resistance to air and water, its insulating properties and long life. Cork cannot be stripped from the tree before it is at least 25–30 years old. The first layer stripped is porous and elastic and of scant commercial use. Only nine to ten years after this first barking process is the true – and profitable – new layer of cork obtained. The trees are then stripped every nine to ten years, and the layers thoroughly seasoned before use.

A barked cork oak tree

The Valle della Luna (Valley of the Moon) near Aggius

⓭ Aggius

Road map C1. 🏔 1,200. **ℹ** Town Hall (079 62 10 60). 🎭 first Sun in Oct: feast days of Santa Vittoria and Madonna del Rosario. **W** aggius.net

Natural features have shaped this village and its surroundings. A granite outcrop dominates the landscape of Aggius, both in the high ground of the Parco Capitza, which towers over the town, and in the amazing labyrinth of rock formations in the nearby Valle della Luna.

Once the dominion of the Doria family from Genoa, and then ruled by the Aragonese, Aggius owes its present prosperity to the quarrying and processing of granite. Local handicrafts are also important to the economy – especially rug-making, every stage of which is carried out using traditional techniques.

The centre of Aggius is a pleasant place to walk; the old stone houses have been lovingly preserved and they are among the most attractive in the Gallura region. On the first Sunday in October traditional festivities are held, including the *di li 'agghiani*, for unmarried men, at which the Gallura *suppa cuata* (bread and cheese soup) is served.

The road to Isola Rossa will quickly bring you to the **Valle della Luna**, with its weird rock formations, which are the legacy of glaciation. On a left-hand curve a dirt road veers right. Follow this almost up to the bridge, then continue along the small road on the right, which leads to the **Izzana Nuraghe** in the middle of the valley.

Rock formations above Aggius

⓮ Berchidda

Road map C2. 🏔 3,400. 🚌 **ℹ** Town Hall (079 70 39 01).

Built on the southern slopes of Monte Limbara, in a hilly landscape which stretches as far as Monte Azzarina, Berchidda is a large village whose economy is based on sheep raising, dairy products, cork processing and viticulture. The leading local wine is Vermentino (one of the best known of Sardinian white wines), and the local pecorino cheese is also of excellent quality.

About 4 km (2 miles) from the centre of Berchidda, a steep climb will take you to the ruins of the **Castello di Montacuto**, which was the fortress of Adelasia di Torres and her husband Ubaldo Visconti before becoming the domain of the Doria and Malaspina families from the mainland. Monte Limbara, the geographical heart of the Gallura region, towers in the background.

Cheese and white Vermentino wine, locally made produce from Sardinia

⓯ Buddusò

Road map C2 & D2. 🏔 6,500. **ℹ** Town Hall (079 715 90 00).

The town of Buddusò is fairly prosperous thanks to sheep farming, granite quarrying and the processing and sale of cork.

The stone-paved streets in the old part of town wind around buildings made of dark stone. In the Roman era the main road from Kàralis (Cagliari) to Olbia crossed the town, then known as Caput Thirsi. The church of **Santa Anastasia** and the paintings in the sacristy are worth a visit. A tour through the **Monti di Alà** is another worthwhile excursion.

Environs
Nearby are **Iselle Nuraghe** (on the road to Pattada) and **Loelle Nuraghe**, towards Mamone.

A cuile, or seasonal shepherd's hut, still a common sight in this region

⓰ San Teodoro

Road map D2. 🏘 2,900. 🛈 0784 86 57 67. 🌐 santeodoroturismo.it

To the south of the Capo Coda Cavallo headland, just opposite the rocky island of Tavolara, the village of San Teodoro has grown rapidly in recent years due to increasing numbers of tourists.

The village also makes an excellent starting point for excursions to the Cinta beach, a long strip of sandy terrain that separates the **Stagno di San Teodoro** from the sea. Fairly close to the Orientale Sarda road, this 200-hectare (494-acre) lake and marsh is one of the few remaining coastal marshes that once lay south of the Bay of Olbia. Mallards and coots are easily sighted on the water. When the birds glimpse a bird of prey or other danger, they

The Island of Tavolara

This island is a mountain of limestone rising from the sea to a height of 500 m (1,640 ft). The eastern side is an inaccessible military zone, but the low sandy area called Spalmatore di Terra has beaches, a small harbour, a couple of restaurants and a few houses. Together with the neighbouring islands of Molara and Molarotto, home to over 150 moufflons, Tavolara is a marine reserve. The granite cliffs are pierced by caves and crevices. Sea lilies grow in the Spalmatore di Terra area and the rock is covered with juniper, helichrysum, rosemary and lentiscus. According to tradition, Carlo Alberto, the king of Piedmont and Sardinia, landed on the island to find the legendary "goats with golden teeth" (a phenomenon caused by a grass they eat), and was so fascinated by the island that he officially dubbed its only inhabitant, Paolo Bertolini, "king of Tavolara". In the summer there is a regular boat service to the island from Olbia *(see p146)* and Porto San Paolo.

The unmistakable profile of the island of Tavolara

gather in large groups and make a loud noise to defend themselves. Grey and red heron as well as Kentish plovers can be seen in search of food. Another common sight is the hovering kestrel, one of Italy's smallest raptors.

Granite outcrops are used as a resting place by ducks.

Kestrel

The clear, still water is rich in food for birds.

Grey heron

The shores are ideal for mud-dwelling creatures.

Lapwing

The Stagno di San Teodoro

The Ruju nuraghe outside the village of Alà del Sardi

⑰ Alà dei Sardi

Road map D2. 🏛 2,000.
ℹ Buddusò Town Hall (079 715 90
00). 🎭 4 Oct: countryside feast day
of San Francesco.

Rocks and maquis, and forests
of enormous cork oaks with the
characteristic marks of recent
stripping, make up the landscape
of Alà dei Sardi and its plateau,
the last tract of the rocky interior
overlooking the Bay of Olbia.

The main street of the village
is lined with the small granite
stone houses characteristic of
this region.

Environs
Not far from Alà dei Sardi,
off the road which leads to
Buddusò, is the **Ruju nuraghe**,
with the remains of a
prehistoric village almost
buried in the scrub. Following
signs to the town of Monti, the
route crosses a sizeable plateau
studded with astonishingly varied
rock formations. At a
fork, the road deviates
for the sanctuary of
San Pietro l'Eremita,
and passes through
some stunning scenery,
with gaps allowing
occasional views of
the sea and the
unmistakable profile of
the island of Tavolara
(see p157) in the
distance. Every year in
August at Ferragosto
(Assumption Day), the
restored Romanesque
church of San Pietro
l'Eremita is crowded
with pilgrims from the
surrounding villages.

⑱ Pattada

Road map C2. 🏛 3,800. ℹ Town
Hall (079 75 51 14). 🎭 29 Aug:
Santa Sabina.

Situated in the middle of a
territory rich in prehistoric
nuraghi and other vestiges of
the past, Pattada is world-
famous for the production
of steel knives, which began
here because of a rich vein
of iron ore which has been
worked for centuries. The
village blacksmiths still carry on
the tradition of making steel
blades, and handles from
animal horn, and dozens of

The Sa Fraigada forest near Pattada

The Knives of Pattada

The best-known style of shepherd's knife made
in Pattada is the *resolza* (the word derives from
the Latin *rasoria*, or razor). The *resolza* is a jack-knife
with a steel blade that may be as much as 14 cm
(5 inches) long. The blacksmiths of Pattada only
use traditional materials. Steel is hammered into
shape in a forge and on an anvil; the handle is
made from wood, or from moufflon, sheep or deer horn. The
production of Pattada knives dates from the mid-19th century, and
the best knives are
still hand-made by
skilled craftsmen.
Among the masters
at work today
some, like Salvatore
Giagu and Maria Rosaria Deroma, draw inspiration
from the oldest types of Pattada knives, such as the
fixed-blade *corrina*, which dates back to the 18th
century. It is not easy to find real Pattada knives on
sale, and you should avoid imitations. Production is a
slow and complicated affair, but it is possible to order
a Pattada knife to be made for you, although this
procedure will take about a year.

Sheath

The handles are
made of wood
or horn.

The blade is
made of hand-
wrought steel.

An assortment of Pattada knives

The artificial lake created by the Rio Mannu at Pattada

imitations of these Sardinian knives can now be found on the Italian mainland.

Environs
In the vicinity of Pattada is the **Fiorentini** – an area of greenery resulting from reforestation – and the ruins of the medieval castle of Olomene.

⑩ Ozieri

Road map C2. 🚗 12,000. 🚌
🛈 Town Hall (079 78 12 00); Pro Loco (079 78 30 13); Comunità Montana del Monte Acuto (0789 44 394).
🎭 second Sun in May: Sant'Antioco di Bisarcio 🔲 **comune.ozieri.ss.it**

Ozieri lies in a natural hollow and its situation is one of the most attractive sights in northeast Sardinia. Both the traditions and architecture here are interesting, and the town has a fascinating history that goes back millennia and has added to the knowledge of the remote pre-nuraghic cultures which developed here.

The fabric and layout of the town are quite varied and blend in well with the slopes of the hills. Among the tall houses the occasional covered roof terrace filled with flowers can be glimpsed. The major sights in the old town are **Piazza Carlo Alberto** and **Piazza Fonte Grixoni**, centred around an ancient fountain. On the edge of the historic quarter is the Neo-Classical **Cathedral**, which contains a splendid 16th-century Sardinian polyptych by the artist

Earthenware found in the Grotta di San Michele

known as the Maestro di Ozieri. The painting depicts the famous miracle of the Sanctuary of the Madonna di Loreto, and reveals Spanish influences as well as traces of Flemish mannerism. The 17th-century San Francesco monastery houses the **Museo Archeologico**, with finds from the archaeological digs in the area. Most of this material belongs to the era of the Ozieri civilization, the predominant culture here from 3500 to 2700 BC. It is also known as

San Michele, from the name of the cave in which major finds were discovered.

The territory surrounding Ozieri is also rich in historic and archaeological sites and ruins, such as the *domus de janas* at Butule, the San Pantaleo necropolis and the dolmen at Montiju Coronas.

The **Grotta di San Michele** is a cave that lies behind the Ozieri hospital, near the track and field stadium (in fact, during the construction of the latter, part of the cave was destroyed). Large quantities of decorated ceramics were found here, as well as human bones, a mother-goddess statuette and pieces of obsidian from Monte Arci. All these finds support the theory that there was some continuity from the earlier Bonu Ighinu culture to the time of the Ozieri.

🏛 **Museo Archeologico di Ozieri**
Piazza Pietro Micca. **Tel** 079 785 10 52.
Open 9am–1pm, 3–7pm Tue–Sun; 9:30am–12:30pm Sun. 🖕 📷

🏛 **Grotta di San Michele,**
Ozieri Hospital. **Open** 10am–1pm, 3–5pm (4–6pm in summer) Tue–Sun.
📷 combined ticket for both sites.

Terraces of houses climbing the slopes of the town of Ozieri

⑳ Tour of the Logudoro

After the fall of the Roman Empire, Sardinia did not return to a central role in the Mediterranean until after the year 1000, when Pisan and Genoese merchants, soldiers and preachers came into contact with the different regional cultures of the island. The Romanesque churches in the north of Sardinia are the result of these encounters. It is difficult to assess how much of each single monument was created by local artists and artisans and how much by those from Pisa and Genoa. Whatever the facts, east of Sassari there is a series of Romanesque churches that has few equals in the rest of mainland Italy.

⑦ **Nostra Signora di Tergu**
This church was built over the remains of a monastery founded by monks from Montecassino in Tuscany.

① **Santissima Trinità di Saccargia**
The Santissima Trinità, built in striped layers of black and white stone, is the most significant example of Romanesque architecture in northern Sardinia. The apse is decorated with frescoes of Christ and the saints. The church was restored in the early 1900s *(see pp162–3)*.

Castelsardo

Valledoria

Sassari

Nuragbe di Camarzu

Ploaghe

② **San Michele di Salvènero (Ploaghe)**
In the 12th century the monks of Vallombrosa built this church near the village of Salvènero, which has since disappeared. The church now stands abandoned in the middle of a series of road interchanges. Restored in the 13th century and again in 1912, this splendid monument needs to attract greater care and respect to safeguard its future.

③ **Santa Maria del Regno (Ardara)**
Consecrated in 1107, this Pisan-Romanesque church is famous for the *Retablo Maggiore di Ardara*, one of the best on the island. The paintings on the altar-step are by the Sardinian Giovanni Muru (1515).

⑥ San Pietro di Simbranos (or delle Immagini)

The traditional name of this church derives from the bas-relief on the façade depicting an abbot and two monks (the *immagini* or "images"). San Pietro, in the Bulzi area, was first built in 1113 and rebuilt in its present form a century later. This isolated and tranquil monument has a particular fascination because of its desert setting among canyons and rocks.

VISITORS' CHECKLIST

Practical Information
Road map C2. Santissima Trinità di Saccargia and Sant'Antioco di Bisarcio: **Open** normal opening hours; San Michele di Salvènero: **Closed** Nostra Signora di Castro: **Open** variable, the *cumbessias* precinct can be visited; Santa Maria del Regno di Ardara:, enquire at priest's house; Nostra Signora di Tergu: **Closed** can usually only be seen from outside; San Pietro di Simbranos: **Open** normal opening hours, or ask Bulzi parish priest.

Lago di Castel Doria

Tempio Pausania

rfugas

Coghinas

Lago del Loghinas

Monte Sassu

Olbia

⑤

Oscbiri

597

Ozieri

597

④

rdara

⑤ Nostra Signora di Castro (Oschiri)

Dominating Lake Coghínas, this church blends Lombard and local architectural elements. It was built in the second half of the 12th century and is surrounded by the *cumbessias* enclosure of pilgrims' houses, built at a later date.

④ Sant'Antioco di Bisarcio (Ozieri)

Sant'Antioco is a combination of Pisan Romanesque and French influences. Sant'Antioco was built from the second half of the 11th century to the late 12th century and was initially the cathedral of the Bisarcio diocese. It differs from the other churches on this tour in its architectural complexity, shown in the unusual two-storey porch, small windows and the decorative detail on the façade.

0 kilometres   5

0 miles   5

Key

— Major road

= Other roads

— River

㉑ Santissima Trinità di Saccargia

Both simple and impressive, Sardinia's most famous Romanesque church stands in the middle of a windswept valley. Its name probably derives from *sa acca argia*, "the dappled cow". According to legend, this animal used to kneel in prayer on the site, which is why there are carvings of the cow on four sides of one of the capitals in the portico. Another account relates how, around the year 1112, the ruler of the region, Constantine, donated the small church to the Camaldolesi monks, who then decided to enlarge it with the help of Tuscan architects, craftsmen and labourers. Initially they added the apse and the bell tower with its alternating layers of black trachyte and white limestone. At a later stage they built the porch, the only one of its kind on a Sardinian church. The austere interior, with a tall, narrow nave lit by small openings or slots in the side walls, is very atmospheric.

Animal Frieze
The severity of the exterior of the church is lightened with sculptures of animals.

★ Façade
Two rows of blind arches adorn the façade, each level decorated with rose windows and multi-coloured diamonds. The central arch has an opening in the form of a cross.

Portico Capitals
The portico is supported by columns with carved capitals. They carry the classic Roman-esque motifs of plants and animals.

★ Carved Cows
It may be that the church was named after the carved cows on this capital, even though the portico was built after the main church.

KEY

① **The campanile** is 41 m (134 ft) tall and each side is 8 m (26 ft) wide.

② **The black and white stripes** reveal Pisan influence.

③ **The aisleless nave** was built after the apse, which dates from 1116.

VISITORS' CHECKLIST

Practical Information
Road map C2.
Tel 347 00 07 882.
Open 9am–6pm (winter:
call in advance). From Sassari,
follow the SS131 for 10 km
(6 miles), then turn off on
the SS597 to Olbia.

Double-lancet Windows
These date from the
late 12th century.

Fresco of Christ
Christ is depicted holding
a book in the act of
benediction.

Monastery Ruins
Only a few black and
white stone archways
are left of the first and
most important
Camaldolese monastery
in Sardinia.

★ The Apse Frescoes
Romanesque frescoes are rare in
Sardinia – these are attributed to
Pisan artists.

❷ Sassari

Sardinia's second most important city commercially, politically and culturally, Sassari lies on a tableland that slopes down to the sea among olive groves and fertile and well cultivated valleys. The city has a long history of invasions, conquests and raids, but also boasts a tradition of stubborn rebellion and uprisings. Pisans, Genoese and Aragonese have all attempted to subdue the city, but the indomitable spirit of the Sassari citizens has always succeeded in asserting independence. The city's hero is a rebel named Carlo Maria Angioj, who headed a revolt in 1796 against the Savoyard government, which had sought to impose a feudal system. Two presidents of the Italian Republic, Antonio Segni and Francesco Cossiga, were born in Sassari, as was the prominent Italian Communist Party leader Enrico Berlinguer *(see pp48–9)*.

The *Li Candareri* festival in Sassari

Exploring Sassari

The old town, with its winding alleyways branching off from the main streets, was once surrounded by walls that ran along present-day Corso Vico, Corso Trinità, Via Brigata Sassari and Corso Margherita. Only a few parts of the city walls (such as the section at the beginning of Corso Trinità) have survived the effects of time, but the old centre has preserved its original layout, even though it is now some-what dilapidated.

A morning should be enough time for a walk around the old town. The main sights are the Duomo (cathedral), the Fontana del Rosello fountain, the churches of Sant'Antonio, Santa Maria di Betlem and San Pietro in Silki, and the Sanna museum.

🏛 Duomo

Piazza Duomo. **Tel** 079 23 20 67.
Open 8:30am–noon, 4–5:30pm daily.
♿

Sassari cathedral is dedicated to San Nicola (St Nicholas). Its impressive Baroque façade is in rather striking contrast to its size and to the small, simple and elegant 18th-century Piazza Duomo with its characteristic semicircular shape. The end result of successive enlargements and changes carried out over the centuries, the Duomo was originally built on the site of a Romanesque church. The base of the façade and bell tower are still intact.

At the end of the 15th century the original structure underwent radical transformation that not only changed its shape but created today's unusual proportions. The side walls were propped up by buttresses decorated with gargoyles of mythical and monstrous animals, while the interior was rebuilt in the Gothic style.

In the late 18th century the upper portion of the façade was radically changed with the addition of rather grand decoration: volutes, flowers, cherubs and fantastic figures. In the middle, the statue of San Nicola is surmounted by the figures of the three martyr saints, Gavino, Proto and Gianuario, set in three niches. At a later stage, an octagonal section decorated with multi-coloured majolica tiles was superimposed on the original Lombard-style lower part of the campanile. The interior, which has been totally restored, has retained its simple Gothic lines despite the presence of lavishly decorated Baroque altars. The choir, the work of 18th-century Sardinian artists, is particularly striking.

The Museo del Duomo, reached through the Cappella Aragonese (Aragonese chapel) on the right, houses the processional standard, a panel painting by an anonymous

Detail of the façade of Sassari Cathedral

The Fontana del Rosello, dating from the Renaissance

VISITORS' CHECKLIST

Practical Information
Road map B2. 120,000..
079 200 8072. last Sun
of month: Antiques Show in
Piazza Santa Caterina; Easter
Week: Maggio Sassarese;
penultimate Sun in May:
Cavalcata Sarda; 14 Aug:
Faradda de li Candareri.

Transport

15th-century artist. There is also a silver statue of San Gavino, embossed using a Mexican technique that was in fashion in the late 17th century.

🎏 Fontana del Rosello

Via Col di Lana.
On the right-hand side of the church of Santissima Trinità, in Piazza Mercato, a small stone stairway known as the Col di Lana will take you to the Fontana del Rosello, the fountain at the lower end of the Valverde gorge.

Unfortunately, very little remains of the steep valley and woods that were once the natural backdrop for this little jewel of late Renaissance art. However, this has not diminished the locals' love for their fountain, which has become one of the city's symbols.

This was once the haunt of the enlightened bourgeoisie and the place where the local water-carriers drew water from the eight lions' mouths sculpted at the base of the fountain.

The fountain was executed in the early 1600s by Genoese artists, who still had a preference for the classical styles of the Renaissance. The base consists of two superimposed white and green marble boxes. The lions' mouths are surrounded by statues symbolizing the four seasons. The original statues were destroyed in the 1795–6 uprisings (see p164) and were replaced in 1828.

In the middle, a bearded divinity, known as Giogli, is surrounded by small towers symbolizing the city. On the top of the fountain are two arches which protect the figure of San Gavino.

Sassari

① Duomo
② Corso Vittorio Emanuele
③ Fontana del Rosello
④ Sant'Antonio Abate
⑤ Santa Maria di Betlem
⑥ Palazzo di Città
⑦ Santa Caterina
⑧ Piazza d'Italia
⑨ Museo Archeologico
    Nazionale

0 metres 300
0 yards 300

For key to symbols see back flap

ⓘ Sant'Antonio Abate

Piazza Sant'Antonio. **Open** 7–10am daily, 4:30–7:30pm Sat.

Dating from the early 1700s, the stately Baroque façade of this church, with its simple elegance and harmonious proportions, dominates the tree-lined square at the end of Corso Trinità.

The upper part of the portal still bears the emblem of the brotherhood responsible for building the church. The Latin cross interior boasts one of the most elegant high altars in Sassari, which bears a carved and gilded wooden altarpiece. The panels were executed in the late 1700s by the Genoese painter Bartolomeo Augusto.

The church stands in Piazza Sant'Antonio, once the site of the old northern gate of the same name, and formerly the hub of the city's commercial and political life. The only vestiges of the past are a part of the medieval city walls, and a battlemented tower to the left of the church.

ⓘ Santa Maria di Betlem

Piazza Santa Maria. **Tel** 079 23 57 40. **Open** 9am–noon, 4:30–6:30pm daily (winter: to 5pm daily).

The church of Santa Maria di Betlem is situated in the square of the same name, at the northwestern entrance to the city. Built by Benedictine monks in 1106, it was later donated to the Franciscans. Unfortunately, the elegant original structure was the subject of frequent rebuilding in the 18th and 19th centuries, and the church has lost its early qualities of lightness and purity of form. The only intact part of the earlier

The Romanesque church of San Pietro in Silki, Sassari

church is the 13th-century façade, decorated with small columns and capitals and pierced by a lovely 15th-century rose window. The Gothic interior, once austere, has been spoiled by the heavy-handed Baroque decoration and altars; yet the original side chapels are intact, each dedicated to a crafts-men's guild as a reminder of the social role the church played in the community. To this day, on 14 August, the date of the *De li Candareri* festivities, the votive candles donated by the various guilds are carried here in procession from the Chiesa del Rosario. The cloister is partly walled in but can still be visited. It contains the 14th-century granite stone Brigliadore fountain, once the source of most of Sassari's water supply.

Detail of an Art Nouveau-style house

ⓘ San Pietro in Silki

Via delle Croci. **Tel** 079 21 60 67. **Open** 7am–noon, 3:30–8pm daily.

The Romanesque church of San Pietro in Silki faces a lovely tree-lined square and was most probably named after the medieval quarter built here in the 1100s. Its simple 17th-century façade has a large atrium leading to the Gothic nave with four side chapels. The first of these was dedicated to the Madonna delle Grazie in the second half of the 15th century. It is named for a statue of the Virgin Mary, found inside a column from the square in front of the church. The statue is one of the best examples of Catalan Gothic sculpture in Sardinia.

On the other side of the square, opposite San Pietro, is the Frati Minori monastery, which houses one of the island's richest libraries. The collections consist of over 14,000 volumes, removed from Franciscan monasteries after their closure.

🚏 Corso Vittorio Emanuele

The city's main street crosses the heart of the old town and connects Piazza Sant'Antonio and Piazza Cavallino. The Corso is lined with 19th-century houses and 16th-century Aragonese buildings, and you can often catch a glimpse of courtyards and interiors that testify to their former splendour. This is Sassari's main shopping street, with shops of all kinds, from clothing to ironmongery.

🏛 Palazzo di Città

Corso Emanuele II 35. **Open** Nov–Apr: 10am–1pm, 5–8pm Tue–Sat. 📷

This Neo-Classical palazzo was built between 1826 and 1829, after the demolition of the pre-existing Municipal House. It was designed by

The church of Santa Maria di Betlem in Sassari

the Piedmontese architect Guiseppe Cominotti, who based the building on the Teatro Carignano in Turin. It features a beautiful small room in the shape of a horse-shoe.

There is an interesting display of local costumes and 19th-century paintings and water-colours illustrating everyday rural and town life, as well as religious and civil events. The Municipal Theatre and the Tourist Board are also housed here.

Hanging on the walls are traditional Sardinian rugs, which resemble abstract paintings with their geometric patterns. There is also fine bobbin lacework and – of interest although not valuable – baskets of dwarf palm wood, terracotta pots and other everyday objects whose design and techniques have been handed down over centuries of tradition. Items on display are for sale.

🏛 Museo Archeologico Nazionale "GA Sanna"

Via Roma 64. **Tel** 079 27 22 03. **Open** 9am–8pm Tue–Sun. 📷 🎧 ♿

The Sassari archaeological museum was donated to the Italian state by the Sanna family, who built these premises in 1931 to house finds collected by Giovanni Antonio Sanna, an important figure in the island's history and director of the local mine.

Two entire storeys are given over to various periods of Sardinian civilizations, from the Neolithic to the Middle Ages. Arrowheads, nuraghic bronze

Entrance to the Museo Nazionale "GA Sanna" in Sassari

statuettes, amphoras, furnishings, weapons, tools, ceramics and jewels are on display in chronological order. On the ground floor, panels illustrate the evolution of Sardinia, and every room has time charts on display.

There are also architectural reconstructions of prehistoric buildings such as dwellings, *domus de janas* (rock-cut tombs) and giants' tombs. In the last hall, among floor plans, sarcophagi and statues there is a reconstructed mosaic floor from a patrician Roman villa in nearby Turris Libisonis (present-day Porto Torres). The mosaic shows lobsters, sea horses, and seals chasing one another in an eternal circle. The next room contains a small art gallery with works by Sardinian artists from the 14th to the 20th centuries.

There is also a traditional crafts section with jewels, costumes, musical instruments and craftsmen's tools, almost all of which are still used in central-northern Sardinia.

🏢 Piazza d'Italia

This large square is laid out at the edge of the 19th-century quarter of Sassari. It is a well-proportioned public space, surrounded by elegant Neo-Classical buildings and with tall palm trees and well-kept flower beds, guarded by a statue of Vittorio Emanuele II.

One of the finest buildings is the Palazzo della Provincia (provincial government building), built in pure Neo-Classical style. The council chamber on the first floor is open to the public. On the walls are 19th-century paintings depicting important events in the city's political history, such as *The Proclamation of the Sassari Statutes* and *Carlo Maria Angioj Entering Sassari (see p164)*. You can also see the adjacent royal apartments, built in 1884 on the occasion of the King of Sardinia's visit. In summer the courtyard is the venue for concerts and plays.

The lovely 19th-century Bargone and Crispi arcades on the northwestern side of Piazza d'Italia shelter the city's oldest bars and pastry shops and lead to Piazza Castello.

⛪ Santa Caterina

Via Santa Caterina. **Tel** 079 23 16 92. **Open** pm for Mass.

This church was built at the end of the 16th century for the Jesuits and combines Sardinian Gothic style with Renaissance elements.

In the interior there are paintings by the artist Giovanni Bilevelt.

Sassari's Piazza d'Italia, framed by the Neo-Classical Palazzo della Provincia

The harbour at Castelsardo

ⓔ Castelsardo

Road map C2. △ 5,500. 🄸 Pro Loco (079 47 15 06). 🄰 Easter Monday: Lunissanti procession.
ⓦ castelsardoturismo.it

Perched on a volcanic headland, Castelsardo has known a number of name changes in its history. The town was founded in 1102 by the aristocratic Doria family from Genoa, and was originally known as Castelgenovese, a name it kept until 1448, when it became Castellaragonese, after the town's new conquerors. The present name dates from 1776.

The town is dominated by the castle (**Castello**), which now houses a museum with exhibits of traditional basket-weaving. Overlooking the sea is the cathedral of Sant'Antonio Abate. The alleyways of the centre

Local basketwork

of town are lined with small shops selling all kinds of local handicrafts. Fish-lovers will do well here, as the local cuisine is based on freshly caught fish and lobsters.

On Easter Monday, the traditional **Lunissanti** procession is held in Castelsardo. The streets are lit by flaming torches, and traditional hooded figures form a slow procession, to the sound of three songs, *Lu Stabat, Lu Jesu* and *Lu Miserere*. These songs are centuries old, and probably date from before Catalan rule. They have been handed down by word of mouth ever since. The solemn procession, one of the most well-known of Sardinia's Easter festivals, ends at the church of **Santa Maria**.

🎦 Castello and Museo dell'Intreccio

Via Marconi. **Tel** 079 47 13 80. **Open** Sep–Jun: 9:30am–1pm, 3–5:30pm daily (to 7:30pm May, Jun & Sep); Jul & Aug: 9am–midnight daily. 🎟

Built in the 13th and 14th centuries, this fortress is now occupied by the **Museo dell'Intreccio** (museum of wickerwork). Local baskets are made from traditional materials such as palm, asphodel and cane. From the castle terraces there are fantastic views; on clear days you can see Corsica.

Sant'Antonio Abate in Castelsardo, its belltower topped by an onion dome

🏛 Cattedrale di Sant'Antonio Abate

Via Seminario. **Open** 8am–6pm daily.
Constructed in the 17th century on the site of an existing Romanesque church, the cathedral has a bell tower roofed with majolica tiles. From the tower there is a splendid view of the water below. The cathedral contains fine 16th-century, carved wooden furnishings.

The town of Castelsardo and the castle above

The Roccia dell'Elefante (Elephant Rock) near Castelsardo

⚑ Santa Maria

Via Vittorio Emanuele. **Open** ask priest for keys.

In the heart of the old town, the upper part of Castelsardo, stands the church of Santa Maria. The building does not have a façade, and entry is gained through the side door. In the interior is a 14th-century crucifix known as the *Cristo Nero* (Black Christ). The church is the focus of the Lunissanti Easter procession, which starts and ends here.

⚑ La Roccia dell'Elefante

To one side of the road near Multeddu, not far from Castelsardo, stands the impressive Roccia dell'Elefante (Elephant Rock). This massive block of dark trachyte rock has been gradually sculpted by the wind into the shape of an elephant with its trunk raised. In ancient times the rock was used as a burial place. At the base you can still see small carved openings for several *domus de janas* (rock-cut tombs).

㉔ Isola Rossa

Road map C1.

The hills of Gallura slope down towards the sea, forming a landscape characterized by rose-coloured crags, sculpted into strange shapes by wind erosion. The small fishing village of Isola Rossa lies on a headland, at the foot of an impressive 16th-century sentinel tower. The village is not an island (*isola*), but was given its name ("red island") after the small, reddish-coloured rock island out in the bay. Fishing boats are drawn up on the beach below the village after each day's catch is brought in.

The coastline either side of Isola Rossa is worth visiting, especially towards the east, where Monte Tinnari overlooks the sea. To the west, the coast gently slopes to meet the mouth of the Rio Coghina, a short distance from Castelsardo.

Environs

A short distance from Isola Rossa is the small agricultural town of **Trinità d'Agultu**, which developed in the late 19th century around the church of the same name. As is so often the case in Sardinia, the simple country church became a sanctuary and pilgrimage site. As a result, it is also an important trade and commercial centre during the associated religious festivities and pilgrimages.

The fishing fleet at Isola Rossa

The Fishing Industry

The Sardinians are historically a nation of shepherds. Despite this, fishing is still an important activity, even though for centuries it has been carried out almost exclusively by non-Sardinian immigrants: people from the island of Ponza at Castelsardo, and Neapolitans, who founded the village of Isola Rossa in the early 20th century. Nowadays a major source of income in these two places is the cultivation of mussels and shellfish. Tuna fishing, once widespread off the northwest coast, no longer survives in northern Sardinia, the small trawlers having been unable to compete with deep-sea fishing, now practised on an industrial scale.

Craftsman at work making a lobster pot

TRAVELLERS' NEEDS

WHERE TO STAY

The legendary allure of Sardinia's beaches has resulted in a boom in tourist facilities, especially along the coast, and visitors can now choose from a wide range of hotels and holiday villages. The exclusive and world-famous hotels built on the Costa Smeralda in the early 1960s cater to the wealthy, but less expensive accommodation is also available. Luxury hotels and resorts are common in the south, while the western coast offers plenty of reliable family-run lodgings. On the eastern coast, comfortable and well-equipped tourist villages are easily found, many offering self-catering as an option. The interior has some excellent hotels, especially in the Gennargentu and Barbagia areas, where travellers can also take advantage of organized excursions. For further information, listings and descriptions of hotels, farm holidays and tourist villages, see pages 174–9.

The Hotel Torre Moresca at Cala Ginepro, Orosei *(see p177)*

Grades of Hotel

As in the rest of Italy, hotels in Sardinia are graded using a star-rating system, which runs from one star for minimum comfort to five stars for luxury accommodation. The four-star category offers first-class service without the very high prices of five-star hotels. Three-star lodgings, especially family-run establishments, sometimes offer better value for your money, but in Sardinia this is generally the exception rather than the rule.

Most Sardinian hotels also have a restaurant that is usually open to non-residents as well. The majority of hotels, whatever their category, provide a range of facilities. Along the coast, for example, hotels are likely to offer beach equipment such as umbrellas and deckchairs.

Holiday Villages

Sardinia's wide variety of holiday villages, mostly on or near the coast range from vast establishments with hundreds of rooms and good facilities and service, to smaller places, which may be more luxurious and expensive. The larger holiday villages offer more than one type of lodging within a single site. Guests can often choose between a serviced apartment (residence) or a normal three-or four-star hotel. Some tourist villages offer all-inclusive packages that may even include drinks at the bar. Tourist villages often require guests to take half- or full-board, as do many hotels on the island. In some resorts guests may choose to rent a self-catering apartment or bungalow with the option of other amenities. These services usually include the use of sports facilities and entertainment, such as a disco or nightclub, a babysitter, beach facilities, swimming pool and various bars and restaurants. Many holiday villages also offer an excellent range of equipment for water sports.

Renting an apartment in a holiday village is a worthwhile alternative to renting a villa, especially if you plan to be on holiday for less than a month. It allows you to be independent while at the same time giving you access to a range of useful services and facilities. At **Villaggio Cugnana Verde**, for example, there are flats available for up to six people, and a host of activities is provided on site. Other holiday villages include **Park Hotel Cala di Lepre & Spa**, **Villaggio Valtur Baia di Conte** and more.

Bed and Breakfasts

Staying in a bed and breakfast is an excellent way to save money and interact with the locals. Usually, about three rooms are rented out per apartment or villa, with either a shared or private bathroom, and

A café in the small square at Porto Cervo

◀ Produce on display in a sweet shop in Cagliari

Plush seating in a guest room at Faro Capo-Spartivento in Baia Chia *(see p176)*

breakfast is provided by the host family. Prices generally start at €25 per room.

Prices

Italian law requires every hotel to place the National Tourist Board price list, with the maximum prices for the current year, behind the door of each room. The prices quoted should never be exceeded. Room prices shown on this list, or quoted by the hotel staff when you book, normally include taxes and service. However, it is advisable to check with staff whether or not breakfast is included in the rate, to avoid misunderstandings.

Hotels on the coast often require guests to take half- or full-board. In low season you could try asking for a bed and breakfast rate, but this is unlikely to be possible during high season. Winter rates are significantly lower than summer rates: in summer prices can easily double. Hotel prices reach their peak in the two middle weeks of August. This is also true of the tourist villages (except that rates here are calculated on a weekly basis).

The location of your hotel will also affect the price. All types of accommodation on the coast are always more expensive than lodgings in the interior. Bear in mind that you may be able to negotiate special rates for groups or for longer stays.

Extras

Generally speaking, guests have to pay separately for drinks consumed with meals, anything taken from the mini-bar in the room, room service as well as telephone calls.

In some cases air-conditioning may be charged as an extra. Glimpses of Sardinia's coast may also be regarded as chargeable and travellers may have to pay extra for rooms that have a sea view. It is always a good idea to verify extras like this when booking or choosing your room. Tipping in hotels is at the visitor's discretion.

Low Season

If you plan to travel to Sardinia in any season other than summer, it is always a good idea to check before-hand on the availability of accommodation. Some hotels are run on a seasonal basis and tend to open around Easter and close in the autumn. The end of the season might depend on unpredictable circumstances such as a sudden turn of bad weather.

Booking and Paying

If you decide to travel in summer, especially in July and August, and want to stay on the coast, book well in advance as the island over-flows with visitors in this period. If you are booking the hotel separately from your travel arrangements, you will almost certainly be asked to pay a deposit. This can be done by credit card or by international money order. Upon arrival, the receptionist will ask for your passport; this is to register travellers with the police – a legal requirement. Guests will be given a receipt at check-out, another legal formality.

The Hotel Hieracon, on the island of San Pietro *(see p176)*

Luxury holiday villas in Porto Cervo, Costa Smeralda

Camping

Camping is the most affordable type of accommodation on the island. Sardinia has a number of good campsites, some of which are located in quiet areas with pleasant views. Most are situated along the coast, sometimes in eucalyptus or pine groves. There are far fewer sites located in the interior. Many have helpful websites, including **La Liccia**, **Baia Blu La Tortuga**, **Cala Gonone**, **International Camping** and **Isola dei Gabbiani**.

As with Sardinian hotels, campsites are much in demand in summer. If you have not booked in advance, you'll need to start looking for a place to stay early in the day.

Some campsites also have a small number of bungalows or chalets with a bathroom and kitchen area. These are often very attractive but be aware that the prices can be steep.

Most campsites are open from Easter to October. Some may be open for the Christmas period, offering bungalows or camper vans with heating.

Camping outside official sites is forbidden, and camping on the beach is particularly frowned on. Guests need permission to camp on private property (from the owner), and in state forests.

Farm Holidays

Agriturismi – farms or wine estates that offer accommodation – are an excellent way to experience Sardinian customs and local traditions. **Agriturismo Li Scopi**, **Il Giglio** and **Le Querce** are just a few of the many options. The accommodation is often basic, but rooms are usually comfortable and quaint. Farmhouses tend not to be situated in isolated countryside – true to tradition, at least half the farms are in villages. Local farmers and shepherds often live in villages and travel some distance to work the fields or take their sheep to pasture.

The highest concentration of *agriturismi* is found around Sassari and Oristano, while there are very few in the Cagliari area. Everyone usually eats at the same table, guests and host family alike, so you will probably feel like part of the family by the time you leave. Meals usually include produce from the farm – cheese, meat, vegetables and even honey – cooked according to local tradition. It is an excellent way to explore the specialities of the region. In general, farms offer accommodation by the week on a half- or full-board basis. Many also organize hikes, horseback riding, mountain biking and canoeing.

It is sometimes possible to eat at an *agriturismo* without being a guest there.

Villa Rental

Renting a house for two weeks or a month is an economical solution for those who want to be unconstrained by hotel or guesthouse mealtimes and routines. This is a good option

A refurbished shepherds' hut at hotel La Essenza in Torpe *(see p178)*

for families with small children. Note that the charge for cleaning is generally the same for a week as for a longer stay.

The local tourist offices are often able to supply lists of private homes available in the area. Travel agents can also arrange this type of accommodation.

Prices are usually quoted on a weekly basis, with a deposit requested. When renting it is advisable to ascertain the exact number of bedrooms as the living room also functions as a bedroom in some houses. Before signing any contract, check if gas, water, electricity and telephone expenses are part of the rent or considered "extras". Make a note of the readings on the meters on arrival if these items are extra.

Adventure Holidays

The great climate and varied scenery of Sardinia make it an ideal location for a sea kayaking or cycling holiday.

Organized off-road mountain bike tours, following the paths and tracks of the island, particularly of the inland areas, are becoming common while road-based holidays are more suitable for the independent traveller. **Saddle Skedaddle** organizes a variety of cycling

tours with accommodation included (usually *agriturismi* or small hotels). For sea kayaking and paddling tours, **Location Sardinia** offers useful information for planning such a trip.

Recommended Hotels

The hotels listed on pages 176–179 cover a huge variety of accommodation options from camping sites and budget hotels to *agriturismo* lodgings and luxury retreats. They are listed by price within each area.

Budget hotels offer great value while bed and breakfasts come with a full breakfast included. Holiday villages are grouped under the resort category. Guests can experience local Sardinian life at an *agriturismo* (farm) while luxury hotels encompass the finest of Sardinia's hotels. There are a couple of historic options and stylish boutique hotels, too.

All rooms have private bathrooms unless otherwise indicated. Book in advance if you plan to stay in high season, and note that many hotels close for the winter.

Establishments highlighted as DK Choice offer something extra special. They might have been chosen for their spectacular location, their original style or for their exceptionally high level of luxury and service, or a combination of these.

Table setting at The Lemon House B&B

DIRECTORY

Holiday Villages

Park Hotel Cala di Lepre & Spa
Località Cala di Lepre, Palau.
Tel 0789 79 00 18.
W hotelcaladilepre.com

Villaggio Cugnana Verde
Cugnana Verde (Olbia).
Map D1 & 2.
Tel 0789 331 94.
W cugnanaverde.net

Villaggio Valtur Baia di Conte
Fertillia (Alghero). **Map** B2.
Tel 079 94 90 00.
W valtur.it

Camping

Baia Blu La Tortuga
Località Vignola Mare, Aglientu. **Map** C1.
Tel 079 60 22 00.
W baiaholiday.com

Cala Gonone
Cala Gonone, Dorgali (Nuoro). **Map** D3.
Tel 0784 931 65.
W camping calagonone.it

International Camping
Località Valledoria.
Map D6.
Tel 079 58 40 70.
W campingvalledoria.com

Isola dei Gabbiani

Località Porto Pollo, Palau (Olbia). **Map** D2.
Tel 0789 70 40 19
W isoladeigabbiani.it

La Liccia
Santa Teresa Gallura.
Map C1.
Tel 0789 75 51 90.
W campinglaliccia.com

Farm Holidays

Agriturismo Li Scopi
Località Li Scopi (San Teodoro). **Map** D2.
Tel 338 976 6350.
W agriturismo liscopi.com

Il Giglio

Strada Prov. 9, Massama (Oristano). **Map** B4.
Tel 349 144 7955.
W agriturismo ilgiglio.com

Le Querce
Località Valli di Vatta, Porto Cervo. **Map** D1.
Tel 0789 992 48.
W lequerce.com

Adventure Holidays

Saddle Skedaddle
Tel +44 191 2651110.
W skedaddle.co.uk

Location Sardinia
Tel +44 1494 601012.
W locationsardinia.com

Where to Stay

Cagliari and the South

ARBUS: Hotel Le Dune di Ingurtosu €€€
Resort **Map** B5
Via Bau 1 – Fraz. Piscinas di Ingurtosu, 9031
Tel 070 97 71 30
Ⓦ leduneingurtosu.it
Simply furnished rooms right on the beach. Small fitness and wellness centre.

DK Choice

BAIA CHIA: Faro Capo Spartivento €€€
Boutique **Map** C6
Viale Spartivento, Domus de Maria, 9010
Tel 070 923 01 10
Ⓦ farocapospartivento.com
This hotel offers unique accommodation in a lighthouse (dating from 1856) perched on an isolated outcropping above deep waters. With only six suites, seclusion is guaranteed. Facilities are world-class, including impeccable staff, a talented chef and an infinity pool.

CAGLIARI: Aurora €
Budget **Map** C6
Salita Santa Chiara 19, 9124
Tel 070 65 86 25
Ⓦ hotelcagliariaurora.it
Centrally located hotel with basic furnishings in clean rooms.

CAGLIARI: Sardinia Domus €
Historic **Map** C6
Via Largo Carlo Felice 26, 9124
Tel 070 65 97 83
Ⓦ sardiniadomus.it
A casual and comfortable B&B located in the historic city centre. Friendly, helpful staff.

CAGLIARI: Sardegna Hotel €€
Mid-range **Map** C6
Via Lunigiana 50, 9122
Tel 070 28 62 45
Ⓦ sardegnahotelcagliari.it
Spacious rooms, some boasting sea views, and ultra-modern bathrooms. Efficient staff.

CALASETTA: Hotel FJBY €
Budget **Map** B6
Via Solferino 83, 9011
Tel 0781 884 44
Ⓦ hotelfjby.it
Located in the historical city centre close to the beach, with elegantly styled rooms.

FLUMINIMAGGIORE: Perdaba €
Agriturismo **Map** B5
Vico III Vittorio Emanuele 15, 9010
Tel 0702 34 78 12
Ⓦ agriturismoperdaba.com
This working farm raises sheep, pigs and cattle. Offers basic, clean rooms with garden views.

GONNOSFANADIGA: Su Murzu e S'Arreposu €
B&B **Map** B5
Via Satta 28, 9035
Tel 0328 287 23 44
Ⓦ murzuearreposu.altervista.org
The rooms at this welcoming B&B are spacious with large windows and a working fireplace.

IGLESIAS: Mare Monti Miniere €
B&B **Map** B5
Via Trento 10, 9016
Tel 0348 331 05 85
Ⓦ maremontiminiere-bb.it
A small B&B with friendly hosts and rooms with washing facilities. Strictly non-smoking.

ISOLA DI SAN PIETRO: Hotel Hieracon €€
Boutique **Map** B6
Corso C. Cavour 62, 9014 Carloforte
Tel 0781 85 40 28
Ⓦ hotelhieracon.com
Old-world charm and views of the marina with sailboats bobbing. Rooms are bright and stylish.

QUARTU SANT'ELENA: Pini e Mare €
Camping **Map** C6
Prov.le per Villasimius, 9045
Tel 0347 116 61 40
Ⓦ piniemare.com
A fully-equipped campsite with single-room and family-style bungalows available.

SANTA MARGHERITA DI PULA: Hotel Costa dei Fiori €€
Resort **Map** C6
SS 195 – km 33, 9010
Tel 070 924 53 33
Ⓦ costadeifiori.it
Intimate resort close to the sea. Stylish rooms and an infinity pool.

SANT'ANTIOCO: Sa Ruscitta €
Agriturismo **Map** B6
Località Cannai, 9017
Tel 0328 761 50 02
Ⓦ agriturismosaruscitta.com
Small *agriturismo* with clean, air-conditioned rooms that overlook the hills and olive groves.

The Eastern Coast

ARBATAX: Hotel La Bitta €€
Resort **Map** D4
Porto Frailis, 8048
Tel 0782 66 70 80
Ⓦ hotellabitta.it
Beach resort with simple facilities. Deluxe rooms feature Jacuzzis.

CALA GONONE: Cala Gonone Beach Village €€
Resort **Map** D3
Viale Bue Marino, 8022
Tel 0784 936 93
Ⓦ calagononebeachvillage.com
Tastefully-designed resort catering to families and business travellers. Has a large pool.

Stylish suite at Faro Capo Spartivento in Baia Chia

DK Choice

DORGALI: Agriturismo Nuelè   €
Agriturismo   Map D3
Località Neulè, 8022
Tel *0380 728 38 87*
W agriturismoneule.com
Ultimate relaxation at a working farm in a protected forest area, just steps from a pristine lake. All lodging is in the farmhouse where hearty breakfasts made with local produce are served.

LOTZORAI: The Lemon House   €
B&B   Map D4
Via Dante 19, 8040
Tel *0339 714 64 96*
W peteranne.it
The friendly and well-informed owners help plan daily activities. Suitable for sport enthusiasts.

OROSEI: Club Hotel Torre Moresca   €€
Resort   Map D3
Località Cala Ginepro, 8028
Tel *0784 91 230*
W torremoresca.it
Cheerful hotel a short walk from the beach. Features a large gym and pool.

OROSEI: Maria Rosaria   €€
Mid-range   Map D3
Via Grazia Deledda 13, 8028
Tel *0784 986 57*
W hotelmariarosaria.it
Clean and spacious rooms with balconies. The restaurant serves delicious traditional fare.

POSADA: Maria Caderina Green Village   €
Budget   Map D2
Loc. Predarva, 8020
Tel *0784 85 30 70*
W greenvillageposada.com
Quiet location in the countryside with traditional furnishings. All rooms have private balconies.

SANTA LUCIA: Villaggio Camping La Mandragola   €
Camping   Map D2
Viale dei Pini, 8029
Tel *078 481 91 19*
W villaggiomandragola.com
Opt for a tent, camper-van pitch or bungalow on this site, set within a pine forest with direct access to the beach.

SINISCOLA: Camping Selema   €
Camping   Map D2
Santa Lucia di Siniscola, 8029
Tel *0342 814 98 01*
W selemacamping.com
Enjoy full-service beach-front camping, ideal for nature- and sports-lovers.

TESONIS: Village Tesonis   €
Camping   Map D4
Loc. Tesonis, Capo Sferracavallo, Marina di Tertenia, Ogliastra, 8047
Tel *0782 90 90 14*
W villaggiotesonis.it
Great for those who love hiking, fishing and diving. All pitches have toilets and hot water.

TORTOLÌ: Hotel Il Vecchio Mulino   €
Budget   Map D4
Via Parigi, 8048
Tel *0782 66 40 41*
W hotelilvecchiomulino.it
Colourful and rustic rooms with a Spanish *hacienda* (ranch) feel. Superb value.

VILLAPUTZU: Agriturismo Marongiu   €
B&B   Map D5
SS 125 – km 72, 9040
Tel *070 997 80 01*
W agriturismomarongiu.it
Stay surrounded by nature in a tranquil setting. All food comes directly from the farm and vegetarian dishes are available.

VILLASIMIUS: Hotel Stella Maris   €€€
Luxury   Map D6
Via dei Cedri 3, 9049
Tel *070 79 71 00*
W stella-maris.com
Excellent value at this seaside resort with a private beach, ample grounds and lovely rooms.

VILLASIMIUS: Tanka Village Hotel   €€€
Resort   Map D6
Viale degli Oleandri 7, 9049
Tel *070 79 51*
W atahotels.it
Immense family beach resort with huge villas. Lots of activities for kids and a well-serviced spa.

Central Sardinia and Barbagia

ARITZO: Sa Muvara Hotel   €€
Boutique   Map C4
Viale Kennedy, 8031
Tel *0784 62 93 36*
W samuvarahotel.com
Large, elegantly furnished rooms set in beautiful surroundings.

BELVÌ: PhillyRea   €
Budget   Map C4
Viale IV Novembre, 8030
Tel *0704 62 92 00*
W phillyreahotel.it
Enjoy a relaxing stay in the centre of Sardinia. A veranda offers panoramic views of the forest and mountains. Rooms are clean.

Unassuming façade of The Lemon House in Lotzorai

FONNI: Il Cinghialetto   €
Budget   Map C3
Via Grazia Deledda, 8023
Tel *0784 576 60*
W ilcinghialetto.it
Modern hotel surrounded by mountains and several nuraghic sites. Friendly, helpful staff.

FONNI: Parco Donnortei   €€
Agriturismo   Map D3
Via San Antonio n.46, 8023
Tel *0784 585 75*
W agriturismodonnortei.com
The highest hotel in Sardinia, with bright rooms. Guides available for hiking tours and horseback riding.

GAVOI: Sa Posada   €
B&B   Map C3
Viale Repubblica 175, 8020
Tel *0784 531 00*
W saposadagavoi.com
Offers clean rooms as well as a shared kitchen for self-catering.

NUORO: Agriturismo Testone   €
Agriturismo   Map D3
Località Testone, Strada Statale 389, 8100
Tel *329 411 5168*
W agriturismotestonenuoro.com
A traditional converted farmhouse, where the hosts serve and sell their own organic produce.

NUORO: Casa Solotti   €
B&B   Map D3
Località Solotti Monte Ortobene, 8100
Tel *0784 33 954*
W casasolotti.it
A charming mountain retreat. Most rooms have terraces, not all have private bathrooms.

NUORO: Su Gologone Hotel   €€
Boutique   Map D3
Località su Gologone, 8025
Tel *0784 28 75 12*
W sugologone.it
Stunning mountain-side lodge with luxurious rooms and rustic decor.

TONARA: Sa Tzia Crara €
B&B **Map** C4
Vico 1 Kennedy n.8, 8039
Tel *0329 161 21 48*
w satziacrara.it
Small, quaint B&B in the heart of the island. Offers clean and modern rooms. Pet-friendly.

DK Choice

TORPE: L'Essenza €€
B&B **Map** D2
Località Cuccu Ezzu
Tel *0333 654 01 40*
w essenzasardegna.com
These four circular stone huts, thatched with tree branches, were once used by shepherds. Brightly painted and decorated in simple, traditional style, they have now also been modernized to include bathrooms and air conditioning. Enchanting views over the valley.

The Western Coast

ALGHERO: Hotel San Francesco €
Historic **Map** B2
Via Ambrogio Machin 2, 7041
Tel *079 98 03 30*
w sanfrancescohotel.com
Small, sober, yet comfortable rooms grouped around a 14th-century cloister; breakfast on a terrace under Gothic arches.

ALGHERO: Hotel Domomea €€
Luxury **Map** B2
Via Vittorio Veneto 47, 7041
Tel *079 973 20 11*
w domomeagroup.com
Attractive rooms with modern bathrooms. Facilities are limited but the rooftop pool is a delightful bonus.

DK Choice

ARBOREA: Hotel Le Torri €
Luxury **Map** B4
Via Sardegna 23, 9092
Tel *0783 800 00 31*
w letorrihotelsardegna.it
In the heart of Arborea this modern hotel has contemporary and spacious rooms, with the option of enjoying a romantic breakfast in bed. Boasts a gym and spa that offers Turkish baths and hydro massages.

BOSA: Mannu Hotel €
Budget **Map** B3
Viale Alghero 28, 8013
Tel *078 537 53 06*
w mannuhotel.it
Spacious, clean rooms with private balconies. The on-site restaurant serves fresh Mediterranean cuisine.

BOSA: Hotel Gabbiano €€
Mid-range **Map** B3
Viale Mediterraneo 5, 8013
Tel *0785 37 41 23*
w hotelalgabbiano.it
Comfortable rooms just a few steps from a windswept bay. Apartments also available.

CABRAS: da Pina €
B&B **Map** B4
Via Alessandria n.19, 9172
Tel *078 339 12 05*
w bbdapina.com
Close to the beach, this quaint B&B has bright rooms. Discounts for children 12 and under. Pet-friendly.

CUGLIERI: Nurapolis €
Camping **Map** B3
Via su Paris de Sa Turre, Santa Caterina di Pittinuri, 9073
Tel *0783 52 283*
w coopsinis.it

This well-equipped campground is just steps from the beach, making it ideal for families and outdoor enthusiasts.

NORBELLO: Nuraghe Ruiu €
Camping **Map** C3
Loc. Sant'Ignazio, 9070
Tel *078 589 61 43*
w nuragheruiu.it
Surrounded by a beautiful forest and rich in wildlife, this campsite offers tent and camper-van pitches, as well as bungalows.

ORISTANO: Eleonora Bed and Breakfast €
B&B **Map** B4
Piazza Eleonora d'Arborea 12, 9170
Tel *0347 481 79 76*
w eleonora-bed-and-breakfast.com
Contemporary rooms with parquet flooring. A great starting point to witness one of Sardinia's best festivals – the Sartiglia.

ORISTANO: Hotel Mistral €
Budget **Map** B4
Via XX Settembre, 34, 9170
Tel *0783 21 03 89*
w hotel-mistral.it
Modern, no-frills lodging in the heart of the old town. A simple outdoor pool; courteous staff.

ORISTANO: Hotel Duomo €€
Historic **Map** B4
Via Vittorio Emanuele 34, 9170
Tel *078 377 80 61*
w hotelduomo.net
This charming 18th-century hotel is an oasis of tranquillity. Rooms are large and elegantly furnished.

TRESNURAGHES: La Terrazza €
B&B **Map** B3
Via Nuraghe 40, 9079
Tel *0339 148 01 10*
w laterrazzabb.com
Experience Sardinian village life in this 18th-century cottage, with just three bedrooms and a suite.

The North and the Costa Smeralda

AGGIUS: il Muto di Gallura €
Agriturismo **Map** C2
Loc. Fraiga, 97011
Tel *079 62 05 59*
w mutodigallura.com
Located in a forest with two suites. Relaxation area with a Jacuzzi, sauna and Turkish bath.

AGLIENTU: Nuraghe Tuttusoni €
Agriturismo **Map** C1
Loc. Portobello di Gallura, 7020
Tel *079 65 68 30*
w nuraghetuttusoni.it

Simply furnished traditional stone hut at La Essenza in Torpe

Fabulous family-run *agriturismo* minutes from a sandy shore. Offers rooms and villas, both with sea views.

BASSACUTENA: Sole e Terra €
Agriturismo **Map** C1
Loc. Funtana d'Alzi, 7020
Tel *0331 584 69 91*
W soleeterra.it
A certified organic farm. The main house features a terrace, lounge, library and shop. Pleasant rooms with balconies.

BUDONI: Sporting Hotel Ottiolu €€
Mid-range **Map** D2
Frazione Agrustos, 8020
Tel *078 484 30 39*
W studiovacanze.it
A contemporary hotel close to the beach with an open-air theatre. Spacious, bright rooms.

CALA DI VOLPE: Hotel Nibaru €€
Mid-range **Map** D1
Loc. Cala di Volpe, 7020
Tel *0789 960 38*
W hotelnibaru.it
Serene hotel with a lovely pool, but also close to the beach. Rooms have mountain views.

ISOLA ROSSA: Marinedda Hotel Thalasso & Spa €€
Luxury **Map** C1
Via Tanca della Torre, 7038
Tel *079 69 41 85*
W hotelmarinedda.com
A stunning hotel with direct access to the Bay of Marinedda. Full-service spa and an excellent restaurant. Impeccable service.

LA MADDALENA: Camping Maddalena €
Camping **Map** D1
Via G.Mary Loc. Moneta, 7024
Tel *078 972 80 51*
W campingmaddalena.it
Organized camping and three different types of bungalows. Close to the town centre.

DK Choice

LA MADDALENA: La Casitta €€€
Luxury **Map** D1
Via Cesare Battisti 2, 7024
Tel *329 370 5621*
W lacasitta.it
This intimate resort, located on a private island, offers ultimate luxury in a natural setting. Two magnificent villas – completely refurbished and exquisitely decorated – come with a butler, chef and maid. Breathtaking views of the sea.

Serene surroundings at La Casitta in La Maddalena

LURAS: Funtana Abbas €
Budget **Map** C1
Loc. San Leonardo, 7020
Tel *079 66 90 00*
W funtanaabbas.it
A spectacular hotel set in acres of forest. Spotless, spacious rooms and excellent service.

OLBIA: Hotel Gallura €
Budget **Map** D2
Corso Umberto 145, 7026
Tel *0789 246 48*
Centrally located hotel with simple rooms and a great restaurant.

OLBIA: Hotel Panorama €€
Mid-range **Map** D2
Via Mazzini 7, 7026
Tel *0789 266 56*
W hotelpanoramaolbia.it
An unassuming 4-star hotel with a panoramic roof terrace and pleasant rooms. Good value.

PITRIZZA: Hotel Pitrizza €€€
Luxury **Map** D1
Porto Cervo, 7021
Tel *0789 93 01 11*
W pitrizzahotel.com
Grand hotel with super-luxe amenities, grounds and stunning views. Private villas also on offer.

PORTO CERVO: La Murichessa €
B&B **Map** D1
Loc. Vaddimala, 7021
Tel *0339 531 65 32*
W lamurichessa.it
Enchanting old-world villa with simple rooms that offer sublime mountain views.

PORTO CERVO: Cervo Hotel €€€
Luxury **Map** D1
Costa Smeralda Resort, 07021
Tel *0789 93 11 11*
W hotelcervocostasmeralda.com
Elegant hotel in a piazza. Boasts a private beach and golf course.

PORTO ROTONDO: Villaggio Baia de Bahas €
Apartments **Map** D1
Località Marana Golfo Di Marinella, 7026
Tel *011 50 47 69*
W baiadebahas.com
Spacious apartments with resort facilities and a sandy beach.

PORTO ROTONDO: Hotel Colonna San Marco €€€
Luxury **Map** D1
Piazzetta San Marco, 7020
Tel *0789 341 10*
W hotelcolonnasanmarco.it
Tastefully furnished hotel with a splendid garden and pool. Close to the port. Boat rental available.

SAN PANTALEO: Petra Segreta Resort €€€
Luxury **Map** D1
Strada Buddeu, 7026
Tel *0346 152 11 87*
W petrasegretaresort.com
Decorated in a rustic style. First-class facilities and spa services.

SAN TEODORO: La Cinta €
Camping **Map** D2
Via del Tirreno, 8020
Tel *078 486 57 77*
W campingsanteodoro.com
Close to a beach, this campsite has a market, bar, volleyball court and bowling alley.

SANTA TERESA DI GALLURA: La Coluccia Hotel €€€
Resort **Map** C1
Via Ulisse, Loc. Conca Verde, 7028
Tel *0789 75 80 06*
W lacoluccia.it
Sleek and minimalistic, with sweeping views from nearly every room. Exquisite pool

SASSARI: Hotel Grazia Deledda €
Business **Map** B2
Viale Dante 47, 7100
Tel *079 27 12 35*
W hotelgraziadeledda.it
Large four-star establishment with comfortable and spacious rooms.

TRINITA D'AGULTU E VIGNOLA: Mediterraneo €
Budget **Map** C1
Loc. Lu Colbu, 7038
Tel *079 68 98 01*
W hotel-mediterraneo.org
Since 1976, this family-run hotel has provided comfortable rooms and excellent service. Superb food.

VALLEDORIA: Monte Istulargiu €
Agriturismo **Map** C2
Loc. Monte Istulargiu - Str. Castelsardo
Tel *0348 724 04 79*
W agriturismomonteistulargiu.com
Colourful rooms and apartments. Located close to the beach.

For more information on types of hotels *see page 174*

WHERE TO EAT AND DRINK

Sardinia is an excellent place to explore and appreciate regional variations in cuisine. Fish and seafood fill restaurant menus along the coast, while meat and stuffed pasta are commonly found in the interior. In fact, restaurants that do not serve typical regional dishes are a rarity. The rhythm for mealtimes is Mediterranean, with lunch served at 1–3pm and dinner at 9–10:30pm. In many cases restaurants often stay open until midnight, especially in summer. The restaurants listed on pages 186–9 have been selected from the best that Sardinia can offer across all price ranges.

Unassuming outdoor seating at Luigi Pomata in Cagliari *(see p186)*

Types of Restaurants

In terms of price, cuisine and atmosphere, there is not much difference between a *ristorante* (restaurant) and a trattoria in Sardinia. Even a fairly expensive restaurant may still be decorated in a functional style. Pizzerias are rarely luxurious, but have the advantage of offering decent eating at lower prices. Choose pizzerias with wood-burning ovens for better quality pizzas. An *enoteca* focuses on wine, usually both regional and national, but almost always has a wide array of savoury snacks and dishes. While the traditional regional cuisine offered in many of Sardinia's restaurants is explained on pp182–3, modern Italian cuisine, served usually in more upmarket restaurants, tends to be more creative, with each chef adding his own innovative twist to classic Italian dishes. The island's seafood restaurants feature mainly lobster, squid, tuna, sardines, mussels and clams, and in the fine-dining establishments, generally in or near resort towns, the best of Italian cuisine is exalted and presented as a work of art on your plate.

Prices and Paying

A three-course meal will cost about €25–€50 per person. In top restaurants the bill may add up to €35–€45 but only rarely will it go above €50 (except in the exclusive areas of the Costa Smeralda). In pizzerias a two-course meal with a beer or half-litre of wine will run to €15–€25. The bill often includes a cover charge, usually €1–€3 per person, and service. Although it isn't customary among the locals to tip, it has become almost expected in the more exclusive resorts. Many restaurants accept major credit cards but, just in case, be prepared to pay in cash, especially at bars, cafés or smaller, family-run places.

Fixed-Price Menus

Some restaurants offer a *menù a prezzo fisso* or *menù turistico* (set menus at fixed prices). *Agriturismi (see p174)* prepare a set menu of local specialities daily, usually including regional dishes such as *porceddu*, or suckling pig, which guests would have to order in advance in restaurants. Upmarket places may offer a menu *degustazione* (tasting menu) giving diners the chance to sample five or six house specialities.

Closing Days

Restaurants close for one day a week – usually Sunday or Monday – except during July and August. Most places also close for one month of annual holidays, usually in winter, except for the restaurants in Cagliari, which are closed in August.

Vegetarian Food

Sardinia is not ideal for strict vegetarians. People who eat fish will not have problems along the coast, although in the interiors the choice may be limited to pasta or soup with fresh bread and cheeses. If you do not see anything suitable on the menu, explain your situation to the waiter. The chef will usually cook you something special – although it may be prepared with meat stock.

Dal Corsaro, one of Cagliari's top restaurants *(see p186)*

The Menu

Restaurants do not always provide a written menu. Instead, a waiter will give a list of the day's dishes at the table and help guests choose. Diners may begin with an *antipasto* (starter) such as sliced sausage, *salumi* or cured meats, grilled vegetables, artichoke hearts or olives. Coastal places offer seafood appetizers such as clams, calamari, cuttlefish, sea anemones and assorted molluscs. This is followed by the *primo* (first course), which may consist of soup, pasta or, occasionally, a rice dish. The *secondo* (second course) will be meat or fish, and may include the famous *porceddu*. Some first courses, such as *pane frattau* (carasau bread in broth) or fregula pasta with clams, make substantial meals. The meal ends with cheese, fruit or dessert, with coffee and perhaps a Sardinian liqueur *(see p185)*.

Reservations

Restaurants are often crowded, particularly in the evening and during the summer. It is advisable to book ahead even in the less expensive establishments, or else arrive fairly early to avoid a long wait.

Wine and Drinks

Most restaurants, even those in the medium-price range, will stock a good selection of regional wines and liqueurs. Some may offer non-Sardinian wines. Almost all restaurants also provide a house wine.

Children

Children are welcome in restaurants, especially family-run ones, where staff are more inclined to prepare half-portions or even special dishes for them.

Smoking

Smoking is banned in all public establishments in Italy. Some places may have terraces or outside tables where smoking is permitted.

Aperitif time in an Alghero bar

Wheelchair Access

Only a few restaurants in Sardinia are equipped with ramps and adapted toilet facilities for the disabled. Some places have steps, but access is not normally a problem. It is a good idea to call the restaurant beforehand to ensure an easily accessible table and assistance when you arrive.

Food Festivals

The best way to get a taste of the real Sardinia is at one of the frequent *sagre* (food festivals). These pleasant occasions are usually dedicated to one particular dish or product, such as wine, cheese or fish. One of the most interesting is the picturesque tuna festival held around the end of May in Carloforte on the Island of San Pietro, where you can try tuna cooked in a multitude of ways. Fish in general is the theme in September at Cagliari's Sagra del Pesce and also in August when Oristano hosts the Festa del Mare. Another popular festival, Sagre della Castagne e delle Nocciole, dedicated to the harvest of chestnuts and hazelnuts, is held in Aritzo in October, while the following month sees the Sagre delle Olive in Gonnosfanadiga, near Cagliari. Various religious and folk festivals held throughout the year usually have a gastronomic element, often including spit-roast *porceddu* – suckling pig.

Recommended Restaurants

The restaurants listed on pages 186–9 have been selected for their good value, interesting cuisine, excellent location and atmosphere. A range of establishments have been included – from pizzerias and traditional places serving classic Sardinian cuisine to restaurants specializing in seafood and fine-dining spots. Be aware that many restaurants close for a month or more in the off season.

Entries highlighted as DK Choice have been selected in recognition of a special feature – this could be an outstanding level of gourmet cuisine, a panoramic view, excellent value or a combination of these. Most of these places are popular with locals and visitors so be sure to book ahead well in advance.

Pane frattau, a dish of stock-softened bread, cheese and tomato sauce

The Flavours of Sardinia

There is a huge contrast between the extravagant lifestyle of Costa Smeralda and the hard lives of Sardinia's farmers and shepherds that inspired the *cucina povera* – a "poor cooking" style of food. But even the most fashionable restaurants serve versions of these simple tasty dishes, the most famous of which is *porceddu*, traditional spit-roasted suckling pig. Remote from the mainland, rugged and dry, the island has a distinctive cuisine, taking its flavours from the herbs that grow on the hillsides. Other popular ingredients include honey, wild-boar ham and salami, goat's and ewe's cheeses and seafood.

Sardinian herbs

Market vendor offering a wide range of local cheeses

Inland Influences

Centuries of seaborne invasion required Sardinians to make the most of available inland ingredients. Vines and olive trees grow everywhere so families made their own wine and oil. Wild herbs flavoured anything that could go into the pot. Rabbit, hare, game birds and even thrushes were easily caught, and lamb or mutton was usually available. Offal is still used, and local specialities include pigs' trotters, cooked in a piquant sauce, and lambs' feet, which are braised in tomato sauce while their intestines are spit-roasted (*cordula*). Porceddu (suckling pig) is spit-roasted over a fire of myrtle and juniper wood and basted until the skin is crisp and the herb-scented meat is tender. Sausages and salami are also made from pork. The meat of the young goats that climb the mountains is cooked with herbs and wine; *capretto al finocchietto* is kid cooked with fennel. Lamb and kid were also roasted by hunters in pits dug in the ground – a technique now reserved for celebrations. Wheat was introduced by the Romans, and bread-making is a local art. Among the many types is the crisp, circular *pane*

Tuna · Mussels · Lobster · Squid · Sardines · Clams

Some of the superb seafood caught in the clear waters around Sardinia

Sardinian Dishes and Specialities

Many local dishes are unique to the island. Sardinian pastas include little ball-shaped *fregula*; similar to couscous, it is often simmered in lamb stock and flavoured with saffron and Pecorino to make *succu*. It is also served with clams, or in broth as a soup. Ravioli-like *culurgiones* may be filled with cheese and fresh mint and served with a tomato sauce, while semolina *gnocchetti* (dumplings) are delicious served with a hearty meat sauce such as *sugo di cinghiale* (wild boar). *Suppa cuata* is layers of bread, grated cheese, nutmeg and parsley, baked in lamb stock. Pork, beans and vegetables go into *favata*, a hearty winter stew. *Stufato di capretto* is a more extravagant dish – a rich casserole made with kid (young goat), wine, artichokes and saffron. Sometimes eggs are added to make a kind of fricassée.

Fresh green figs

Pesce Spada alla Sardegna is a swordfish steak with a sauce of tomatoes, wine, mint, saffron and chilli.

Tresses of vine-ripened tomatoes hanging on a local produce stall

tuna are grilled with herbs or fried in a semolina-flour batter. Risottos, pasta dishes and fish soups make use of the plentiful squid, cuttlefish, anchovies and shellfish. Octopus, prawns, mussels, clams, scallops and squid are boiled and dressed in oil and vinegar as *antipasti*. *Burrida* is fish marinaded in vinegar with walnuts and parsley, and *bottarga* is the dried and salted roe of grey mullet or tuna, which may be served sliced as an *antipasto* or grated over pasta.

carasau, that shepherds would take to work with them. When moistened and topped with a sauce, Pecorino cheese and egg, it is called *pane frattau*. Pecorino is Sardinia's most renowned cheese: soft when young, it hardens with age and is then used grated. *Pecorino pepato* contains peppercorns. Other cheeses include *fiore Sardo* and *dolce Sardo*. Soft ricotta is used in savoury and sweet dishes.

Cosmopolitan Coasts

The Romans, Arabs, Genoese and Spanish who colonized the island brought with them their culinary influences. Saffron, an Eastern import, still adds colour and perfume to numerous savoury and sweet recipes. The west coast has Catalan-influenced dishes that stem from the era of Spanish

rule. *Panadas* are savoury pies filled with meat or cheese and vegetables; the most popular type is stuffed with eel *(panada di anguillas)*. Lobster *alla Catalana*, stewed with vinegar, onion and tomatoes, is a typical dish from Alghero. Mullet, sea bass, bream, swordfish and

Newly harvested olives ready to be taken to the mill for pressing

SARDINIAN SWEETS

Soft almond nougat is a speciality of Tonara. Many Sardinian biscuits and sweets were originally made for religious festivals:

Aranciata or Aranzada Preserved orange peel with honey and nuts.

Caschettes Rose-shaped nut- and honey-filled pastries, given to brides at weddings.

Gianchittos Toasted almond and lemon peel meringues

Papassinos Walnut, raisin and almond biscuits.

Sebadas Ricotta and citrus peel fritters, covered in honey.

Sos guelfus Balls of almond or hazelnut paste.

Sospiri di Ozieri Iced almond paste and citrus sweets, wrapped in bright paper.

Malloreddus are *gnocchi*-like dumplings served with a fresh tomato sauce and minced sausage meat.

Agnello alla zafferano, saffron- and garlic-scented lamb stew, is shown here served with *fregula* pasta.

Pardulas (or *casadinas*) are fresh cheese pastries that are flavoured with cinnamon, saffron and lemon.

What to Drink in Sardinia

Grapevines first came to Sardinia from the eastern
Mediterranean, where the Phoenicians had long cultivated
vineyards. The warm climate tends to yield very ripe grapes,
which are then turned into strong, deeply coloured wines.
Lighter, fruity *novellos* are also worth trying. Good-quality
Sardinian wines are widely available in shops, but it also
pays to go directly to the suppliers. All types are made, from
red *(rosso)*, white *(bianco)* and rosé *(rosato)* to rich dessert
wines. Many qualify for the status of *denominazione di origine
controllata* (DOC), with guaranteed provenance and quality
standards. Sardinian wines are almost always made from a
single grape variety. Perhaps the best-known is Vernaccia
di Oristano, the first to gain DOC status in Sardinia.

Old winemaking equipment, now largely
superseded by modern techniques

Slightly
sparkling Sinis

Vernaccia

Grape harvesting

Recommended Whites

· **Cantina Sociale della
Riforma Agraria, Alghero**
Vermentino di Sardegna
Aragosta
· **Cantina Sociale Gallura**
Vermentino
· **Tenuta Sella & Mosca,
Alghero**
Terre Bianche

White Wines

The white wines of Sardinia
go well with fish and
seafood dishes, and some
are sturdy enough to go with
meat dishes such as pork.
Nuragus is a widely planted
white grape, producing rather
neutral, soft and fruity wines.
Vermentino is also widely
grown and the wines have
more complex flavours. Both
Vermentino di Sardegna and
Vermentino di Gallura, made
mostly around Sassari and
Nuoro province, tend to be
fairly strong. There is also a
sparkling version. DOC
Vermentino from Cala Viola
and Usini is very good. The
Campidano area produces
the fruity, dry white Semidano.

Red Wines

The best-known red wine is
Cannonau, which is usually full-
bodied and strong, although
some lighter versions are made.
Most Cannonau is produced in
the province of Nuoro in eastern
Sardinia. It goes well with roast
meat and game. Another wine
to drink with game and mature
cheese is Monica di Sardegna,
a dry red with intense perfume
that should be drunk young.
Less common but equally good
DOC reds are the light, dry
Mandrolisai, Campidano di
Terralba and Carignano del
Sulcis. Other reds, such as Tanca
Farrà di Alghero and Terre Brune
del Sulcis, blend Sardinian and
imported grape varieties. The
most expensive Sardinian red
wine is Turriga.

Cannonau
grapes

Nieddera rosé
and Cannonau

Recommended Reds

· **Azienda Giuseppe
Cabras, Nuoro**
Cannonau
· **Tenuta Sella & Mosca,
Alghero**
Anghelu Ruju
· **Attilio Contini, Cabras**
Nieddera

Dessert Wines

Sardinia produces a number of sweet dessert wines, both white and red. Besides mature white Vernaccia and sweet red Cannonau, there is Moscato di Sardegna, made from Muscat grapes and bottled at three years old. It is sweet but has good acidity, and an alcoholic content of 15°. Tempio Pausania Muscat tends to be lightly fizzy, while the Cagliari version is strong and sweet. The red Girò di Cagliari and amber-coloured Nasco are also strong and sweet. Two dessert wines made from semi-dried grapes come from the Alghero area: Torbato and the port-like Anghelu Ruju, both produced with Cannonau grapes. The Bosa and Cagliari Malvasia wines are similar to Vernaccia.

Cantina Sociale della Vernaccia at Oristano

Sparkling Vernaccia Malvasia di Bosa

Vernaccia grapes

Malvasia grapes

Moscato grapes

Harvesting black grapes from Cannonau vines

Recommended Dessert Wines

· *Centro Enologico Sardo, Villacidro*
Malvasia

· *Centro Enologico Sardo, Villacidro*
Moscato Dolce (Muscat)

· *Fratelli Serra, Zeddiani*
Vernaccia

· *Meloni Vini, Selargius*
Malvasia di Cagliari

· *Cantina Sociale Dolianova*
Moscato di Cagliari

Digestivi

The best-known spirit made in Sardinia is *abbardiente* (named from the Spanish *aguardiente*), a *grappa* or eau de vie. Among the best are those made from the strong-tasting Cannonau and the more delicate Malvasia. Grappa here is also called *fil'e ferru* (iron wire), from the wire used to mark hiding places for illegally produced grappa. There is a variety of flavourings used in grappa, such as the combination of wild fennel, juniper and thistle. The most famous liqueur, however, is Mirto, both red and white, made with wild myrtle leaves and berries. The Sardinians' favourite is Zedda Piras.

Cork-covered bottles with characteristic decorative motifs

Where to Eat and Drink

Cagliari and the South

DK Choice

CAGLIARI: La Stella Marina di Montecristo €€
Seafood   **Map** C6
Via Sardegna 140, 9124
Tel *347 578 89 64*   **Closed** *Sun*
This simple restaurant serves superlative traditional fish dishes at very reasonable prices. The setting is humble, but the atmosphere is warm and welcoming, and the staff courteous. On Thursdays, in addition to seafood, wild game is on offer. The restaurant is very popular so be sure to book ahead.

CAGLIARI: Su Cumbidu €
Enoteca   **Map** C6
Via Napoli 13, 9124
Tel *070 67 07 12*
Su Cumbidu means "invitation" in Sardinian dialect and this cozy wine bar, with its attentive service, lives up to its name. Savoury snacks complement a vast selection of local wines.

CAGLIARI: Antica Hostaria €€
Traditional   **Map** C6
Via Cavour, 9124
Tel *070 66 58 70*
Hidden in a winding warren of picturesque backstreets, this surprisingly elegant place serves Sardinian dishes and classic Italian favourites. The ample wine list features local and mainland Italian labels.

CAGLIARI: Trattoria Lillicu €€
Seafood   **Map** C6
Via Sardegna 78, 9124
Tel *070 65 29 70*   **Closed** *Breakfast*
Old-fashioned trattoria serving rustic, fish-based fare on basic, marble-topped tables. The food is fresh and good, but the prices may seem a bit high considering the simple interior.

CAGLIARI: Dal Corsaro €€€
Fine Dining   **Map** C6
Viale Regina Margherita 28, 9124
Tel *070 66 43 18*   **Closed** *Sun*
Sardinian specialities are creatively reinterpreted by the chef at this family-owned, sophisticated restaurant. Archways, mirrors and prettily framed prints enhance the dining experience.

CAGLIARI: Luigi Pomata €€€
Modern   **Map** C6
Viale Regina Margherita 18, 9124
Tel *070 67 20 58*   **Closed** *Sun*
In addition to the tempting seafood dishes, each interpreted with a modern twist on tradition, a sushi bar makes this fun restaurant a well-rounded choice. It is advisable to make reservations in advance.

CALASETTA: Da Pasqualino €€
Traditional   **Map** B6
Viale Regina Margherita 85, 9011
Tel *078 18 84 73*
Unassuming little trattoria with a relaxed vibe, offering mostly seafood dishes prepared using traditional local recipes. Specialities include tuna dishes and lobster. Good local wines.

CARLOFORTE: Da Nicolo €€
Seafood   **Map** B6
Corso Cavour 32, 9014
Tel *0781 85 40 48*   **Closed** *Winter*
Proudly interpreting the local cuisine of the area – a surprising combination of North African, Ligurian and Sardinian flavours – this restaurant serves up unusual dishes, many based on fresh tuna.

CARLOFORTE: Al Tonno di Corsa €€€
Seafood   **Map** B6
Via Marconi 47, 9014
Tel *0781 85 51 06*
As suggested by the name, tuna is the star of the show at this characterful restaurant with warm and bright rooms set out on two levels. The speciality here is *musciame* or sun-dried tuna.

PORTOSCUSO: La Ghinghetta €€€
Seafood   **Map** B6
Via Cavour 20, 9010
Tel *0781 50 81 43*
Just steps from the sea, this tiny restaurant serves super-fresh seafood in the same village where it is caught. Try the prawn tartare with quails' eggs and caviar, then a gourmet dessert.

SANT'ANTIOCO: Moderno-da Achille €€
Traditional   **Map** B6
Via Nazionale 82, 9017
Tel *0781 831 05*
The talented chef at stylish Moderno-da Achille expertly prepares excellent Sardinian fare. A touch of Oriental influence livens up the menu. Welcoming atmosphere.

TEULADA: Ristorante Sebera €€
Traditional   **Map** C6
Via San Francesco 8, 9019
Tel *070 927 08 76*
For a hotel restaurant, the atmosphere here is refreshingly charming. The menu items are staples of Sardinian cuisine, and the service is attentive. *Spaghetti ai frutti di mare* (seafood pasta) is a particular favourite.

The Eastern Coast

ARBATAX: Il Faro €€
Traditional   **Map** D4
Via Porto Frailis, 8048
Tel *0782 66 74 99*
The interior of this seaside restaurant is rather plain, but there are great views from the sunny terrace facing the shore. Simple, time-honoured dishes fill the menu, many based on fish.

BAUNEI: Il Golgo €€
Traditional   **Map** D4
Loc. Golgo, 8040
Tel *337 811 828*
Rustic and inviting, this restaurant serves authentic local cuisine, such as their speciality, *porceddu*. Sit outside to enjoy the mountain views, or inside by the open fire in cooler weather.

Casual dining space at Luigi Pomata in Cagliari

CALA GONONE: Il Pescatore €€
Seafood   Map D3
Via Lungomare dell'Acqua Dolce 1, 8022
Tel *0784 931 74*
Highlights at this charming seaside spot include swordfish carpaccio and octopus salad. Good local wines.

DORGALI: Il Colibrì €€
Traditional   Map D3
Via Floris 7, 8022
Tel *0784 960 54*   **Closed** *Breakfast*
Sardinian dishes are prepared lovingly using ancient recipes. The wild game is excellent – in particular the *cinghiale* (wild boar) – and the desserts are home-made.

DORGALI: Ispinigoli €€
Traditional   Map D3
SS 125 – Loc. Ispinigoli, 8022
Tel *0784 952 68*   **Closed** *Breakfast*
The menu here features dishes based on wild game, but there are also many vegetarian options along with an ample wine list. Conveniently located close to the stunning Ispinigoli caves.

OROSEI: Su Barchile €€
Traditional   Map D3
Via Mannu 5, 8028
Tel *0784 988 79*
Located in the heart of the old town, Su Barchile has a versatile seasonal menu featuring varieties of seafood, wild game and vegetarian specialities.

POSADA: Da Marco e Caterina €€
Seafood   Map D2
Viale Mario Melis s/n, 8020
Tel *0784 85 45 82*
Cheerful trattoria, run by a husband and wife, that exudes passion for the native cuisine. Tasty dishes have a great balance of traditional and modern flavours.

SANTA MARIA NAVARRESE: Ristorante Nascar €€
Seafood   Map D4
Via Pedras s/n, 8040
Tel *0782 61 53 14*
This romantic place, attached to a small hotel, has a low-lit garden with glass tables and wicker armchairs set among the trees. A particular favourite is the *fregula*, a Sardinian version of couscous.

SANTA MARIA NAVARRESE: Sa Cadrea €€
Seafood   Map D4
Via Pedralonga 23, 8040
Tel *0784 261 51 12*
This unassuming restaurant offers superb *fritto misto* (seafood in batter), seafood salad and local prosciutto. Hamburgers and

Beautifully presented food at Ristorante Nascar in Santa Maria Navarrese

sandwiches are also on the menu. There are breathtaking sea views from the terrace.

TORTOLÌ: Da Lenin €€
Seafood   Map D4
Via Matteotti 24, 8048
Tel *0348 544 55 55*
Despite a relatively simple dining room, this restaurant serves fabulous seafood dishes made with traditional and seasonal recipes. The service is warm and professional.

VILLASIMIUS: Da Barbara €€
Seafood   Map D6
Localita' S.P.76, Solanas, 9049
Tel *070 75 06 30*
It is worth making a short trek to find this family-run gem and dine with the locals. Delicious, traditional fish-based dishes are prepared and served with a smile.

VILLASIMIUS: Il Moro €€
Traditional   Map D6
Loc. Villaggio dei Mandorli, 9049
Tel *070 79 81 80*
A quaint restaurant with an open fireplace and lots of exposed wood. The menu has a wide selection of traditional Sardinian recipes. There is a spacious terrace for outdoor dining.

Central Sardinia and Barbagia

GAVOI: Santa Rughe €€
Traditional   Map C3
Via Carlo Felice 2, 8020
Tel *0784 537 74*   **Closed** *Wed*
Exposed stone walls and wood-beamed ceilings make this rustic place all the more intimate. It serves local specialities such as pasta with wild boar ragù and local salami, plus pizza and delicious pastries.

NUORO: Canne al Vento €€
Fusion   Map D3
Via Giuseppe Biasi 159, 8100
Tel *0784 20 17 62*   **Closed** *Sun*
This simple and homey restaurant is where typical Sardinian recipes meet modern Mediterranean cuisine, and the results are fantastic. The wine list is stellar and the service is warm and attentive.

NUORO: Il Portico €€
Modern   Map D3
Via Monsignor Bua 13, 8100
Tel *0784 21 76 41*
Top-class cuisine at affordable prices is offered here, in the heart of Nuoro's old town. Traditional local dishes including pasta and seafood are given a modern twist.

NUORO: Ristorante Tascusi €€
Traditional   Map D3
Via Aspromonte 13, 8100
Tel *0784 37 287*
Sardinian art on the walls echoes the culinary arts of Barbagia on the menu – try the antipasti, the *culurgiones* pasta and *seadas*, a local dessert of cheese pastries topped with honey.

NUORO: Il Rifugio €€
Traditional   Map D3
Via Antonio Mereu 28, 8100
Tel *0784 23 23 55*
Genteel service in an atmospheric setting. The menu features an ample variety of Sardinian dishes; try one of the specialities featuring sheep's cheese. The pizza is excellent too.

OLIENA: CiKappa €€
Traditional   Map D3
Corso Martin Luther King 2, 8025
Tel *0784 28 80 24*
Local dishes presented with style and detail. An impressive variety of seafood as well as meat dishes, and in the evenings there are inventive pizzas as well.

For more information on types of restaurants *see page 180*

OLIENA: Su Gologone €€€
Fine Dining Map D3
Località su Gologone, 8025
Tel *0784 28 75 12*
Set amid lush, gorgeous gardens
this exquisite restaurant serves
Sardinian cuisine paired with
excellent wines. The *pasticceria*
creates delicate confections.

ORGOSOLO: Il Portico €
Traditional Map D3
Via Giovanni XXIII 34, 8027
Tel *078 440 29 29*
Authentic flavours and local
ingredients are the key draws at
this trattoria. Sardinian favourites
as well as plenty of pizzas on offer.

DK Choice

**ORGOSOLO: Ai Monti del
Gennargentu** €€
Traditional Map D3
Località Settiles, 8027
Tel *078 440 23 74* **Closed** *Nov–
Easter*
An elegant restaurant situated
high in the mountains offering
a mouthwatering range of
quality meats, cooked to
perfection over an open fire.
For a truly unique experience,
take a guided excursion into
the wilderness and relish a
traditional lunch of lamb stew,
roast pork, bread and cheese
with local shepherds.

OTTANA: Il Platano €€
Traditional Map C3
Via Ghitti 83, 8020
Tel *0784 755 64*
Quality food, especially the fish.
The decor leaves a little to be
desired, but the mountain views
are fantastic. Pizzas also available.

The Western Coast

ALGHERO: Trattoria Cavour €
Seafood Map B2
Via Cavour 110, 7041
Tel *079 973 87 62*
This simple trattoria is one of the
best on the island for scrumptious
fish. Squid ink risotto, fish soup
and *fritto misto* (seafood in batter)
are the highlights.

ALGHERO: Il Ghiotto €
Enoteca Map B2
Piazza Civica 23, 7041
Tel *079 97 48 20*
A casual wine bar with interesting
local labels and a vast selection
of tasty dishes, both hot and cold.
Fritto misto (seafood in batter) is
excellent. Outdoor seating on a
charming piazza.

ALGHERO: Al Vecchio Mulino €€
Traditional Map B2
Via Don Deroma 3, 7041
Tel *079 97 72 54* **Closed** *Mon dinner;
Tue*
In a rustic spot in the centre of
the old town, this place whips up
traditional delights such as fried
sea urchins and Catalan lobster.
Tasty pizzas are also available.

DK Choice

ALGHERO: Al Tuguri €€
Seafood Map B2
Via Maiorca 113, 7041
Tel *079 97 67 72* **Closed** *Sun*
Booking ahead is advisable
here, as the few tables at this
cozy restaurant, converted
from a centuries-old house,
are very much in demand. The
staff are welcoming, service is
smooth, and guests can
watch their fish or meat being
grilled in the open kitchen.
There's an excellent wine list,
packed with local vintages.

**ALGHERO: Osteria
Barcellonetta** €€
Traditional Map B2
Via Gioberti 31, 7041
Tel *079 97 32 079*
This intimate restaurant in the
old town exudes old-style
charm. Seafood tops the menu
but you'll also find gnocchi with
a rich wild boar sauce.

**BOSA: Mannu da
Giancarlo e Rita** €€
Seafood Map B3
Viale Alghero 28, 8013
Tel *0785 37 53 07*
Only the freshest ingredients are
used at this stylish restaurant, in
a family-run hotel. Fish dominates
the menu but meat dishes are
also abundant. Try the town
speciality, lobster.

ORISTANO: Cocco E Dessi €€
Traditional Map B4
Via Tirso 31, 9170
Tel *0783 25 26 48*
This central spot has an elegantly
retro atmosphere and a vast
menu with good vegetarian
choices, pizzas and delicious
desserts. Try *fregula alle arselle*
(local couscous with mussels).

ORISTANO: Craf da Banana €€
Traditional Map B4
Via De Castro S. A. 34, 9170
Tel *0783 42 01 82*
Wild game is the house speciality
at this welcoming restaurant,
popular with locals for its homely
cooking. Try the mixed grill for the
widest range of options.

ORISTANO: Da Giovanni €€
Fine Dining Map B4
Via Colombo 8 – Torre Grande, 9170
Tel *0783 220 51* **Closed** *Mon*
An elegant restaurant with an
impeccable reputation. The
talented local chef interprets
traditional Sardinian recipes with
flair. All fish is caught fresh locally.
Superb wine list.

PORTO TORRES: Li Lioni €€
Traditional Map B2
Veccia SS131 direzione Sassari, 7046
Tel *079 50 22 86*
Four brothers run this inviting
restaurant with lots of old-world
charm; many dishes are prepared
in a fine wood-burning oven.
Non-carnivores beware: meat
dishes are the speciality here.

STINTINO: Silvestrino €€€
Seafood Map B2
Via Sassari 14, 7040
Tel *079 52 30 07*
Located in a small hotel just steps
from the sea, this restaurant serves
authentic local dishes. Seafood is
the main attraction, and the
lobster is particularly good.

Charming interior of Su Gologone in Oliena

Key to Price Guide *see page 186*

The North and the Costa Smeralda

ARZACHENA: I Frati Rossi €€€
Seafood   **Map** D1
Località Pantogia, 7021
Tel *0789 943 95*
A chic restaurant perched in the hills overlooking the sapphire sea. The impressive wine list features regional, national and international labels.

BAIA SARDINIA: Corbezzolo €€
Seafood   **Map** D1
Piazzetta della Fontana, 7021
Tel *0789 998 93*
There are two dining options here: a family-friendly pizzeria on the pedestrianized piazza, or fine seafood in the airy dining room and on terraces over- looking the sea. Great service.

LA MADDALENA: Locanda del Mirto €€
Seafood   **Map** D1
Loc. Punta della Gatta, 7024
Tel *0789 73 90 56*
Tibetan-style gazebos dot the restaurant for intimate dining. An open kitchen serves excellent seafood and a few meat dishes.

OLBIA: Antica Trattoria Pizzeria €€
Pizzeria   **Map** D2
Via Terme, 1, 7026
Tel *0789 240 53*
Fabulous pizzas with a variety of traditional and unusual toppings, including mixed seafood. The decor is simple but quaint.

OLBIA: Vecchia Gallura €€
Traditional   **Map** D2
Localita' Scopa (Palau), 7020
Tel *0789 70 81 94*
Located in a stone house covered with ivy, this restaurant is a picturesque spot to sample local cuisine. The set menu of either meat or fish is excellent value.

PORTO CERVO: Hivaoa €€
Pizzeria   **Map** D1
Via della Marina, 7021
Tel *0789 914 51*
White tables and fresh linen on a breezy covered terrace. Pizza is just the beginning: excellent seafood and pasta too. The *frutti di mare antipasto* spread is a must.

PORTO CERVO: Cipriani €€€
Fine Dining   **Map** D1
Via Rocce Sul Pevero Localita' Golfo Pero, 7020
Tel *0789 941 92*
With its white sofas, chandeliers and luxurious gold accents this restaurant defines glamour.

Glamorous dining at Cipriani in Porto Cervo

The dishes are delectable and original, the wine list is stellar and the house cocktails legendary.

PORTO CERVO: Gianni Pedrinelli €€€
Fine Dining   **Map** D1
Loc. Piccolo Pevero, 7021
Tel *0789 924 36*   **Closed** *Nov– Feb*
The menu at this restaurant offers mostly meat and game dishes but many seafood options are also available. Do not miss the house speciality, *porcettu allo spiedo* (spit-roast suckling pig). A lovely space with simple, classic furnishings.

PORTO CERVO: Il Pescatore €€€
Seafood   **Map** D1
Porto Cervo, 7020
Tel *0789 31 62 24*
One of the oldest restaurants in this exclusive port town, and the only one offering *pied dans l'eau* (right on the water) dining. Heavenly dishes but small portions. Book ahead.

PORTO CERVO: Spinnaker €€€
Seafood   **Map** D1
Res. Alba Ruja, Liscia di Vacca, 7020
Tel *0789 912 26*
One of the Costa Smeralda's best-known restaurants, serving innovative fish pasta dishes, such as black ravioli stuffed with salt cod or farfalline with celery and mullet roe. The portions, however, are on the small side.

PORTO ROTONDO: Da Giovannino €€
Fine Dining   **Map** D1
Piazza Quadra 10, 7026
Tel *0789 352 80*
Watch out for celebrities at this high-profile restaurant while sampling the excellent Mediterranean cuisine. Highlights include the scampi sushi with lemon juice and the grilled squid.

DK Choice

PORTO ROTONDO: Pedristellas €€
Traditional   **Map** D1
Via Monte Ladu, 7026
Tel *0377 236 92 01*
The name of this extraordinary restaurant, which translates to "rocks and stars", refers to its magnificent rock garden, dotted with old pine trees. The placement of tables and even the meandering garden paths were designed to complement the glorious setting. The menu has an abundance of seafood and meat specialities in the typical Sardinian tradition.

PORTO ROTONDO: Stella di Gallura €€
Traditional   **Map** D1
Loc. Monte Ladu, 7026
Tel *0789 344 02*
A modern, elegant restaurant close to the beach. The menu is filled with typical Sardinian dishes from both land and sea as well as excellent pizzas. Opt for poolside dining.

SASSARI: Il Cenacolo €€
Traditional   **Map** B2
Via Ozieri 2, 7100
Tel *079 23 62 51*
A centrally located, elegant place whipping up all of the best regional specialities. Seasonal menu and friendly service.

SASSARI: L'Antica Hostaria €€
Traditional   **Map** B2
Via Cavour 55, 7100
Tel *079 20 00 66*
Charming, slightly old-fashioned restaurant in the modern town. The chef is Sicilian: don't miss his authentic cassata ice-cream. Long list of Sardinian wines.

For more information on types of restaurants *see page 180*

SHOPS AND MARKETS

Sardinia produces a great variety of handicrafts that are hard to find in other regions of Italy. Among these are hand-woven rugs, linen napkins, *pibbiones* (embroidered fabrics) and baskets. Traditional materials and techniques are used for all these products, and while some are still made in the traditional style, others have been adapted to more modern tastes. Crafted goods are often made to a very high standard of design and workmanship, and include coral and filigree pins and brooches, pottery and crockery, and items made from cork and wrought iron.

In the larger towns and tourist resorts, traditional souvenirs are sold, such as ashtrays in the shape of nuraghi, costumed dolls and seashell pictures. Specialities such as pecorino cheese, salted mullet roe, sweets and wine are also worth trying.

Opening Hours

Shops in Sardinia generally open at 9am, close at 1pm for lunch and reopen 4:30–8pm (5–8:30pm or later in summer). Large supermarkets and larger clothes stores are open throughout the day. In the cities most shops close for a few weeks in August, while on the coast they tend to open on a seasonal basis (June to September).

A potter at the wheel producing traditionally shaped vessels

How to Pay

The majority of the larger shops and department stores accept credit cards, but it is advisable to check in advance. The smaller shops and artisan's workshops will generally prefer payment in cash. You must get a receipt (*scontrino*) when you pay; it is required by law and you may be asked to produce it as you leave the shop. It will also be needed should you want to change purchased articles later on.

Department Stores

The main department store in Cagliari is **La Rinascente** in Via Roma. Other large stores are **Upim** and **Standa**, which you will also find in other Sardinian towns and cities. Large shopping centres have grown up on the outskirts of towns, with a wide selection of goods on offer, from shoe shops and clothing stores to supermarkets and fast-food restaurants.

Handicrafts

Local handicrafts are on sale all over Sardinia. In the villages, women display their wares, such as baskets, rugs or ceramics, outside their homes.

Shops that belong to the *Istituto Sardo Organizzazione Lavoro Artigianale* (**ISOLA**), Sardinian Institute of Handicrafts, offer quality products from the local craftsmen's cooperatives, including rugs, tablecloths, leather, jewellery, baskets, pottery, carved wood and wrought-iron objects.

Local handicrafts for sale in a certified ISOLA shop

All ISOLA products carry a special seal of quality guaranteeing their origin and authenticity.

You can find some good bargains at the *Fiera del Tappeto* (Carpet Fair), which is held at Mogoro in late July–August. Handicrafts can also be purchased at holiday farms. Other useful addresses can be found at www.regione.sardegna.it/isola.

A fish stall in Cagliari's covered market, San Benedetto

Regional Specialities

Gastronomic specialities in Sardinia are sold in the food section of supermarkets as well as in delicatessens and specialist shops or directly from the producers.

The **Mercato Coperto di San Benedetto** in Cagliari is the largest covered market in Italy. It offers an excellent choice of regional delicacies. *Bottarga* (mullet roe) can be bought at **Vaghi**, on Via Bayle, which also sells sea urchin pâté. Salted *bottarga* can be bought from the manufacturer at

San Francesco's feast day celebrated at Lula with barbecued *porceddu*

A dish of typical Sardinian honey

Fratelli Manca in Cabras. Smoked fish is on sale at **Sarda Affumicati** in Buggerru.

Cakes and sweets are also a Sardinian speciality and a fine selection is on offer in several shops, including **Sorelle Piccioni** in Quartu Sant'Elena, **Colomba Codias** in Olbia and **Acciari** at Porto Torres. A visit

to a winery (*cantina*) to taste the wines before buying can prove both interesting and good value. It is sometimes possible to taste wines in a wine shop (*enoteca*).

Visit www.sardegnaturismo. it/en/offerta/enogastromia for useful addresses of shops and workshops.

DIRECTORY

Handicrafts

Alghero
Centro Forme
Via Lamarmora 64/66.
Tel 079 97 53 52.
🔲 centroforme-alghero.it

Cagliari
ISOLA
Via Bacaredda 184.
Tel 070 40 47 91.
🔲 regione.sardegna.it/isola

Olbia
Sardartis srl
SS125, km 313.
Tel 0789 669 33.
🔲 sardartis.it
Cerasarda
Circonvallazione Nord.
Tel 0789 56 73 11.
🔲 cerasarda.it

Oristano
Cooperativa Su Trobasciu
Via Gramsci 1, Mogoro.
Tel 0783 99 05 81.
🔲 sutrobasciu.com

Porto Cervo
ISOLA
Sottopiazza.
Tel 0789 94 428.

Sant'Antioco
Cooperativa Sant'Antioco Martire
Lungomare Vespucci 30.
Tel 0781 820 85.

Sassari
ISOLA
Viale Mancini. Tel 079 23 01 01.

Regional Specialities

Alghero
Sella & Mosca
I Piani. Tel 079 99 77 00.
🔲 sellaemosca.com

Buggerru
Sarda Affumicati
Località Sa Colombera.
Tel 0781 549 14.
🔲 sardaffumicati.com

Cabras
Fratelli Manca
Via Cima 5. Tel 0783 29 08 48.
🔲 orodicabras.it

Cagliari
Mercato San Benedetto
Via Cocco Ortu. Tel 070 667 56 14.

Olbia
Colomba Codias
Via Australia 12.
Tel 0789 682 26.

Ozieri
Pasticceria Pietro Pinna
Via Pastorino 35.
Tel 079 78 74 51.

Porto Torres
Acciaro
Corso Vittorio Emanuele 36. Tel 079 51 46 05.
🔲 baracciaro.it

Quartu Sant'Elena
Sorelle Piccioni
Via Marconi 312.
Tel 070 81 01 12.
🔲 sorellepiccioni.com

Sassari
Fratelli Rau
Via Gorizia 7.
Tel 079 29 22 64.

Tonara
Salvatore Pruneddu
Via Porru 5. Tel 0784 638 05.

Wine

Cabras
Azienda Attilio Contini
Via Genova 48.
Tel 0783 29 08 06.
🔲 vinicontini.it

Cagliari
Antica Enoteca Cagliaritana
Scalette Santa Chiara.
Tel 070 65 56 11.
🔲 enoteca-cagliaritana.it

Jerzu
Jerzu Antichi Poderi
Via Umberto I 1.
Tel 0782 700 28.
🔲 jerzuantichipoderi.it

Olbia
Cantina della vigne di Piero Mancini
Tel 0789 50 71 7.
🔲 pieromancini.it

Oristano
Cantina Sociale della Vernaccia
Loc. Rimedio.
Tel 0783 33 383.
🔲 vinovernaccia.com

Quartu Sant'Elena
Cantina Sociale
Via Nazionale, Maracalagonis.
Tel 070 78 98 65.
🔲 cantinaquartu.com

Sant'Antioco
Cantine Sardus Pater
Via Rinascita 46.
Tel 0781 800 274.
🔲 cantinesarduspater.it

Sennori
Tenute Dettori
Tel 079 51 27 72.
🔲 tenutedettori.it

Serdiana
Cantina Argiolas
Via Roma 28/30.
Tel 070 74 06 06.
🔲 argiolas.it

What to Buy in Sardinia

Sardinia offers a great variety of traditional island products and local handicrafts, ranging from handwoven rugs, bedspreads and pillowcases to baskets woven in asphodel, reed or raffia. Some of the finest baskets are made in Flussio and Castelsardo. Other household articles, such as kitchenware and tableware, are made of cork or ceramics, materials which are also used to make large plates, statues and bas-reliefs. Filigree jewellery production is widespread and worn by the women for festivals and weddings; the best is made in Alghero and Bosa.

Gold buttons

Pin and earrings

Filigree pendant

Jewellery

Traditional Sardinian jewellery, such as earrings, brooches and buttons, often worn with local dress, is made of filigree and coral. Goldsmiths also make bracelets and necklaces in modern designs, including elegant coral spirals.

Circular amphora

Flower vase

Cork ice bucket

At Calangianus, in the Gallura region of the Costa Smeralda, cork is used to make numerous household articles such as boxes, umbrella stands, bowls and ice buckets.

Vases and jugs made to a modern design

Pottery

Sardinian pottery is hand-thrown and glazed with natural colours. The most common articles are vases, plates and jugs and the designs are simple and fluid. Some potters have modified traditional designs to suit modern tastes.

Basket-weaving is an ancient craft that is still widely practised. Baskets are made of straw, raffia, dwarf palm, asphodel, corn sheaves or wicker in delicate, natural colours.

Rug made in Nule

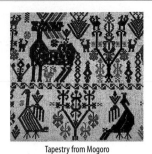

Tapestry from Mogoro

A *pibbiones* rug

Rugs and Tapestries

Among the typical hand-woven articles are woollen rugs, linen bedspreads and napkins, and tapestries. The rugs are made from coloured wool with lively geometric or floral designs. The pibbiones rugs consist of an embroidered raised pattern knitted with small needles on neutral coloured fabric.

Wood carving is an ancient Sardinian tradition. The most common articles produced are chests, kitchen implements, chopping boards and ceremonial masks.

Carved mask

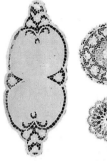

Lacework from Dorgali

Lace-making is a rare craft that requires great skill. At Oliena you can find delicate shawls made of black silk embroidered with bright colours. At Bosa you can still see women making filet lace.

Gastronomic Delicacies

Typical Sardinian products include cakes and cheeses which vary from region to region. Other specialities include jam, wine and liqueurs, such as myrtle (mirto) and lemon (limoncino), salted mullet roe and vegetables in oil.

Typical Sardinian cakes

Salted mullet roe

Myrtle liqueur

Typical Sardinian delicacies

SURVIVAL GUIDE

PRACTICAL INFORMATION

Beaches and clean blue sea are the principal attractions for visitors to Sardinia, and the coastline, especially in the northeast, gets very crowded from early July to late August. Visiting the island out of season can have its advantages, apart from avoiding the bustling crowds. The weather can be very hot in midsummer and visits to the towns and countryside, rich in history, ancient culture, old traditions and spellbinding scenery, are all the more easily appreciated in spring, early summer and autumn. In Sardinia, the familiar problems of funding and staffing for monuments and museums occur here as on the mainland. Do not be surprised to see signs such as *chiuso per restauro* (closed for restoration). Provision of information for travellers is far from perfect but is improving; there are now more tourist offices, opening at regular hours, able to provide maps and guides to help you plan your time. Attempts to speak Italian, however halting, are always appreciated.

Bathers cooling off in the Mediterranean as temperatures soar in summer

When to Visit

In July and August practically the whole of Italy goes on holiday and everywhere is overcrowded, in particular the ferries to and from Olbia and Cagliari, and the seaside hotels and resorts. Prices are much higher and you need to plan your visit ahead to make sure of accommodation. The most crowded areas are the Costa Smeralda, the beaches near the Golfo di Cagliari and the area around Stintino.

The best months to visit the beautiful interior are May, June and September. Spring is particularly delightful, when flowers are in bloom.

In winter the cold can be quite intense, especially at higher altitudes.

Tourist Information

Tourist information facilities in Sardinia are currently undergoing a substantial change. The local tourist offices (Azienda Autonoma di Soggiorno e Turismo) have been abolished, along with the provincial tourist offices (Entre Provinciale Per il Turismo), so tourism is now the responsibility of the comune (local town council) and the local Pro Loco (Town Hall). Some Sardinian towns have already set up new tourism offices – mainly those in well-established tourist areas – while others are in the process of doing so.

In the meantime, local papers – *L-Unione Sarda, La Nuova Sardegna* and *Il Sardegna* are useful sources of information, providing complete day-by-day listings of activities and events.

There are also useful websites aimed at tourists in Sardinia. Two of the best are www.sardinia.net and www.sardiniapoint.it. They list holiday accommodation, events and festivals.

Immigration and Customs

European Union (EU) residents and visitors from the United States, Canada, New Zealand, Australia, Japan, need no visa for up to three months but must have one for a longer stay. Non-European Union citizens must carry a valid passport with them, while for EU citizens an ID with photo will suffice. It is however, adviseable to check the requirements before travelling. Non-EU citizens can bring in either 400 cigarettes or 100 cigars or 500 grams of tobacco, 1 litre of spirits, 2 litres of wine and 50 grams of perfume. Valuable goods may be imported only for strictly personal use.

Snowy scene in the interior, not unusual in midwinter

◀ Motorcycles parked on a narrow street in Cagliari

Shops, Banks and Post Offices

This guide provides the opening hours for the island's museums and archaeological sites. Shops are open from 8 or 9am to 1pm and from 3:30 or 4pm (in winter) or 5pm (in summer) to 7 or 8pm from Monday to Saturday, with one early closing day during the week. Banks are open from Monday to Friday from 8:30am to 1:30pm and 2:30pm to 3:30pm. Small post offices are open from 8am to 1:15pm, while larger offices open until 6:45pm (1:15pm on Saturday). The Italian national telephone company, Telecom Italia, runs both coin-operated and card *(scheda*

An elegant shop offering
Sardinian handicrafts

telefonica) public phones in all towns. For English-language information on post office services, visit www.poste.it.

Museums and Monuments

Normally museums and archaeological zones are open every day except Monday. However, in winter, some sites close in the afternoon and, in summer, opening hours are extended.

Museum entrance fees vary and, in line with EU rules, there are discounts or free entry for children, young people under 18, senior citizens and group bookings.

Churches in the interior are usually closed in the middle of the day and may only be open for mass. If a church is closed, the parish priest *(parroco)* or sexton may open it for you as a special favour for a short visit. A small contribution to church funds will always be welcome in return for assistance.

Festivals

Sardinia's festivals have a very long history and are colourful and unusual affairs. The busiest times of year for seeing traditional festivals

Traditional rituals, still part of the community year in Sardinia

are Carnival, Easter and 15 August. Town halls provide information on feast days and festivals, and dates are also given in the information for each town in this guide. For an overview of the main festivals and events in Sardinia, see pages 30–33.

Disabled Travellers

Unfortunately, special facilities for the disabled are rare, even in the larger towns, and touring can be quite a frustrating experience for wheelchair users.

For further information on advice and assistance for the disabled, contact the offices of the Sardinian provinces.

DIRECTORY

Sardinian Provinces

Provincia del Medio Campidano
w provincia.mediocampidano.it

Provincia di Cagliari
w provincia.cagliari.it

Provincia di Carbonia-Iglesias
w provincia.carboniaiglesias.it

Provincia di Nuoro
w provincia.nuoro.it

Provincia di Ogliastra
w provinciaogliastra.gov.it

Provincia di Olbia Tempio
w provincia.olbia-tempio.it

Provincia di Oristano
w provincia.or.it

Provincia di Sassari
w provincia.sassari.it

Embassies and Consulates

Australia
Roma. **Tel** 06 852 721.

Canada
Roma. **Tel** 06 85 444 2911.

United Kingdom
Cagliari. **Tel** 070 82 86 28.
Roma. **Tel** 06 42 20 00 01.

United States
Roma. **Tel** 06 94 80 37 77.

Italian Tourist Offices Abroad

1 Princes Street, London W1B 2AY, United Kingdom.
Tel 020 740 812 54.
w enit.it
w italiantouristboard.co.uk

110 Yonge Street, Suite 503, Toronto, Ontario M5C 1T4, Canada.
Tel 416 925 4882.
w italiantourism.com

630 Fifth Ave, Suite 1965, New York, NY 10111, United States.
Tel 212 245 5618.
w italiantourism.com

Country Codes

To call Italy from these countries, dial the code and then the number.

Australia
Tel 00 1139.

Canada
Tel 011 39.

United States
Tel 011 39.

United Kingdom
Tel 00 39.

Personal Security and Health

On the whole, Sardinia is a safe place for visitors and only a few precautions are needed for a pleasant stay. There is some petty crime, so take extra care of money and belongings in the busy passenger terminals of the ports and in cities. Do not leave valuables in your car if the parking place is unsupervised. On the whole, rural areas are generally safer than cities. During the summer, forest fires are a very serious problem, so be sure to follow the instructions of the local police or firemen should an emergency arise. If you fall ill, the nearest pharmacy *(farmacia)* is a good first stop.

in the undergrowth of the maquis, and the main enemy of the firemen is the wind, which is capable of carrying the fire a long way in a very short time. Fire-fighting is carried out by the local fire brigades as well as the state forest rangers, volunteers and specially equipped fire-fighting planes positioned in key areas of the island.

Medical Treatment

Should you need medical assistance during your stay, Sardinia has a network of hospitals and casualty departments *(pronto soccorso)*, as well as pharmacies which can dispense advice as well as medicines. European Union nationals are entitled to Italian medical care, but you need to carry an EHIC card.

In all the tourist resorts there is a *Guardia Medica* (emergency treatment centre) equipped to give medical attention to summer visitors. These seasonal surgeries are often closed in the winter and, in an emergency in low season, you will have to go to one of the main hospitals.

Pharmacies in Sardinia are open from Monday to Friday, 9am–1pm and 4–7pm and Saturday morning. Lists of the night and holiday opening rotas for the local area are carried on the chemist's door.

Credit Cards and Lost Property

It is never a good idea to carry a lot of cash with you. The major credit cards (Visa, MasterCard, American Express and Diners Club) are accepted by the majority of shops, restaurants and hotels on the island. It is reasonably easy to find automatic cash dispensers *(bancomat)* in all the large cities, but interest will be charged on currency exchange withdrawals, so you may prefer to carry travellers' cheques as well.

Generally speaking, it is safe to park where you like, as car theft is not common, especially in small towns. However, if anything is stolen, go immediately to the local police or carabinieri to report the theft; you will need the report for the insurance claim.

Fire, a constant danger, spreading rapidly across the dry, scrubby vegetation

Fire Hazards

Unfortunately, forest fires are a real problem in Sardinia, especially in the summer. Except for the rare cases of

accidental fire that may be caused by a thrown-away cigarette, most fires on the island are started deliberately. In some instances forest and brush are destroyed to make way for more grazing land but, more often than not, the motive is to clear space for new buildings. In an attempt to halt the practice, a law has been passed prohibiting construction in areas destroyed by fire, but even this has not stopped arsonists. In the dry heat of summer, fire spreads rapidly

Fire Prevention Rules

1. Always take care to extinguish cigarettes before discarding them.
2. Never light a fire except in areas where this is explicitly permitted.
3. If you see a fire, you must report it to the local firemen.
4. Do not stop or park your car to watch a fire; you may block the roads and interfere with fire-fighting operations.
5. Pay attention to the wind direction: it is highly dangerous to be downwind of a fire, as it may spread quite rapidly and catch you unawares.

Policemen on horseback at the Poetto beach near Cagliari

Countryside Codes

During your stay you are likely to spend a good deal of time exploring outdoors, so be prepared for any problems that may occur.

In the summer, whether you are on the beach or in the interior, be wary of too much sun, as it may cause serious burns and sunstroke. If it is windy, you may not be aware you are burning.

If a storm breaks and you need to take shelter, do not head for isolated trees or rocky peaks, which may attract lightning.

Although you cannot simply camp wherever you like, you can make private arrangements with landowners to pitch your tent away from official camping sites. Make sure you take away all your rubbish and do not light fires.

Bear in mind that grazing in the open countryside is still quite common in Sardinia: pigs, sheep, cows and horses may well decide to see whether campers have anything good to eat in their tents. In hilly areas sheepdogs should be

Livestock often graze on fields near campsites.

avoided, since they are trained to chase away any potential intruders.

While walking or trekking in the countryside you may come across gates or fences barring your way. It is always a good idea, if possible, to ask whether you can go through. Having done so, remember to close the gate so that animals are unable to escape. If you plan a lengthy hike, make sure you carry enough water with you, as villages may be few and far between. Lastly, despite the wildness, there are no poisonous snakes.

DIRECTORY

Emergency Telephone Numbers

Directory Enquiries
Tel 89 24 24.

Fire (Vigili del Fuoco)
Tel 115.

General Emergencies (Polizia di Stato)
Tel 113.

Medical Emergencies
Tel 118.

Mountain Emergencies (Soccorso Alpino)
Tel 118 (ask for Soccorso Alpino).

Nautical Information
Tel 196.

Police (Carabinieri Pronto Intervento)
Tel 112.

Road Emergencies (Soccorso Stradale)
Tel 116.

Currency

The euro (€) is the common currency of the European Union. It went into general circulation on 1 January 2002, originally for 12 participating countries, of which Italy was one. EU members using the euro as sole official currency are known as the Eurozone. Several EU members have opted out of joining this common currency. Euro notes are identical throughout Eurozone countries, each including designs of fictional architectural structures and monuments. The coins, however, have one side (the value side) that is the same throughout the Eurozone and one with an image unique to each country. Both coins and notes are exchangeable in each participating euro country.

Euro bank notes have seven denominations. The €5 note (grey in colour) is the smallest, followed by the €10 note (pink), €20 note (blue), €50 note (orange), €100 note (green), €200 note (yellow) and €500 note (purple). The euro has eight coin denominations: €1 and €2; 50 cents, 20 cents, 10 cents, 5 cents, 2 cents and 1 cent. The €2 and €1 coins are silver and gold in colour. The 50-, 20- and 10-cent coins are gold. The 5-, 2- and 1-cent coins are bronze.

Euro notes

Using Banks

Bank opening hours are usually 8:30am–1:30pm and 3–4:30pm from Monday to Friday. All banks close at weekends and on public holidays. Credit cards, once regarded with suspicion in Sardinia, are now accepted without question by hotels, restaurants and shops, especially those in the tourist areas. All the major credit cards are accepted, the most popular cards being Visa and MasterCard. You will not have difficulty in finding an automatic cash dispenser (bancomat) in all the larger towns and in some of the smaller villages.

Water Sports

Despite the impressive beauty of its interior, Sardinia's fame is more strongly associated with the sea. The development of the tourist industry means that the island now offers a good range of facilities for water sports, in particular sailing, windsurfing and scuba diving. There are diving centres and sailing schools in almost all the coastal resorts, and many of the holiday villages are well-equipped for water sports. Canoeing is a different matter, since the lack of navigable rivers limits your choice in the interior, and sea canoeing is only practised in a few places along the coast.

Scuba diving in the crystal-clear waters of the Mediterranean

Sailing along the rocky inlets of the coast; a challenging but rewarding pastime

Sailing

With its marvellous sea and coastline, Sardinia is regarded as a paradise for boating of all kinds, whether your preferred style is a billion-dollar luxury yacht on the Costa Smeralda or a simple dinghy for hire from one of the more affordable centres. The conditions vary considerably and even experienced sailors find the Sardinian coast a challenge because of the strong and variable winds. A good source of useful information for a sailing holiday is volume 1A of *Portolano del Mediterraneo* (Mediterranean Pilot's Book), which is published by the Istituto Idrografico della Marina Militare. Another useful publication is the pamphlet *I Porti Turistici della Sardegna* (Sardinian Yacht Harbours), available from all tourist information offices. You need permission from the harbour master to moor in most of Sardinia's harbours.

Scuba Diving

The coastline offers plenty of opportunities for experienced divers. Among the most famous spots for diving are the coasts of Asinara and Gallura, Capo Caccia, Carloforte, the Golfo di Orosei and the area around the island of Tavolara. Many diving centres – often based at sports shops – organize diving trips. You can also buy or rent diving equipment and get advice on diving sites.

Windsurfing

Windsurfing equipment is available for hire at almost all the tourist beaches. Some of the sailing centres also offer boards for hire and can organize lessons.

Windsurfing in the open sea, taking advantage of Sardinia's strong winds

DIRECTORY

Windsurfing Beaches

The following beaches are the best on the island for windsurfing (see pp22–3)

Bosa Marina
Poetto – Cagliari
Calagrande – Isola di Sant'Antioco
Saline – Isola di Sant'Antioco
Monti d'a Rena – La Maddalena
Porto Massimo – Lu Muddalena
Porto Taverna – Porto San Paolo
* Lotzorai*
Marinella – Olbia
Porto Istana – Olbia
Torre Grande – Oristano
Porto Pollo – Palau
Capo Testa – Santa Teresa di Gallura
La Cinta – San Teodoro
Putzu Idu – San Vero Milis
Platamona - Sorso
La Pelosa – Stintino

The Centro Velico Caprera sailing school

The safety rules for sailing also apply to this sport: the winds can be very strong and fickle (especially the mistral), so do not go too far out.

Canoeing

Although there are very few navigable rivers for canoeing in the interior – and the variable weather makes practising the sport even more difficult – you can canoe in the lakes or along certain stretches of the coast.

Other Sports

There are numerous coves along the Sardinian coasts where you can explore the rocks and the water and observe the varied marine life. Snorkelling is perhaps best left to the experienced: strong winds and currents can easily create difficult and dangerous conditions.

Subaqua fishing with a harpoon and aqualung is not permitted but freshwater fishing is possible in the lakes and reservoirs. You will need a permit to fish in the rivers.

In some holiday villages water-based tours are offered to guests, and some also provide dinghies in which to explore the coastline.

Canoeing in the fabulous Cala Sisine cove

DIRECTORY

Sailing and Windsurfing Centres

Carloforte Yacht Club
Tel 328 893 4596.
W carloforteyachtclub.org

Centro Velico Caprera – La Maddalena
Localita Punta Coda Caprera. Tel 02 8645 2191.
W centrovelico caprera.it

Circolo Nautico Arbatax
W circolonautico arbatax.org.

Circolo Nautico Olbia
Molo Brin 6.
Tel 0789 261 87.

Circolo Nautico Oristano
Porticciolo Turistico Torregrande.
Tel 335 524 2203.
W circolonautico oristano.it

Club Nautico La Maddalena
Via G Cesare 20.
Tel 0709 72 79 05.

Windsurfing Club Cagliari
Marina Piccola.

W windsurfingclub cagliari.org

Windsurfing Vela Club Portoscuso
Via Marco Polo 1.
Tel 340 123 2144.

Yacht Club Alghero
Tel 079 95 20 74.
W yachtclubalghero.it

Yacht Club Cagliari
Marina Piccola.
Tel 070 37 03 50.
W yachtclubcagliari.it

Yacht Club Costa Smeralda – Porto Cervo
Porto Cervo.
Tel 0789 90 22 00.
W yccs.it

Yacht Club Porto Rotondo
Tel 0789 340 10.
W ycpr.it

Diving Centres

Air Sub Service – Villasimius
Tel 070 79 20 33 or 070 50 68 63 (winter).
W airsub.com

Anthias
Palau. Tel 0789 86 311 or 339 891 79 67.
W anthiasdiving.com

Aqua Diving Center Puntaldia
Puntaldia, San Teodoro.
Tel 0784 86 43 90 or 348 511 23 33.

Areamare Diving
Cannigione.
Tel 338 822 11 35.
W areamare.com

Centro Sub Isuledda Compagnia dell'Avventura
Cannigione, Arzachena.
Tel 0789 862 53 or 392 947 4246.
W lacompagniadell avventura.com

Centro Sub Tavolara
Porto San Paolo.
Tel 0789 403 60.
W tavolaradiving.it

Isla Diving
Carloforte.
Tel 335 46 25 02.
W isladiving.it

Karibu Diving Center
c/o Hotel Capo Caccia.
Tel 079 94 66 66 or 329 928 2836.

L'Argonauta Diving Center
Cala Gonone.
Tel 0784 930 46 or 347 530 40 97.
W argonauta.it

Orso Diving Club – Poltu Quato
Porto Cervo.
Tel 0789 990 01 or 331 289 4697.
W orsodiving.com

Oyster Sub Diving Center
Palau.
Tel 0789 70 20 70.
W oystersub.com

Proteus Diving Center
Tel 327 530 53 55.
W lnx.proteusdiving.it

Tanka Village Diving Center – Villasimius
Tel 070 79 54 64 or 338 674 14 74.
W subcentertanka.com

Canoeing

Cardedu Kayak
Cardedu, Ogliastra.
Tel 0782 75 185 or 348 936 9401.
W cardedu-kayak.com

Federazione Italiana Canoa Kayak
Cagliari. Email crsardegna @federcanoa.it.
W federcanoa.it

Team Kayak Sardegna
Cagliari. Tel 335 608 4313.
W teamkayaksardegna.com

Outdoor Sports

Neglected for years because attention was focused on tourist development along the coast, the interior landscape of Sardinia offers plenty of opportunity to practise outdoor sports. The countryside can be explored on foot or on horseback – riding centres have made great advances in recent years and are in great demand. Facilities for hiking and rock climbing are good and increasing numbers of mountain climbing routes are in the process of being marked out.

The Su Rei riding centre in Sulcis

Horse Riding

Sardinia is ideally suited for trekking and horse riding. Horses have long been an integral part of the island's culture, as the animal has been part of local life since Phoenician times: many of the religious feast days and festivities include breakneck rides and horse races.

The many isolated minor roads, mule tracks and paths, far away from traffic and noise, particularly in the interior, are ideal for pleasant rides, and many are not too difficult for beginners.

There are nearly a hundred Sardinian equestrian clubs and centres, large and small, offering facilities for this sport. Most are equipped to organize lessons and rides for beginners as well as extended treks for experienced riders.

Most of the stables and clubs are located near Cagliari, Nuoro and Oristano, but there has been an increase in the number of holiday farms (see p174) offering horse riding and riding excursions for their guests, whatever their ability. Supramonte, Giara di Gesturi and the Valle della Luna are three of the most interesting and popular destinations for those who love long treks in the Sardinian countryside.

Rock Climbing

In the 1960s the Italian mountaineer Alessandro Gogna published *Mezzogiorno di Pietra* (Midday Stone), which opened up the possibilities for rock climbing in Sardinia. Since those days enthusiasm for the sport has grown considerably, and today the island's most challenging rocks and cliffs are tackled by climbers from all over Italy and Europe. Among the most popular climbing areas are Supramonte (Surtana, l'Aguglia), the cliffs at Iglesiente (Domusnovas), where hand- and foot-holds have been placed, and the Isili area in Nuoro province.

Essential reading for rock climbers who decide to come here is *Pietra di Luna* (Moon Stone) by Maurizio Oviglia, the most up-to-date guide to rock climbing in Sardinia.

Additional information can be obtained at the **Sezione di Cagliari del Club Alpino Italiano**. Programmes are organized by a number of companies, including **Barbagia Insolita** and **Keya**. Climbing lessons are available from **Rock & Sun**.

Cliffs at the seaside with facilities for rock climbing

Walking and Trekking

Wild mountains, hills dotted with prehistoric ruins, forests and maquis vegetation make up most of the terrain in the interior of Sardinia. The countryside is rugged but unspoilt and ideal for walking, hiking and more strenuous treks. However, facilities are few and far between, clearly signposted footpaths are rare and there are very few refuges or stopping places. It is always advisable to carry an up-to-date map and to take plenty of water when walking.

The most rewarding and popular areas are Supramonte, the Gennargentu massif and the Sulcis area (which offers an unusual blend of hiking and industrial archaeology). Some stretches of the steep coastline are more suited to those with climbing experience.

In the Supramonte area experienced mountaineers can even tackle the wild and precipitous Su Gorroppu gorges. The trek takes a couple of days and special rock climbers' equipment is needed in order to make it down the vertical walls of the falls. This

The Selvaggio Blu Route

Its very name – Wild Blue – is the best possible description of this difficult route along the Golfo di Orosei, starting from Santa Maria Navarrese and ending at Cala Luna. The Selvaggio Blu was conceived by Mario Verin and Peppino Cicalò in the late 1980s. The course requires excellent physical condition and preparation (since part of it consists of stretches of rock climbing, some of the descents are achieved by abseiling and you have to walk with a heavy load because of the distance between water supply sources) but the rewards are some of the most spectacular views of the Sardinian coast. The town of Baunei publishes a guide to Selvaggio Blu; for information, or if you are interested in buying the book, call 0782 61 08 23.

A stretch of the Selvaggio Blu trail

particular excursion is, therefore, not suitable for beginners. Whether walking or climbing, or a combination of both, make sure you have the best map possible to hand (a good map is published by IGM). You should also carefully calculate the time the tour will take and how much food and water will be needed, as it is possible to walk for kilometres without stumbling across a village.

Caving

The mountains of Sardinia are riddled with dozens of fascinating caves to be explored, some of which have tourist facilities. The temperature inside is likely to be relatively high, more or less the yearly average of the surrounding area. Bear in mind that some of the difficult caves, such as the Golgo abyss (at Su Sterru),

the Grotta Verde at Capo Caccia or the Su Palu cave near Orosei, are only open to experienced spelunkers.

Golf Courses

Sardinia has some famous golf courses, including the one at the **Pevero Golf Club** in Porto Cervo, designed by the architect Robert Trent Jones. This 18-hole golf course is internationally known for its tournaments.

Other Sports

The island's sports activites are not confined to the mountains and caves in its interior. More traditional sports such as tennis, football, swimming and five-a-side football can be pursued in the many sports grounds and courts throughout the island.

The golf course at Pevero in Porto Cervo, on the Costa Smeralda

DIRECTORY

Horse Riding

La Posada del Cavallo
Posada. **Tel** 0784 85 41 16.
W posadacavallo.it

Cooperative Goloritze
Ogliastra.
Tel 368 702 89 80.
W coopgoloritze.com

Horse Country
Arborea. **Tel** 0783 80 500.
W horsecountry.it

Idee Natura in Sardegna
Capoterra, Cagliari.
Tel 070 711 212.
W ideenatura insardegna.it

Walking Tours

Cooperativa Goloritze
Baunei. **Tel** 368 702 89 80.
W coopgoloritze.com

Barbagia Insolita
Oliena. **Tel** 0784 28 60 05.
W barbagiainsolita.it

Club Alpino Italiano
Cagliari. **Tel** 070 66 78 77.
W caicagliari.it

Compagnia dell'Avventura
Cannigione. **Tel** 0789 862 53. W lacompagnia dellavventura.com

Cooperativa Ghivine
Dorgali. **Tel** 338 834 1618.
W ghivine.com

Cooperativa Turistica Enis
Oliena. **Tel** 0784 28 83 63.
W coopenis.it

Escursioni in Sardegna
Cala Gonone. **Tel** 349 672 7750.
W escursioniinsardegna.com

Keya
Orosei.
Tel 348 6530 682/683.
W keya.eu

Nordic Walking
W nordicwalking sardegna.it

Rock & Sun
Tel (from UK) 0203 390 0351.
W rockandsun.com

Scoprisardegna
Porto Torres.
Tel 328 456 46 82.
W scoprisardegna.com

Zente
Dorgali. **Tel** 349 666 2264.
W zente.it

Caving

Federazione Speleologica Sarda
Iglesias. **Tel** 0781 306 64.
W www.federazione speleologicasarda.it

Società Speleologica Italiana
Via Zamboni 67, Bologna.
Tel 051 25 00 49.
W ssi.speleo.it

Golf Courses

Tanka Village
Villasimius. **Tel** 070 7951.
W atahotels.it/tanka

Is Molas Golf Club
Pula. **Tel** 070 924 10 06.
W ismolas.it

Pevero Golf Club
Porto Cervo.
Tel 0789 95 80 00.
W golfclubpevero.com

TRAVEL INFORMATION

Sardinia is served by Europe's major airlines, including British Airways, the Sardinian Meridiana and the Italian carrier, Alitalia. Low-cost flights are available from Ryanair and easyJet. In addition, many charter flights operate in summer, often with low fares or as part of a package deal. During summer there are also more direct flights available. If no direct flights or suitable connections are available, Alitalia and Meridiana provide regular domestic flights from Italy's mainland cities throughout the year. The island is also served by an excellent network of ferries from ports on the Italian mainland. Slower ferries offer a long crossing, with berths for overnight trips, whereas the faster and more expensive ferry lines can almost halve the travelling time. During the peak summer season of July and August it is not easy to find places on passenger and, in particular, car ferries, so make sure to book your place well in advance.

Arriving by Air

The main airports in Sardinia are Cagliari's **Elmas** airport, Alghero's **Fertilia** airport and the **Olbia-Costa Smeralda** airport. These are not far from their respective city centres and offer taxi services as well as public transport into town. In Alghero, for example, a bus runs according to the flight timetable, linking the airport to the city centre (call 079 95 04 58 for details). In the summer there is also a coach service from Olbia-Costa Smeralda airport to the towns on the Costa Smeralda.

    Alitalia and the Sardinian airline **Meridiana** serve Cagliari and Olbia from a number of Italian cities, providing links to major European capitals. Meridiana also flies daily from Gatwick to Cagliari via Florence. **British Airways** flies

Aeroplane coming into land at Olbia-Costa Smeralda airport

from London Heathrow to Cagliari. Low-cost airline **Ryanair** serves Alghero direct from London Stansted, East Midlands and Liverpool airports, while **easyJet** serves Olbia from London Gatwick and Cagliari from London Luton.

    Long-haul passengers will almost inevitably have to change in an Italian mainland or other European city. If you are travelling from the United States, American, United Airlines and Delta offer direct flights to Rome or Milan where you can get a connection to one of the island's airports. Canadian Airlines flies from Canada and Qantas flies from Australia. Alitalia also has a regular service between these countries and Rome.

Passenger waiting area, Olbia-Costa Smeralda airport

A Tirrenia line car ferry

Tickets and Fares

If you are based in the UK, Ryanair and easyJet usually provide the cheapest flights. However, it is also worth scouring the small ads of news-papers for cut-price charters and discounted scheduled flights. Fares vary greatly during the year, but the most expensive periods are summer, Christmas and Easter holidays. Meridiana offers low-season economy flights.

For intercontinental flights the most economical option is to take a budget flight to London, Berlin or Barcelona and get a Ryanair or easyJet flight from there to the island.

Ferry Services

Sardinia is easily reached by ferry from Italy's mainland ports which are accessible by train. The crossing can be long (16 hours from Naples to Cagliari, 7 hours between Civitavecchia and Olbia), although the more expensive ferry lines offer a faster service. For overnight crossings, passengers can book a cabin. Ferry services leave from Civitavecchia, Fiumicino, Naples, Genoa, Livorno, Palermo and Trapani. They dock at Sardinia's tourist ports of Arbatax, Cagliari, Olbia, Golfo Aranci, Palau and Porto Torres. **Sardinia Ferries**' fast service connects Livorno and Civitavecchia with Golfo Aranci in just over four hours. **Tirrenia** offers a similar service from La Spezia and Civitavecchia to Olbia (a four- to five-hour trip). There are also ferries from Bonifacio in Corsica, bound for Santa Teresa di Gallura and between Palau and Porto Vecchio in Corsica during the high season. **Moby** sails from mainland Italy to the Sardinian port of Olbia and between Bonifacio (Corsica) and Santa Teresa di Gallura.

Package Holidays

Most travel agencies, both in Italy and abroad, offer holidays to Sardinia. The sea and coast are the greatest attractions, but there are also options for holidays in the interior. Many holiday villages provide a wide range of entertainment and sports facilities, including diving and windsurfing, sailing lessons and horseback riding.

A Moby ferry

DIRECTORY

Airlines

Alitalia
International & Domestic flights
Tel 89 20 10.
Flmas airport, Cagliari
Tel 070 24 00 79.
Fertilia airport, Alghero
Tel 89 20 10.
w alitalia.com

British Airways
Tel 0844 493 0787 (UK).
Tel 02 6963 3602 (Italy).
w ba.com

easyJet
Tel 0843 104 5000 (UK).
Tel 199 201 840 (Italy).
w easyjet.com

Meridiana
Information/reservations
Tel 89 29 28.
Elmas Airport, Cagliari
Tel 89 29 28 or 0789 526 82.
Costa Smeralda Airport, Olbia **Tel** 89 29 28 or 0789 526 82.
Rome **Tel** 89 29 28.
Milan **Tel** 89 29 28.
w meridiana.it
UK 17 Leighton Place, London NW5 2QL.
Tel 0871 222 9319.

Ryanair
Tel 0871 246 0000 (UK).
Tel 899 552 589 (Italy).
w ryanair.com

Ferry Companies

Grandi Navi Veloci
Information/reservations
Tel 010 209 4591.
w gnv.it

Moby
Tel 199 303 040.
w moby.it

Corsica Sardinia Ferries
Information/reservations
Tel 199 400 500.
w corsica-ferries.co.uk

Tirrenia
Information/reservations
Tel 892 123
w tirrenia.it

Train Companies

Ferrovie dello Stato
Tel 892 021.
w trenitalia.com

Getting Around Sardinia

Many of Sardinia's roads are characterized by an interminable number of curves and tight bends: annoying if you are in a hurry, but pleasant if you're on holiday and can take time to enjoy the scenery. With the exception of a few major roads, such as the SS131 which connects the four corners of the island, the roads wind their way over hills and across plains so that, even though the traffic outside the towns is light, always calculate plenty of time when planning a tour. The empty roads, on the other hand, are perfect for cyclists.

A flock of sheep blocking a country road

Travelling by Car

Given the inefficient public transport system, and the spectacular natural scenery, travelling by car is the best way to become acquainted with the island.

It is important, however, to be aware of the issues that may occur. Minor roads will often be blocked by flocks of sheep, adding to your travel time. Road signs are not always clear and may be missing just when you need them most. Should this occur, the best thing to do is to ask someone on the way – Sardinians will happily help. Another potential problem is petrol, as there are not many filling stations in the interior. Lastly, you will often find yourself forced to take difficult dirt roads, particularly when looking for an out-of-the-way church or archaeological site.

Always carry a good, up-to-date road map. One of the best is published by the Touring Club Italiano, to a scale of 1: 200.000. Keep your vehicle and identity documents (including driving licence) with you in the car at all times, since the police often do spot checks.

Renting a Car

Most international car rental companies are represented in Sardinia, with offices in the main port towns (Olbia, Cagliari, Porto Torres) and in the airports of Cagliari Elmas, Olbia-Costa Smeralda and Alghero Fertilia. Hertz offers discounts for those who fly with Meridiana and Ryanair.

A number of holiday companies offer fly-drive deals.

Rules of the Road

The speed limits are 50 km/h (30 mph) in town and 90 km/h (55 mph) on major roads. Seat belts are required, and motor cyclists, moped riders and passengers must wear helmets.

Parking

In winter, parking at the beach is normally free. In summer, car park attendants charge by the hour, half a day, or a full day. The Costa Smeralda has the highest charges. Cagliari's Poetto beach always has free parking.

Boat Hire

In many ports it is possible to charter yachts, from one day to one week. The prices may include a crew or simply the use of the boat. Hiring a boat enables you to see the island away from the busy resorts. For information, make enquiries with the harbour authorities or boat owners.

Cycling and Mountain Biking

The quiet roads along the coast or the stunning countryside in the interior are ideal for long trips by bicycle. If you prefer more arduous exercise, the steeper mountain roads are suitable for mountain bikes. Tourist offices will have suggestions for local bicycle routes and several associations exist with information about off-road tours by mountain bike. Cyclists should wear high-visibility clothing.

Train Travel

Sardinia has an efficient – if sometimes slow – railway service. There are several daily departures from Cagliari to Sassari, Porto Torres and Olbia, and the journey takes between 3 and 4 hours. Most journeys necessitate a change of train at Oziere-Chilivani.

A car on a single-track road travelling through the Sardinian countryside

A bicycle tour among the olive groves near Sassari

Local trains running between Cagliari, Iglesias and Carbonia depart regularly, as do trains between Alghero and Sassari. Fares are surprisingly cheap: €17 one-way between Cagliari and Olbia.

A train ride in true late-19th-century style, such as on the Mandas–Sòrgono route *(see p113)*, is an enjoyable and relaxing way to see the island's stunning scenery, which has fascinated travellers for many centuries. In spring and summer, the **Azienda Regionale Sarda Trasporti** (ARST) organizes train services from Mandas to Sorgono, Seui and Arbatax on the *trenino verde* *(see pp96–7)*. "Vintage" wagons dating from 1913 are pulled by steam locomotives from the 1930s.

Travelling by Coach

The Azienda Regionale Sarda Trasporti (ARST) network covers most towns, cities and resorts in Sardinia. In order to meet the needs of the ever-growing number of visitors, ARST has issued a special tourist pass *(biglietto turistico)*, available to non-residents only, between 1 June and 30 September. The pass allows you to travel on all ARST coaches, and can be purchased for a period of 7 (€40), 14 (€70), 21 (€100) or 28 (€130) days.

Other bus companies operate within specific towns or provinces. Tickets are sold in newspaper kiosks and at tobacconists, as well as bus stations. For more information, contact the local tourist office.

The narrow-gauge train known as the *trenino verde*

DIRECTORY

Renting a Car

Avis
Tel 199 100 133.
[w] avisautonoleggio.it

Europcar
Tel 199 30 70 30.
[w] europcar.it

Hertz
Tel 070 24 00 37.
[w] hertz.it

Maggiore
Tel 199 15 120.
[w] maggiore.it

Mountain Biking

Cicloexpress
Alghero.
Tel 079 98 69 50.
[w] cicloexpress.com

Dolcevita Bike Tours
Pula.
Tel 070 920 98 85.
[w] dolcevitabiketours.com

Federazione Ciclista Italiana
Tel 070 66 32 43.
[w] federciclismo.it/sardegna

Mountain Bike Club Taxus Baccata
Gonnasfanadiga.
Tel 070 979 98 64.
[w] taxusbaccata.it

Sardinia Cycling
Quartu Sant'Elena.
[w] sardiniacycling.com

Skedaddle
[w] skedaddleitalia.it
[w] skedaddle.co.uk

Team Spakkaruote Sud West Sardinia
Carbonia.
[w] spakkaruote.it

Train Travel

Trenitalia
Tel 892 021, 199 30 30 60 (disabled users).
[w] trenitalia.com

ARST Information Offices

Tel 800 86 50 42.
[w] arst.sardegna.it

Cagliari
Tel 070 409 83 24.

Gùspini
Tel 070 97 02 36.

Lanusei
Tel 078 24 02 92.

Nuoro
Tel 078 429 08 00.

Olbia
Tel 078 955 30 00.

Oristano
Tel 078 335 58 00.

Sassari
Tel 079 263 92 00.

General Index

Page numbers in **bold** refer to main entries

Phrase Book

In an Emergency

Help!	**Aiuto!**	eye-**yoo**-toh
Stop!	**Fermate!**	fair-**mah**-teh
Call a doctor.	**Chiama un medico**	kee-**ah**-mah oon **meh**-dee-koh
Call an ambulance.	**Chiama un' ambulanza**	kee-**ah**-mah oon am-boo-**lan**-tsa
Call the police.	**Chiama la polizia**	kee-**ah**-mah lah pol-ee-**tsee**-ah
Call the fire brigade.	**Chiama i pompieri**	kee-**ah**-mah ee pom-pee-**air**-ee
Where is the telephone?	**Dov'è il telefono?**	dov-**eh** eel teh-**leh**-foh-noh?
The nearest hospital?	**L'ospedale più vicino?**	loss-peh-**dah**-leh pee-**oo** vee-**chee**-noh?

Communication Essentials

Yes/No	**Si/No**	see/noh
Please	**Per favore**	pair fah-**vor**-eh
Thank you	**Grazie**	**grah**-tsee-eh
Excuse me	**Mi scusi**	mee **skoo**-zee
Hello	**Buon giorno**	bwon **jor**-noh
Goodbye	**Arrivederci**	ah-ree-veh-**dair**-chee
Good evening	**Buona sera**	**bwon**-ah **sair**-ah
morning	**la mattina**	lah mah-**tee**-nah
afternoon	**il pomeriggio**	eel poh-meh-**ree**-joh
evening	**la sera**	lah **sair**-ah
yesterday	**ieri**	ee-**air**-ee
today	**oggi**	**oh**-jee
tomorrow	**domani**	doh-**mah**-nee
here	**qui**	kwee
there	**la**	**lah**
What?	**Quale?**	**kwah**-leh?
When?	**Quando?**	**kwan**-doh?
Why?	**Perchè?**	pair-**keh**?
Where?	**Dove?**	**doh**-veh?

Useful Phrases

How are you?	**Come sta?**	**koh**-meh stah?
Very well, thank you.	**Molto bene, grazie.**	**moll**-toh **beh**-neh grah-tsee-eh
Pleased to meet you.	**Piacere di conoscerla.**	pee-ah-**chair**-eh dee coh-**noh**-shair-lah
See you later.	**A più tardi.**	ah pee-**oo** tar-dee
That's fine.	**Va bene.**	va **beh**-neh
Where is/are...?	**Dov'è/Dove sono...?**	dov-**eh**/dov-eh **soh** noh?
How long does it take to get to...?	**Quanto tempo ci vuole per andare a...?**	kwan-toh **tem**-poh chee voo-**oh**-leh pair an-**dar**-eh ah...?
How do I get to...?	**Come faccio per arrivare a...?**	koh-meh **fah**-choh pair arri-**var**-eh ah...?
Do you speak English?	**Parla inglese?**	**par**-lah een-**gleh**-zeh?
I don't understand.	**Non capisco.**	non ka-**pee**-skoh
Could you speak more slowly, please?	**Può parlare più lentamente, per favore?**	pwoh par-lah-reh pee-**oo** len-ta-**men**-teh pair fah-**vor**-eh?
I'm sorry.	**Mi dispiace.**	mee dee-spee-**ah**-cheh

Useful Words

big	**grande**	**gran**-deh
small	**piccolo**	**pee**-koh-loh
hot	**caldo**	**kal**-doh
cold	**freddo**	**fred**-doh
good	**buono**	**bwoh**-noh
bad	**cattivo**	kat-**tee**-voh
enough	**basta**	**bas**-tah
well	**bene**	**beh**-neh
open	**aperto**	ah-**pair**-toh
closed	**chiuso**	kee-**oo**-zoh
left	**a sinistra**	ah see-**nee**-strah
right	**a destra**	ah **dess**-trah
straight on	**sempre dritto**	**sem**-preh **dree**-toh
near	**vicino**	vee-**chee**-noh
far	**lontano**	lon-**tah**-noh
up	**su**	**soo**
down	**giù**	**joo**
early	**presto**	**press**-toh
late	**tardi**	**tar**-dee
entrance	**entrata**	en-**trah**-tah
exit	**uscita**	oo-**shee**-ta
toilet	**il gabinetto**	eel gah-bee-**net**-toh
free, unoccupied	**libero**	**lee**-bair-oh
free, no charge	**gratuito**	grah-**too**-ee-toh

Making a Telephone Call

I'd like to place a long-distance call.	**Vorrei fare una interurbana.**	vor-**ray far**-eh oona in-tair-oor-**bah**-nah
I'd like to make a reverse-charge call.	**Vorrei fare una telefonata a carico del destinatario.**	vor-**ray far**-eh oona teh-leh-fon-**ah**-tah ah **kar**-ee-koh dell dess-tee-nah-**tar**-ree-oh
I'll try again later.	**Ritelefono più tardi.**	ree-teh-**leh**-foh-noh pee-oo **tar**-dee
Can I leave a message?	**Posso lasciare un messaggio?**	**poss**-oh lash-ah-reh oon mess-**sah**-joh?
Hold on.	**Un attimo, per favore**	oon **ah**-tee-moh, pair fah-**vor**-eh
Could you speak up a little please?	**Può parlare più forte, per favore?**	pwoh par-**lah**-reh pee-**oo** for-teh, pair fah-**vor**-eh?
local call	**telefonata locale**	te-leh-fon-**ah**-tah loh-cah-leh

Shopping

How much does this cost?	**Quant'è, per favore?**	kwan-**teh** pair fah-**vor**-eh?
I would like...	**Vorrei...**	vor-**ray**
Do you have...?	**Avete...?**	ah-**veh**-teh...?
I'm just looking.	**Sto soltanto guardando.**	stoh sol-**tan**-toh gwar-dan-doh
Do you take credit cards?	**Accettate carte di credito?**	ah-chet-**tah**-teh kar-teh dee **creh**-dee-toh?
What time do you open/close?	**A che ora apre/ chiude?**	ah keh or-ah **ah**-preh/kee-oo-deh?
this one	**questo**	**kweh**-stoh
that one	**quello**	**kwell**-oh
expensive	**caro**	**kar**-oh
cheap	**a buon prezzo**	ah bwon **pret**-soh
size, clothes	**la taglia**	lah **tah**-lee-ah
size, shoes	**il numero**	eel **noo**-mair-oh
white	**bianco**	bee-**ang**-koh
black	**nero**	**neh**-roh
red	**rosso**	**ross**-oh
yellow	**giallo**	**jal**-loh
green	**verde**	**vair**-deh
blue	**blu**	bloo

Types of Shop

antique dealer	**l'antiquario**	lan-tee-**kwah**-ree-oh
bakery	**il forno/il panificio**	eel forn-oh/eel pan-ee-fee-**fee**-koh
bank	**la banca**	lah **bang**-kah
bookshop	**la libreria**	lah lee-breh-**ree**-ah
butcher	**la macelleria**	lah mah-chell-eh-**ree**-ah
cake shop	**la pasticceria**	lah pas-tee-chair-**ee**-ah
chemist	**la farmacia**	lah far-mah-**chee**-ah
delicatessen	**la salumeria**	lah sah-loo-meh-**ree**-ah
department store	**il grande magazzino**	eel **gran**-deh mag-gad-**zee**-noh
fishmonger	**il pescivendolo**	eel pesh-ee-ven-**doh**-loh
florist	**il fioraio**	eel fee-or-**eye**-oh
greengrocer	**il fruttivendolo**	eel froo-tee-**ven**-doh-loh
grocery	**alimentari**	ah-lee-men-**tah**-ree
hairdresser	**il parrucchiere**	eel par-oo-kee-**air**-eh
ice cream parlour	**la gelateria**	lah jel-lah-tair-**ree**-ah
market	**il mercato**	eel mair-**kah**-toh
newsstand	**l'edicola**	leh-**dee**-koh-lah
post office	**l'ufficio postale**	loo-**fee**-choh pos-**tah**-leh
shoe shop	**il negozio di scarpe**	eel neh-**goh**-tsioh dee **skar**-peh
supermarket	**il supermercato**	eel su-pair-mair-**kah**-toh
tobacconist	**il tabaccaio**	eel tah-bak-**eye**-oh
travel agency	**l'agenzia di viaggi**	lah-jen-**tsee**-ah dee vee-**ad**-jee

Sightseeing

art gallery	**la pinacoteca**	lah peena-koh-**teh**-kah
bus stop	**la fermata dell'autobus**	lah fair-**mah**-tah dell **ow**-toh-booss
church	**la chiesa**	lah kee-**eh**-zah
	la basilica	lah bah-**seel**-i-kah
closed for holidays	**chiuso per le ferie**	kee-**oo**-zoh pair leh **fair**-ee-eh
garden	**il giardino**	eel jar-**dee**-no
library	**la biblioteca**	lah beeb-lee-oh-**teh**-kah
museum	**il museo**	eel moo-**zeh**-oh
railway station	**la stazione**	lah stah-tsee-**oh**-neh
tourist information	**l'ufficio di turismo**	loo-**fee**-choh dee too-**ree**-smoh

Numbers

1	uno	oo-noh
2	due	doo-eh
3	tre	treh
4	quattro	kwat-roh
5	cinque	ching-kweh
6	sei	say-ee
7	sette	set-teh
8	otto	ot-toh
9	nove	noh-veh
10	dieci	dee-eh-chee
11	undici	oon-dee-chee
12	dodici	doh-dee-chee
13	tredici	tray-dee-chee
14	quattordici	kwat-tor-dee-chee
15	quindici	kwin-dee-chee
16	sedici	say-dee-chee
17	diciassette	dee-chah-set-teh
18	diciotto	dee-chot-toh
19	diciannove	dee-chah-noh-veh
20	venti	ven-tee
30	trenta	tren-tah
40	quaranta	kwah-ran-tah
50	cinquanta	ching-kwan-tah
60	sessanta	sess-an-tah
70	settanta	set-tan-tah
80	ottanta	ot-tan-tah
90	novanta	noh-van-tah
100	cento	chen-toh
1,000	mille	mee lch
2,000	duemila	doo-eh mee-lah
5,000	cinquemila	ching-kweh mee-lah
1,000,000	un milione	oon meel-yoh-neh

Time, Days, Months, Seasons

one minute	un minuto	oon mee-noo-toh
one hour	un'ora	oon or-ah
half an hour	mezz'ora	medz-or-ah
a day	un giorno	oon jor-noh
a week	una settimana	oona set-tee-mah-nah
Monday	lunedí	loo-neh-dee
Tuesday	martedí	mar-teh-dee
Wednesday	mercoledí	mair-koh-leh-dee
Thursday	giovedí	joh-veh-dee
Friday	venerdí	ven-air-dee
Saturday	sabato	sah-bah-toh
Sunday	domenica	doh-meh-nee-kah
January	gennaio	jen-nah-yo
February	febbraio	feb-bra-yo
March	marzo	mar tzo
April	aprile	a-pree-leh
May	maggio	mah-jo
June	giugno	joo-nyo
July	luglio	loo-lyo
August	agosto	ag-os-toh
September	settembre	set-tem-bre
October	ottobre	ot-toh-bre
November	novembre	no-vem-bre
December	dicembre	dee-chem-bre
Spring	primavera	pree-mah-veh-ra
Summer	estate	es-tah-te
Autumn	autunno	ow-toon-noh
Winter	inverno	een-vair-no
Christmas	Natale	nah-tah-le
Christmas Eve	la Vigilia di Natale	vee-jee-lya dee nah-tah-le
Good Friday	Venerdí Santo	ven-air-dee san-toh
Easter	Pasqua	pas-kwa
New Year	Capodanno	kah-poh-dan-noh
New Year's Eve	San Silvestro	san seel-ves-tro
Whitsun	Pentecoste	pente-kos-te

Travelling

adult	l'adulto	ad-ool-toh
airport	l'aeroporto	a-air-oh-por-toh
baggage claim	il ritiro bagagli	ree-tee-roh bah-gal-yee
boarding card	la carta d'imbarco	kar-tah deem-bar-koh
boat	la barca	bar-kah
booking office	la biglietteria	beel-yet-teh-ree-ah
bus	l'autobus	ow-toh-booss
bus stop	la fermata dell'autobus	fer-mah-tah del-ow-toh-booss
check-in desk	l'accettazione	achet-ah-tzyoh-neh
luggage	i bagagli	bah-gal-yee
child (male)	il bambino	bam-bee-noh
child (female)	la bambina	bam-bee-nah
coach (bus)	la corriera	kor-ree-air-ah
connection	la coincidenza	ko-een-chee-den-tza

Couchette	la cuccetta	koo-chet-tah
customs	la dogana	doh-gah-nah
delay	ritardo	ree-tar-doh
domestic	nazionale	natz-yoh-nah-leh
exit gate	l'uscita	oo-shee-tah
fare	la tariffa	tah-reef-fah
ferry	il traghetto	trah-get-toh
first class	prima classe	pree-mah klas-seh
flight	il volo	voh-loh
left luggage	il deposito bagagli	deh-poh-zee-toh bah-gal-yee
lost property	l'ufficio oggetti smarriti	oof-fee-cho ojet-tee zmar-ree-tee
luggage trolley	il carrello	kar-rel-loh
non-smoking	non fumatori	nohn foo-mah-toh-ree
passport	il passaporto	pas-sah-por-toh
platform	il binario	bee-nah-ree-o
railway	la ferrovia	fer-roh-vee-a
reservation	la prenotazione	pre-noh-tatz-yoh-neh
return ticket	andata e ritorno	an-dah-tah ay ree-tor-no
seat	il posto	poss-toh
second class	seconda classe	sek-on-da klas-seh
single ticket	solo andata	soh-loh an-dah-tah
smoking	fumatori	foo-mah-toh-ree
station	la stazione	statz-yoh-neh
supplement	il supplemento	soop-leh-men-toh
taxi	il taxi	tak-si
ticket	il biglietto	beel-yet-to
timetable	l'orario	oh-rah ry oh
train	il treno	treh-no
underground	la metropolitana	met-roh-poh-lee-tah-nah

Motoring

Fill her up	il pieno	eel pyeh-noh
Do you do repairs?	Effettua riparazioni?	ef-fet-tua ree-paratz-yoh-nee?
I'd like to hire a car	Vorrei noleggiare una macchina	vor-ray noh-ledg-ah-re oona mah-keena
automatic	con il cambio automatico	kon eel kam-bee-oh ow-toh-mah-tee-koh
boot	il portabagagli	porta-bah-gal-yee
car	l'automobile, la macchina	ow-toh-moh-bee-leh mah-kee-nah
car ferry	il traghetto	trah-geh-toh
diesel oil	gasolio	gaz-oh-lyo
garage (repairs)	il meccanico	mek-ah-neeko
four-star petrol	benzina super	ben-dzee-na soo-per
licence	la patente	pah-ten-teh
motorbike	la motocicletta	moh-toh-chee-kleh-ta
motorway	l'autostrada	ow-toh-strah-da
petrol	la benzina	ben-dzeenà
petrol station	la stazione di servizio	statz-yoh-neh dee sair-veetz-yo
ring road	raccordo anulare	rak-or-do an-oo-lah-re
road	la strada	strah-da
traffic lights	il semaforo	sem-ah-foh-roh
unleaded petrol	benzina senza piombo	ben-dzeena sen-dza peeom-boh

Signs you may see on the Road

accendere i fari	ach-en-deh-reh ee fah-ree	headlights on
caduta massi	kah-doo-tah mah-see	falling rocks
divieto di accesso	dee-vyeh-toh dee ach-eh-so	no entry
divieto di sosta	dee-vyeh-toh dee sos-tah	no stopping
dogana	dog-ah-nah	customs
escluso residenti	es-kloo-so reh-zi-den-ti	residents only
ghiaccio	gyah-cho	ice
lavori in corso	lah-voh-ree een kor-so	roadworks
nebbia	neb-bya	fog
parcheggio a pagamento	par-kej-yo a pah-gah-men-toh	paying car park
parcheggio custodito	par-kej-yo koo-sto-dee-toh	car park with attendant
pedaggio	peh-daj-oh	toll
pericolo	peh-ree-koh-loh	danger
rallentare	rah-lehn-tah-reh	reduce speed
senso unico	sen-tzo oo-nee-ko	one way
uscita camion	oo-shee-tah kah-myon	works exit
zona pedonale	dzoh-na peh-doh-nah-leh	pedestrian area

Staying in a Hotel

Do you have any vacant rooms?	**Avete camere libere?**	ah-**veh**-teh **kah**-mair-eh **lee**-bair-eh?
double room	**una camera doppia**	oona **kah**-mair-ah **doh**-pee-ah
with double bed	**con letto matrimoniale**	kon **let**-toh mah-tree-moh-nee-**ah**-leh
twin room	**una camera con due letti**	oona **kah**-mair-ah kon **doo**-eh **let**-tee
single room	**una camera singola**	oona **kah**-mair-ah **sing**-goh-lah
room with a bath, shower	**una camera con bagno, con doccia**	oona **kah**-mair-ah kon **ban**-yoh, kon **dot**-chah
I have a reservation.	**Ho fatto una prenotazione.**	oh **fat**-toh oona preh-noh-tah-tsee-**oh**-neh
balcony	**balcone**	bal-**coh**-neh
breakfast	**prima colazione**	**pree**-ma coh-lah-**tzyoh**-neh
key	**la chiave**	lah kee-**ah**-veh
porter	**il facchino**	eel fah-**kee**-noh
room service	**servizio in camera**	ser-**vitz**-yoh een **cah**-meh-rah

Eating Out

Have you got a table for…?	**Avete una tavola per… ?**	ah-**veh**-teh oona **tah**-voh-lah pair…?
I'd like to reserve a table.	**Vorrei riservare una tavola.**	vor-**ray** ree-sair-**vah**-reh oona **tah**-voh-lah
the bill, please.	**il conto, per favore.**	**kon**-toh pair fah-**vor**-eh
I am a vegetarian.	**Sono vegetariano/a.**	**soh**-noh **veh**-jeh-tar-ee-**ah**-noh/nah
beer	**la birra**	**bee**-rah
bread	**il pane**	**pah**-neh
bottle	**la bottiglia**	bot-**teel**-yah
breakfast	**la prima colazione**	pree-mah koh-lah-tsee-**oh**-neh
butter	**il burro**	**boor**-roh
carafe	**la caraffa**	kah-rah-**fah**
child's portion	**una porzione per bambini**	portz-**yoh**-neh pair bam-**bee**-nee
coffee	**il caffè**	kaf-**feh**
cover charge	**il coperto**	koh-**pair**-toh
cup	**la tazza**	**tat**-zah
dessert	**il dessert**	des-**ser**
dinner	**la cena**	**cheh**-nah
dish of the day	**il piatto del giorno**	pee-**ah**-toh dell **jor**-no
first course	**il primo**	**pree**-moh
fixed price menu	**il menù a prezzo fisso**	meh-**noo** ah **pret**-soh **fee**-soh
fork	**la forchetta**	for-**ket**-tah
glass	**il bicchiere**	bee-kee-**air**-eh
half-litre	**da mezzo litro**	da **met**-zoh **lee**-troh
knife	**il coltello**	kol-**tel**-loh
litre	**un litro**	**lee**-troh
lunch	**il pranzo**	**pran**-tsoh
main course	**il secondo**	seh-**kon**-doh
medium (meat)	**al punto**	al **poon**-toh
menu	**il menù**	meh-**noo**
milk	**il latte**	**lat**-teh
pepper	**il pepe**	**peh**-peh
plate	**il piatto**	p-**yat**-toh
rare (meat)	**al sangue**	al **sang**-gweh
receipt (in bars)	**lo scontrino**	skon-**tree**-noh
(in restaurants)	**la ricevuta**	ree-cheh-**voo**-tah
restaurant	**il ristorante**	rees-toh-**ran**-teh
salad	**l'insalata**	een-sah-**lah**-tah
salt	**il sale**	**sah**-leh
sandwich	**il panino**	pan-**ee**-noh
serviette	**il tovagliolo**	toh-val-**yoh**-loh
snack	**lo spuntino**	spoon-**tee**-noh
soup	**la minestra**	mee-**nes**-trah
spoon	**il cucchiaio**	koo-kee-**eye**-oh
starter	**l'antipasto**	an-tee-**pas**-toh
sugar	**lo zucchero**	**dzoo**-keh-roh
tea	**il tè**	teh
teaspoon	**il cucchiaino**	kook-yah-**ee**-noh
tip	**la mancia**	**man**-cha
vegetables	**il contorno**	eel kon-**tor**-noh
waitress	**la cameriera**	kah-mair-ee-**air**-ah
waiter	**il cameriere**	kah-mair-ee-**air**-eh
water	**l'acqua**	**ak**-wah
fizzy/still	**gassata/naturale**	gah-**zah**-tah/ nah-too-**rah**-leh
well done (meat)	**ben cotto**	ben **kot**-toh
wine	**il vino**	**vee**-noh
wine list	**la lista dei vini**	**lee**-stah day **vee**-nee

Menu Decoder

abbacchio	ab-**ak**-yoh	spring lamb
acciughe	ach-**oo**-geh	anchovies
aceto	ach-**eh**-toh	vinegar
acqua minerale gassata/ naturale	**ah**-kwah mee-nair-**ah**-leh gah-**zah**-tah/ nah-too-**rah**-leh	mineral water fizzy/still
aglio	**al**-ee-oh	garlic
agnello	ah-**niell**-oh	lamb
al forno	al **for**-noh	baked
alla griglia	ah-lah **greel**-yah	grilled
albicocche	al-bee-**kok**-eh	apricots
ananas	**an**-an-ass	pineapple
anatra	**an**-at-rah	duck
anguria	an-**goo**-rya	water melon
antipasti	ahn-ti-**pas**-ti	starters
aperitivo	apeh-ree-**tee**-voh	aperitif
aragosta	ara-**goss**-tah	lobster
arancia	ah-**ran**-cha	orange
aringa	ah-**reen**-gah	herring
arrosto	ar-**ross**-toh	roast
asparagi	as-**pah**-rah-ji	asparagus
baccalà	bak-al-**la**	dried cod
basilico	bas-**ee**-lee-ko	basil
besciamella	besh-ah-**mel**-ah	white sauce
birra	**beer**-rah	beer
bistecca	bees-**tek**-ka	steak
bottarga	bot-**ahr**-gah	salted mullet roe
branzino	bran-**zee**-no	sea bass
brasato	bra-**sah**-toh	braised beef
bresaola	breh-**sah**-oh-lah	slices of cold, wind-dried beef with oil and lemon
brioche	bri-**osh**	type of croissant
brodo	**broh**-doh	clear broth
budino	boo-**dee**-noh	pudding
burro	**boor**-oh	butter
caffè	kah-**feh**	espresso coffee
caffè corretto	kah-**feh** koh-**reh**-toh	espresso coffee with a dash of liqueur
caffè lungo	kah-**feh** **loon**-goh	weak espresso coffee
caffè macchiato	kah-**feh** mak-**yah**-toh	espresso coffee with a dash of milk
caffè ristretto	kah-**feh** ree-**streh**-toh	strong espresso coffee
caffelatte	kah-**feh**-**lah**-teh	half coffee, half milk
calamari	kah-lah-**mah**-ree	squid
calzone	kal-**zoh**-neh	folded pizza filled with tomato and mozzarella
camomilla	kah-moh-**mee**-lah	camomile tea
cannella	kan-**el**-ah	cinnamon
cannelloni	kan-eh-**loh**-nee	stuffed pasta tubes
cappuccino	kap-oo-**chee**-noh	coffee with foaming milk
carciofi	kar-**choh**-fee	artichokes
carne	**kar**-neh	meat
carote	kar-**roh**-teh	carrots
castagne	kas-**tan**-yeh	chestnuts
cavolfiore	kavol-**fyoh**-reh	cauliflower
cavolo	**kah**-voh-loh	cabbage
cefalo	**che**-fah-loh	grey mullet
cernia	**cher**-nya	grouper (fish)
ciambella	cham-**bella**	ring-shaped cake
cicoria	chih-**kor**-ya	chicory
ciliege	chil-**yej**-eh	cherries
cioccolata	choc-ch-**lah**-tah	chocolate
cipolle	chip-**oh**-leh	onions
coniglio	kon-**ee**-lyo	rabbit
contorni	kon-**tor**-nee	vegetables
coperto	kop-**er**-toh	cover charge
coppa	**koh**-pah	cured pork, sliced finely and eaten cold
cordula	**kor**-doo-lah	Sardinian spit-roasted plaited lamb entrails
cotoletta	kot-oh-**let**-ta	pork or lamb chop
cozze	**kot**-zeh	mussels
crema	**kreh**-mah	custard dessert
crespella	**kres**-pel-lah	savoury pancake
crostata di frutta	kros-**tah**-tah dee **froo**-tah	fruit tart
datteri	**dat**-eh-ree	dates
digestivo	dee-jes-**tee**-voh	digestive liqueur
dolci	**dol**-chi	desserts, cakes
espresso	es-**pres**-soh	strong black coffee
fagiano	fah-**jah**-noh	pheasant
fagioli	fah-**joh**-lee	beans
fagiolini	fah-joh-**lee**-nee	long, green beans
fegato	**feh**-gah-toh	liver
fettuccine	feh-too-**chee**-neh	ribbon-shaped pasta
fichi	**fee**-kee	figs
filetto	fee-**leh**-toh	fillet (of beef)
finocchio	fee-**noh**-kyo	fennel
formaggio	for-**maj**-yo	cheese
fragole	**frah**-goh-leh	strawberries
frappé	frap-**eh**	whisked fruit or milk drink with ice
fregula	**freh**-goo-lah	small, granular pasta
frittata	free-**tah**-tah	type of omelette
fritto	**free**-toh	deep fried
fritto misto	**free**-toh **mees**-toh	seafood in batter
frittura di pesce	free-too-rah dee **pesh**-eh	variety of fried fish
frutta	**froo**-tah	fruit
frutta secca	**froo**-tah sek-kah	dried fruit
frutti di mare	**froo**-tee dee **mah**-reh	seafood
funghi	**foon**-g-ee	mushrooms

gamberetti	gam-beh-**reh**-tee	shrimps
gamberi	**gam**-beh-ree	prawns
gamberoni	gam-beh-**roh**-nee	king prawns
gelato	gel-**ah**-toh	ice cream
gnocchi	**nyok**-ee	small flour and potato dumplings
gorgonzola	gor-gon-**zoh**-lah	strong, soft blue cheese
granchio	**gran**-kyo	crab
granita	gra-**nee**-tah	drink with crushed ice
grissini	gree-**see**-nee	thin, crisp breadsticks
insalata	een-sah-**lah**-tah	salad
involtini	een-vol-**tee**-nee	meat rolls stuffed with ham and herbs
lamponi	lam-**poh**-nee	raspberries
latte	**lah**-teh	milk
lattuga	lah-**too**-gah	lettuce
leggero	leh-**jeh**-roh	light
legumi	leh-**goo**-mee	pulses
lenticchie	len-**teek**-yeh	lentils
lesso	**less**-oh	boiled
lepre	**leh**-preh	hare
limone	lee-**moh**-neh	lemon
lingua	**leen**-gwa	tongue
macedonia di frutta	mach-eh-**doh**-nya dee **froo**-tah	fruit salad
maiale	mah-**yah**-leh	pork
mandarino	man-dah-**ree**-noh	mandarin
mandorla	**man**-dor-lah	almond
manzo	**man**-dzo	beef
mascarpone	mah-skar-**poh**-neh	soft, sweet cheese
mela	**meh**-lah	apple
melanzane	meh-lan-**zah**-neh	aubergines
melone	meh-**loh**-neh	melon
menta	**men**-tah	mint
merluzzo	mer-**loo**-tzoh	cod
minestrone	mee-nes-**troh**-neh	thick vegetable soup
mirtilli	meer-**tee**-lee	bilberries
more	**mor**-eh	blackberries
nasello	nah-**seh**-loh	hake
nocciole	noch-**oh**-leh	hazelnuts
noce moscata	**noh**-che mos-**kah** tah	nutmeg
noci	**noh**-chi	walnuts
olio	**oh**-lyo	oil
orata	oh-**rah**-tah	gilthead bream
origano	oh-**ree**-gah-noh	oregano
ossobuco	os-oh-**boo**-ko	stewed shin of veal
ostriche	**os**-tree-keh	oysters
pane	**pah**-neh	bread crisp, circular bread
carasau	cah-rah-**sahw**	
panino	pah-**nee**-noh	filled roll
panna	**pah**-nah	cream
parmigiana di melanzane	par-mee-**jah**-nah dee meh-lan-zah-neh	aubergine, tomato, mozarella and parmesan bake
parmigiano	par-mee-**jah**-noh	parmesan cheese
pasticcio	pas-**tich**-oh	pasta and meat bake
patate	pah-**tah**-teh	potatoes
pecorino	peh-coh-**ree**-noh	strong, hard ewe's milk cheese
penne	peh-**neh**	pasta quills
pepe	**peh**-peh	pepper (spice)
peperoncino	peh-peh-**ron**-chee-noh	cayenne pepper
peperoni	peh-peh-**roh**-nee	peppers
pera	**peh**-rah	pear
pesca	**pes**-kah	peach
pesce	**pesh**-eh	fish
piselli	pee-**seh**-lee	peas
polenta	poh-**len**-tah	boiled cornmeal with meat or vegetables
pollo	**poh**-loh	chicken
polpette	pol-**peh**-teh	meatballs
polpettone	pol-peh-**toh**-neh	meatloaf
pomodori	poh-moh-**doh**-ree	tomatoes
pompelmo	pom-**pel**-moh	grapefruit
porceddu	por-**ched**-doo	roast suckling pig
porri	**poh**-ree	leeks
prezzemolo	pretz-**eh**-moh-loh	parsley
primi piatti	**pree**-mee **pyah**-tee	first courses
prosciutto cotto/crudo	pro-**shoo**-toh **kot**-toh/**kroo**-doh	ham cooked/cured
prugne	**proo**-nyeh	plums
radicchio	rah-**deek**-yo	red chicory
ragù	rah-**goo**	mince and tomato sauce
ravanelli	rah-vah-**neh**-lee	radishes
ravioli	rah-vee-**oh**-lee	square-shaped egg pasta filled with meat
razza	**rah**-tzah	skate
ricotta	ree-**kot**-tah	white, soft cheese
ripieno	**ree**-pyeh-noh	stuffed
riso	**ree**-soh	rice
risotto	ree-**soh**-toh	rice cooked in stock
rognone	ron-**yoh**-neh	kidney
rosato	roh-**sah**-toh	rosé wine
rosolato	roh-soh-**lah**-toh	fried
rosmarino	ros-mah-**ree**-noh	rosemary
salame	sah-**lah**-meh	salami
sale	**sah**-leh	salt
salsa	**sal**-sah	sauce
salsiccia	sal-**see**-cha	sausage
salvia	**sal**-vya	sage
scaloppine	skah-loh-**pee**-neh	veal escalopes
seadas	say-**ah**-dahs	sweet cheese and lemon fritters
secco	**seh**-koh	dry
secondi piatti	seh-**kon**-dee **pyat**-ee	main courses
sedano	**seh**-dah-noh	celery
selvaggina	sel-vah-**jee**-nah	game
semifreddo	seh-mee-**freh**-doh	ice cream and sponge dessert
senape	**seh**-nah-peh	mustard
seppie	**sep**-pee-eh	cuttlefish
servizio compreso	ser-**vitz**-yo com-**preh**-soh	service charge included
servizio escluso	ser-**vitz**-yo es-**cloo**-so	service charge not included
sogliola	**sol**-yoh-lah	sole
sorbetto	sor-**bet**-oh	sorbet
speck	sp-**ek**	cured, smoked ham
spezzatino	spetz-ah-**tee**-noh	stew
spiedini	spyeh-**dee**-nee	meat or fish on a spit
spinaci	spee-**nah**-chee	spinach
spremuta	spreh-**moo**-tah	freshly squeezed juice
spumante	spoo-**man**-teh	sparkling wine
stufato	stoo-**fah**-toh	casserole
tacchino	tak-**ee**-noh	turkey
tagliatelle	tah-lyah-**teh**-leh	flat strips of egg pasta
tartine	tar-**tee**-neh	small sandwiches
tartufo	tar-**too**-foh	ice cream covered in cocoa
tè teh	tea	
tiramisù	tee-rah-mee-**soo**	dessert of coffee-soaked sponge, Marsala and mascarpone
tisana	tee-**zah**-nah	herbal tea
tonno	toh-**noh**	tuna
torta	**tor**-tah	tart, cake
torta salata	**tor**-tah sah-**lah**-tah	savoury flan
tortellini	tor-teh-**lee**-nee	stuffed pasta shapes
triglia	**tree**-lya	red mullet
trippa	tree-**pah**	tripe
trota	**troh**-tah	trout
uova	oo-**wo**-va	eggs
uova sode	oo-**wo**-va **soh**-deh	hard-boiled eggs
uva	**oo**-va	grapes
verdura	ver-**doo**-rah	vegetables
vino	**vee**-noh	wine
vino bianco	**vee**-noh **byan**-ko	white wine
vino da dessert	**vee**-noh dah deh-**ser**	dessert wine
vino da pasto	**vee**-noh dah **pas**-toh	table wine
vino da tavola	**vee**-noh dah **tah**-voh-lah	table wine
vino rosso	**vee**-noh **ros**-soh	red wine
vitello	vee-**tel**-loh	veal
vongole	**von**-goh-leh	clams
zafferano	zah-fair-**ah**-noh	saffron
zucca	**dzoo**-kah	pumpkin
zucchero	**dzoo**-kair-oh	sugar
zucchine	dzoo-**kee**-neh	courgettes
zuppa	**dzoo**-pah	soup
zuppa inglese	**dzoo**-pah een-**gleh** seh	trifle

Acknowledgments

Dorling Kindersley would like to thank the following organizations and people whose contributions have made the preparation of this book possible:

Special Assistance

Agriturismo di Lucia Sotgiu, Agriturismo Sa Perda Marcada, Hertz, Claire Littlejohn, Hotel Mediterraneo, Greca Mattan, Meridiana, Anna Chiara Montefusco, Filomena Rosato, Anna Sacripanti, Terranostra Sardegna.

Design and Editorial

Additional Picture Research Ellen Root
Revisions and Relaunch Team Louise Abbott, Beverley Ager, Gillian Allen, Robert Andrews, Jennifer Avventura, Claire Baranowski, Uma Bhattacharya, Emma Bird, Samantha Borland, Antonugo Cerletti, Michelle Clark, Michelle Crane, Cooling Brown, Felicity Crowe, Vivien Crump, Fay Franklin, Anna Freiberger, Camilla Gersh, Vinod Harish, Mohammad Hassan, Elinor Hodgson, Annette Jacobs, Jasneet Kaur, Rupanki Kaushik, Vincent Kurien, Sarah Lane, Georgina Matthews, Alison McGill, Tiffany Parks, Helen Peters, Piero Pirosu, Gillian Price, Lee Redmond, Azeem Siddiqui, Tarini Singh, Ellie Smith, Susana Smith, Tiziana Tuveri, Sylvia Tombesi-Walton, Helen Townsend, Conrad van Dyk, Nikhil Verma, Ingrid Vienings, Catherine Waring.

Additional Photography

Ian O'Leary

Picture Credits

Key: a = above; b = below; c = centre; f = far; l = left; r = right; t = top.

All the photographs were taken by the photographic agency Overseas S.r.l., except for the following:

Alamy Images, London: Arco Images 14tc; Claudio H. Artman 10c, 96cl; Marco Casiragh 179tc; Authors Image/Mickael David 182cl; CuboImages srl/Marco Casiraghi 150cla, 181br, 199tr; Renato Granieri 32c; Robert Harding Picture Library Ltd/J Lightfoot 13tr; Yadid Levy 188br; Enrico Spanu 187tr; Specialpictures.nl 204b; Tim E White 123t; Andrew Woodley 174t; **Fabrizio Ardito, Rome:** 28tr, 28br, 29cr, 36cr, 37bl, 37br, 41t, 63bl, 86b, 87b, 89bl, 89cr, 100b, 103c, 103cr, 106b, 108tr, 108bc, 109tl, 110tl, 110cr, 110b, 112c, 115tl, 115cr, 120tr, 120cl, 123cl, 124tc, 125t, 128tl, 128c, 128b, 129tl, 154tl, 154b, 155tr, 155cr, 155br, 155cla, 156tl, 157tl, 159cr, 160tr, 160c, 160b, 161tl, 161cr, 161b, 162tr, 162c, 162clb, 163tl, 163b, 168cr, 169tl, 169crb. **Fabio Braibanti, Milan:** 150br, 190cl, 193bl, 193tr, 193crb. **Cipriani Porto Cervo:** 189tr.

Corbis: David Fleetham 23br, 87cr; Owen Franken 183c; Michelle Garrett 183tl. **Fabio De Angelis, Milan:** 36tr, 36cra, 147bl, 192c, 193cr. **Dreamstime.com:** Alkan2011 52clb, 116; Massimo Campanari 204cr; Ana Del Castillo 10bl, 14br; Jeanne Coppens 12t; Marta Fernandez 53br; Frhojdysz 200tr; Filip Fuxa 206br; Neptune Grotto 14bl; Irakite 194-5; Elisa Locci 10cr, 15tr; Marmo81 15bl; Fabio Medda 21b, 97cr; Nico Smit 75tl. **La Essenza:** 174bl, 178bl. **European Commission:** 199b. **Faro Capo Spartivento:** 173t, 176br. **Foto Carfagna + Associati, Rome:** 137br. **Cristina Gambaro, Milan:** 29b, 74cl, 74c, 95cr, 112tl, 113cl, 144bl. **Getty Images:** Walter Bibikow 50-1; Andy Christiani 170-1; Riccardo Deiana Photography 2-3; Katja Kreder 142; Andrew Peacock 98; DEA/A. VERGANI 158tl. **Robert Harding Picture Library:** Bruno Morandi 18. **Il Dagherrotipo:** Marco Melodia 13bl. **Ilisso edizioni, Nuoro:** 163cra, 163crb; **Image Bank, Milan:** 55bc, 131t, 134t. **The Lemon House:** 175br, 177tr. **Antonio Mannu, Sassari:** 36bl, 45br, 47cr, 52tr, 56cl, 76tl, 99b, 106clb, 107tl, 117b, 121tl, 121cra, 121crb, 122cl, 122bl, 123cl, 125tl, 130tr, 130cr, 130bl, 131cr, 132tl, 133cr, 133b, 138cl, 138br, 139tl, 140t, 140bl, 158br, 158bl, 161cr, 161br, 164cl, 164br, 166tr, 166bl, 167tc, 167b, 191tr. **Moby Lines Ferry, Italy:** 205cr. **Luigi Pomata:** 180cla, 186br. **Alfio Elio Quattrocchi, Cagliari:** 26tr, 43t, 46cl, 57tr, 66b, 110tr, 113cr, 149tl, 153tl, 169br, 192bl, 193br. **Raccolta Delle Stampe Achille Bertarelli, Milan:** 35b, 40, 41c, 41bl, 42b. **Francine Reculez, Milan:** 182, 183, 193bc. **Sardegna Turismo:** 143b. **Superstock:** DeAgostini 8-9; Ana del Castillo/age fotostock 54; Peter Eberts/age fotostock. **Trenino Verde:** 53crb, 97bl, 113cla, 207cr. **Tirrenia Di Navagazione S.P.A, Italy:** 205tl. **Ufficio Stampa Del Comune Di Cagliari:** Enzo Pinna 49crb.

Front Endpaper:
Dreamstime.com: Alkan2011 Lbc; **Getty Images:** Andy Christiani Rtr; Katja Kreder Ltl; Andrew Peacock Ltr; **Superstock:** Ana del Castillo/age fotostock Rbc.

Cover Picture Credits
Front and Spine - 4corners: Johanna Huber / SIME
All other images © Dorling Kindersley. For further information see: ***www.dkimages.com***

Special Editions of DK Travel Guides

DK Travel Guides can be purchased in bulk quantities at discounted prices for use in promotions or as premiums. We are also able to offer special editions and personalized jackets, corporate imprints, and excerpts from all of our books, tailored specifically to meet your own needs.

To find out more, please contact:
in the United States **SpecialSales@dk.com**
in the UK **travelspecialsales@uk.dk.com**
in Canada DK Special Sales at **general@tourmaline.ca**
in Australia **business.development@pearson.com.au**

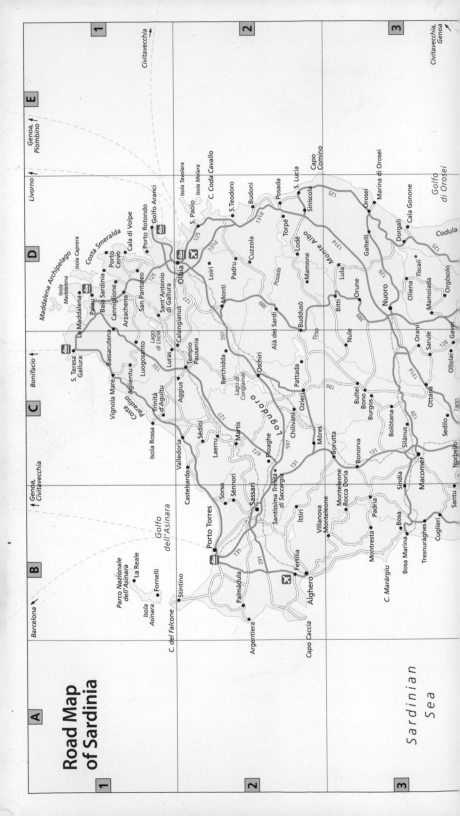

Road Map of Sardinia